European politics today

In this new textbook Geoffrey Roberts and Patricia Hogwood provide an up-to-date introduction to the political system and processes of western Europe. They show that political decisions are not made in a vacuum, but in the context of specific historical developments, geographical constraints and social demands.

The book begins with an overview of the features and events which have shaped the political landscape of Europe. The authors go on to discuss liberal democracy, historical sources of conflict between countries, electoral systems, political parties and interest groups, government and parliament. The final section of the book looks at federalism and EU decision-making and sums up with a look at how western liberal democracies in Europe have attempted to provide stable government while remaining responsive to changes in society.

Geoffrey K. Roberts is Reader in the Department of Government, University of Manchester; Patricia Hogwood is visiting Research Fellow in the Department of Government, University of Strathclyde

D0645517

Politics Today
Series Editor: Bill Jones

Other titles in the series

Forthcoming titles

European politics today

Geoffrey Roberts and
Patricia Hogwood

Manchester University Press

Manchester and New York

distributed exclusively in the USA by St. Martin's Press

Published by Manchester University Press
Oxford Road, Manchester M13 9NR, UK
and Room 400, 175 Fifth Avenue, New York, NY 10010, USA

Distributed exclusively in the USA
by St. Martin's Press, Inc., 175 Fifth Avenue, New York,
NY 10010, USA

British Library Cataloguing-in-Publication Data
A catalogue record for this book is available from the British Library

Library of Congress Cataloging-in-Publication Data

Roberts, Geoffrey K.
  European politics today / Geoffrey Roberts and Patricia Hogwood.
      p.   cm. – (Politics today)
  Includes bibliographical references.
  ISBN 0-7190-4362-X. – ISBN 0-7190-4363-8
    1. Europe, Western – Politics and government.   2. Europe – Politics and
  government – 1989–   I. Hogwood, Patricia.   II. Title.
  III. Series: Politics today (Manchester, England)
  JN94.R63   1997
  320.94′09′049 – dc20   96-17959
                                                                        CIP

ISBN 0 7190 4362 X *hardback*
      0 7190 4363 8 *paperback*

First published 1997

01 00 99 98 97   10 9 8 7 6 5 4 3 2 1

Typeset by Best-set Typesetter Ltd., Hong Kong
Printed in Great Britain by Bell & Bain Ltd., Glasgow

Contents

List of Tables

Preface

This textbook is intended as an introduction to the political systems and processes of western Europe. Political decisions are not made in a vacuum, but in the context of specific historical developments, geographical constraints and social demands. The book begins with an overview of the features and events which have shaped the political institutions and decision-making processes of western Europe (Chapter 1). Chapter 2 introduces the concept of liberal democracy and its particular relevance for the countries of our study. Politics is rooted in conflicting interests: Chapter 3 identifies the common historical sources of political conflict in western Europe and explores new issues which might help to shape the political agenda in the near future.

The next three chapters are devoted to the processes of representation. Chapter 4 describes the electoral systems currently in use in western European countries and explains their implications. Chapters 5 and 6 examine the 'linkage organisations' – political parties and interest-groups – which provide means of representation for the interests of citizens within the political process. The main institutions of government are compared in Chapters 7 (executive government) and 8 (parliaments). Since the Second World War, there has been a growing awareness that citizens must sometimes be protected from flawed, corrupt or domineering government. Chapter 9 is concerned with the means which have been devised to protect the citizen.

Chapters 10 and 11 look beyond central government in western Europe. Chapter 10 explores the theme of subnational government. It contrasts federal and unitary states, considering the issues of decentralisation and the devolution of government powers. Chapter 11 is concerned with supranational decision-making within the European Union. It describes the evolution and main institutions of the European Union, and the way in which its decisions affect the countries and citizens of western Europe. Finally, Chapter 12 evaluates the ongoing attempt by western European liberal democracies to provide stable government while remaining responsive to the demands of change in society. It examines some of the problems and challenges faced by European democracies throughout the postwar period and those which seem certain to be relevant in the immediate future.

The book is designed to be used in a flexible manner. Each chapter is self-contained in terms of content and the use of abbreviations or foreign terms. A glossary of these terms and abbreviations is provided towards the back of the book for easy reference. To avoid overloading the chapters with too much explanatory detail, a series of concise 'country profiles' is provided as an appendix. These supply details of each political system in a standard format, for easy comparison. The book can be read from start to finish, as an introduction to politics in western Europe. Alternatively, students might prefer to concentrate on one or more of the themes outlined above, or to refer to a particular chapter.

The chapters are intended as introductory material. For those readers who wish to investigate themes more deeply, a selection of further reading relevant to the chapter topics is listed at the conclusion of each chapter. A list of more general works, including books specialising in the politics of particular countries and reference sources, is provided after the glossary.

A word of warning: any book about contemporary politics soon falls prey to new political developments. Inevitably, some aspects of this book will have become dated even before it is published. General elections, political crises, constitutional amendments, new policies, new parties, new personalities will soon render some of the points and several of the examples obsolete. This is inescapable for a book about contemporary politics, but it does not pose an insuperable problem. Change is what makes politics interesting, after all. The main themes of the book – political culture, political institutions and political processes – are slow to change, and the reader will be able to apply current political examples to the general points made in each chapter.

Also, no politics textbook can pretend to be completely comprehensive. The countries of eastern Europe have not been included in the scope of the book. These countries of the former communist bloc are all now, in different ways and with different degrees of commitment and success, developing as democracies. However, as noted in Chapter 12, their democratic regimes are still very much in flux and their economies are not yet comparable to those of western European states. At this time, the western European model of liberal democracy is still quite distinctive and is worth studying separately from the emerging democracies of eastern Europe. With the exception of the chapters exploring the historical context of politics in western Europe, the book has a contemporary focus and concentrates on the period since the end of the Second World War.

Readers will notice that priority is given in the book to the United Kingdom, France and Germany. The size and historical and contemporary importance of these countries make them worth studying in some detail. Also, these are the countries which feature most often and most prominently in courses of comparative European politics at universities and colleges. The book will be useful to students of the language, society and culture of any of those countries. The book is not limited to these three countries, though; it makes frequent reference to other European countries where they offer interesting examples. These include the Irish and Dutch electoral systems; Italian and Spanish regional government; Swiss and Belgian federalism; and special features of the political systems of Sweden and Finland.

The book is very much a collaborative undertaking. However, the primary responsibility of authorship for each chapter is indicated in the table of contents. Patricia Hogwood was responsible for the country profiles. Geoffrey Roberts produced the glossary and index. The authors would like to thank the following friends and colleagues for reading various draft chapters of the book and making helpful and constructive suggestions: Laura Cram; Peter Cullen; John Davnall; Kris Deschouwer; David Farrell; Tom Mackie; James Mitchell. No responsibility for what we have produced in any way devolves on those colleagues. Had we been able to include *all* of their suggestions, this would no doubt have been a better book – in several volumes!

Geoffrey K. Roberts and Patricia Hogwood
April 1996

1

Politics in western Europe: contexts and patterns

Politics shapes the lives of all of us. It affects our welfare, our prosperity, our health and security. Sometimes – in very dramatic fashion when politics leads to war, revolution or civil war – it can be a matter of life and death.

Of course, politics alone does not determine all the developments and changes which a society experiences, let alone everything which affects the various life-styles and life-chances of every individual. Social and cultural factors, the physical environment, the interplay of commercial and financial institutions, the chance incidences of disease or infirmity are just some of the influences outside politics which affect our lives. But politics involves the deliberate attempt to steer and shape those other influences in particular ways for particular purposes. Politics can be about extending, defending or defining national boundaries and negotiating relationships with other countries. It can be about subsidising particular businesses, such as national airlines. It can attempt to find ways to control crime. It can be about entering into multinational free-trade areas, such as the European Economic Community (EEC) or the European Free Trade Association (EFTA). It may be concerned with the provision of health care and social insurance. It can, through regulation, seek to improve the quality of the air we breathe and the water we drink, impose controls on financial institutions, and set safety standards for road vehicles, passenger aircraft, railways and ferries.

So politics can be of vital importance to everyone. The history of Europe over the past two centuries demonstrates how significant politics can be.

That significance is sometimes shown in dramatic form. The French Revolution which began in 1789, the processes of unification which formed the powerful states of Italy and Germany in the late nineteenth century, the two world wars, Mussolini's 'March on Rome' in 1922 and seizure of power in 1925, the Spanish Civil War which began in 1936, the colonels' coup in Greece in 1967, the opening of the Berlin Wall in 1989: these are some of the more famous examples. Any of them would provide subject-matter for a gripping film or television documentary. But sometimes equally significant political developments are more evolutionary, more diffuse in their impact. These include, for example, the formation of the European Community (EC) and European Union (EU) (see Chapter 11); the creation of the welfare state in various countries and in differing formats; arguments about the most appropriate forms of constitutional design in West Germany in 1948–49, in France in 1958, in post-Franco Spain of the mid-1970s, or in Italy in the early 1990s; or adaptations of socialist and social democratic politics to the collapse of communist regimes in eastern Europe.

Whether in the dramatic or the more evolutionary mode, western European politics has often been associated with and affected by personalities, some of whom have become well known beyond their own national frontiers, and a few of whom have acquired almost mythical status. Napoleon, Garibaldi and Bismarck in the nineteenth century; Franco, de Valera, Mussolini, Hitler and Churchill before the Second World War; de Gaulle, Brandt, Thatcher and Le Pen since the Second World War: all are names familiar to people in many countries, and all became famous through politics. This does not mean that politics is only, or even primarily, controlled by 'great men' or 'great women'. It does mean, though, that personalities can make a difference to political outcomes and that personalities can become symbols for political programmes of various kinds, ranging from Napoleon's or de Gaulle's versions of France's destiny, to

Hitler's vision of Germany's dominance in Europe and Brandt's *Ostpolitik*[1] or Margaret Thatcher's brand of conservatism. Some critics complain that television and the popular press now exaggerate the effects of personalities on political outcomes, so that other influences – economic cycles of expansion and recession, technological innovation, international relations, for instance – are downplayed or ignored. Certainly, whatever one's views about the significance of personality and leadership in politics, reading biographies can provide an interesting way of learning about, and understanding, the political trends and events which were associated with, say, Adolf Hitler, Konrad Adenauer, Jean Monnet, Charles de Gaulle, or Harold Wilson.

Besides the 'personality' factor, three other types of influence need mention in this introduction to European politics. They provide contexts within which day-to-day political events occur, and are important for the explanation and analysis of those events. These contextual factors are: the pattern of political structures and organisation; history; and geography.

Day-to-day politics in European states will of course be affected by the patterns of political structures and the forms of political organisation which exist in each state. Several aspects of these patterns of structure and organisation will be explored in detail in later chapters. Suffice it here to mention the differences between unitary and federal forms of state organisation; the degree of separation between parliamentary and presidential tendencies in government; the type of electoral system employed to elect parliaments; arrangements for the representation of interests; and the possibility of direct influence by the public on policy issues through referenda.

A good history book can be of considerable utility in understanding the politics of European countries and their regions, as well as the international relations between European countries. States, like individual personalities, are the products – even sometimes the prisoners – of their histories. Some aspects of their political arrangements, their political agendas and their policies cannot be understood at all without reference to the past. Consider the Gibraltar issue for Anglo-Spanish relations; the

Northern Ireland question for Britain and Ireland; Greek sensitivity regarding the Macedonian state in former Yugoslavia; or the impassioned debate in Germany concerning the desirability of deploying its military forces outside its own territory. Indeed, most contemporary political issues and much of the patterning of the political structures of any country can be better appreciated if some knowledge of that country's history is available. Examples could include: the special concern of French politicians that riots by students and trade unionists should not lead to a rerun of the events of 1968; the responses of German politicians to manifestations of right-wing extremism; regionalist problems in Spain and Belgium; and the whole question of the political integration of the eastern and western parts of Germany.

Geography matters, because the location of the territory of a country, relative to other countries and relative to factors such as climate and access to the sea, can and often has affected the political options available to the government of that country. The 'off-shore island' locations of Ireland and Great Britain; the position of Germany at the centre of Europe; Italy's peculiar shape and its extension from the cool north, bordering alpine regions of France, Switzerland and Austria, down to the hot south, close to Africa's northern shores; the dependency of Iceland on its fisheries; the location of Finland relative to the former USSR: these are all examples of the linkage between geography and politics. In a surprisingly large number of instances, political problems, political issues, even the political arrangements of a society, can be understood so much better with the aid of a good map.

The shaping of the political map

One important thread running through the two centuries of European history since the French Revolution is the definition and redefinition of national boundaries.

Comparing the political map of western Europe in 1996 with that which existed two hundred years earlier or which came into existence after the Congress of Vienna at the end of the revolutionary-Napoleonic period, it is clear that certain features are more or less common to both. Great Britain, France, Spain and Portugal, Sweden and Denmark (apart from the status of Norway) have recognisably changed little since the end of the eighteenth century. Other features are very different, however. Ireland (minus the six counties which remained part of the United Kingdom (UK) after the post-First World War partition) is a 'new' state. Belgium broke away from the Netherlands in 1830. Norway declared itself independent in 1814, though not until 1905 did it finally separate from Swedish rule. Austria is a post-First World War remnant of the former heterogeneous Austro-Hungarian empire. Germany and Italy were each formed after complicated, dramatic and bloody unification processes in the mid-nineteenth century.

The idea of national self-determination in the nineteenth century and (sponsored by US president Woodrow Wilson in the post-First World War peace settlement) in the early twentieth century, was influential in creating today's political map of Europe. The geopolitical strategies and outcomes of the 1930s and 1940s, associated with the Second World War, produced for a time a stable pattern of European states during the period of the 'cold war'. This pattern broadly consisted of western Europe allied to the USA (with a few neutral states, such as Sweden, Ireland, Austria and Switzerland), confronting a set of states under USSR hegemony. It included a Germany in which one part was a republic linked to the western system of alliances, another part a republic tied to the Soviet system of communist states, and the former capital, Berlin, was itself divided and possessed a very peculiar semi-independent status.

The fabled 'visitor from Mars', investigating the politics and economics, the cultures and societies of these western European states, would fail to appreciate the interplay of political, economic, social and cultural developments simply by confining analysis to what has occurred within the boundaries of the states themselves. Why, for example, should France possess a 'Foreign Legion'? Why should Britain play its peculiar game – cricket – against teams from Australia, the Indian subcontinent or southern parts of Africa, but not against Italy, Spain or parts of North Africa? Why should Spain have military bases in North Africa? Why should the Netherlands have close links to South Africa and islands in southern Asia? The explanation is that these states all had colonial and imperial possessions. Such overseas expansion affected the politics, trade, culture and military strategies and resources of many Eurpean states during much of this period. Examples include British involvement in the Indian subcontinent and Malaya; the Suez crisis in 1956; Britain's retreat from several African former colonies; the Falklands War; and Britain's scheduled relinquishment of Hong Kong. The French were affected by problems in Indo-China and Algeria. Belgian withdrawal from the Congo, Portugese withdrawal from Angola and its other African dependencies, and Dutch withdrawal from the East Indies, as well as patterns of immigration to those states from former overseas possessions, are other examples of this link between national politics and overseas expansion. The formation of western European trading areas (EFTA and the EEC), was another significant development that affected the politics, economics and societies of the western European states concerned.

A review of the historical forces which have contributed to the shaping of the current political map of western Europe could take any of a dozen or more significant dates as a starting-point. Certainly the extension of the Roman Empire, the spread of Christianity, the invasion of Muslim influences, the Reformation and the Thirty Years War, the voyages of discovery across the Atlantic and beyond the equator are just a few of the trends that have contributed to the way Europeans now live, how they are governed and the definition of the national boundaries within which they are grouped together as peoples.

Having, though, to select one date in order to show how the peoples of western Europe have reached their present situation, the outbreak of the French Revolution commends itself for many reasons. It affected profoundly ideas about the relationship between peoples and their governments. It challenged the rights of monarchs to rule without restriction by a constitution or parliament and of the church to retain its specially privileged status *vis-à-vis* governments. It led to the Napoleonic conquests, from which the map of Europe emerged redesigned as though shaken in a kaleidoscope. The spread of revolutionary ideas by the printed or spoken word and by French military conquests gave impetus to notions of national identity and desires for political unity in many regions, leading eventually to the creation of 'new' countries such as Belgium, Germany, Italy, Norway and Ireland. It defined and disseminated the principle of 'sovereignty of the people', which was to become a central feature of liberal democracy (see below). And it established the precedent in modern times of revolution as the instrument of 'last resort' for dissatisfied people – in France especially, but for other countries potentially.

So the ideals of the French Revolution provided a foundation for the principles of liberal democracy. This concept will be further defined and explored in Chapter 2. Here it is only necessary to note the different velocities with which western European states evolved towards what are now remarkably similar patterns of democratic politics. Table 1.1 gives examples of the timing of the adoption of current constitutions, and the attainment of universal suffrage (noting that, at first, 'universal' was taken to mean 'all adult males'!). What such a tabular representation cannot show with any chronological precision are developments such as the evolvment of a competitive and democratic party system, the establishment of a free and critical press, the promotion of a literate, sophisticated electorate or the shaping of a galaxy of interest groups, citizens' associations and movements as part of a plural society. Yet these provide the flesh on the skeleton of constitutional and electoral provisions to give shape to the liberal democratic political order in western Europe.

The central idea of liberal democracy is that a constitutional order should exist which defines and delimits the scope of political power exercised by political institutions. Individuals should have civic rights which are protected against arbitrary acts of governmental institutions through the rule of law. The government and parliament should be representative of the people, who

Table 1.1   Dates of current constitutions and introduction of
              democratic suffrage[a]

Country	Date of current constitution[b]	Introduction of democratic voting rights	
		Men	Women[c]
Austria	1929	1907	1918
Belgium	1994	1893	1948
Denmark	1953	1849	1908
Finland	1919	1906	1906
France	1958	1848	1945
Germany	1949	1871	1919
Greece	1975	1844	1952
Iceland	1944	1915	1915
Ireland	1937	1923	1923
Italy	1948	1912	1945
Luxembourg	1868	1918	1918
Netherlands	1815	1917	1919
Norway	1814	1905	1913
Portugal	1976	1822[d]	1970[d]
Spain	1978	1869	1931
Sweden	1975	1919	1919
Switzerland	1874	1848	1971
United Kingdom	–	1918	1918/1928[e]

[a] The franchise refers to national elections only.
[b] Some countries had democratic constitutions which preceded that
currently in force (e.g. Belgium, France, Germany).
[c] Date of introduction of the female franchise is when it was granted
on the same terms as men.
[d] Voters were required to be literate in order to qualify for the
franchise.
[e] Women over the age of thirty were given the right to vote in 1918;
in 1928 they received the right to vote on the same terms as men.

should be able to participate regularly through competitive and
fair elections in the choice of their representatives. These ideas
are developed further in Chapter 2 and particular aspects are
also treated in later chapters.

The development of such a liberal democratic order followed no prescribed path, and was different in each and every state. The ideals of the French Revolution, and its written constitution as a supreme source of authority in substitution for that of a divinely appointed monarch, were of course influential as model and precedent. (So were the ideals and constitutional provisions of the American 'freedom fighters', after a different kind of struggle than that of the original French revolutionaries.) But because the historic, political and economic context was different in each case, the path from some form of absolutist rule to liberal democracy has also been different. This can be shown by a brief review of the way in which liberal democracy has become established in Britain, France, Germany, Italy and Spain.

In Britain, the process has been gradual and generally non-violent, stretching from 1832 to the present day. The principal stages have been: the extension of the franchise (and the crucially important introduction of the secret ballot to keep voting 'honest'), a displacement of monarchical power by that of cabinet government based on parliamentary majorities, the emergence of a sophisticated extra-parliamentary form of party organisation (given impetus by the rise of the Labour Party in the twentieth century), and the erosion of the legislative powers of the House of Lords. The most remarkable aspect of this process – in contrast to that in all other western European countries – is that it has occurred without the stimulus of a revolution, foreign occupation, or independence struggle. So (to the regret of some reformers) there has been no occasion to introduce a codified, written constitution (see Chapter 2), and no opportunity to replace the remnants of the old, aristocratic form of government (such as the monarchy, the House of Lords, even the electoral system) by a more modern, more 'rational', set of political institutions.

By contrast, France has undergone a switchback course of change from monarchical absolutism to mob rule, from military dictatorship which transmuted itself into Napoleon's self-bestowed 'imperial' rule to restored monarchy and renewed republics, from occupation by the German military to two varieties of post-Second World War republic. These numerous regime changes have been associated with changes in the right to vote, the growth of political parties, various degrees of parliamentary or monarchical or presidential power, with a variety of electoral systems and with a continuing penchant for direct action by interests resentful about some policy – or lack of it.

Germany, too, has experienced a distinctive path to liberal democracy. German unification was achieved by the diplomatic craft of Bismarck and based on military rather than constitutional strategies, under the hegemony of the Prussian monarchy. Though political parties developed and the right to vote was extended in the nineteenth century, it is difficult to justify applying the term 'democracy' to German politics before the invention of the Weimar Republic in 1919, after the First World War had swept away Germany's monarchies. The failure of the Weimar democracy led to its replacement by the dictatorial Third Reich. This regime eliminated, forcefully, all traces of liberal democracy in Germany, and Hitler's military ambitions led to the Second World War. Following Germany's unconditional surrender in 1945, the western occupying powers fostered in their part of Germany a limited form of liberal democracy, which culminated in 1949 in the Basic Law, a provisional constitution pending the reunification of Germany, when it was assumed that the German people would devise and adopt their own form of liberal democracy. However, when at long last that day of reunification arrived – much later than the drafters of the 1949 Basic Law had expected but much earlier than anyone in 1989 could have imagined – the provisional constitution of the Federal Republic was regarded as being so satisfactory that it was adopted, unamended in its essentials, for the new, reunified Germany.

Italy's story of the development of liberal democracy parallels that of Germany in several ways. A dictator, Mussolini, in the 1920s deliberately destroyed the democratic order which had been developed following the unification of Italy. Like Hitler, he led his fascist-governed state into the Second World War. Following the Allied invasion of Italy in 1943, Mussolini was overthrown (though still ruling in North Italy under German protection until his execution by partisans in 1945). At the end of the Second World War, the monarchy was abolished in favour of a republic, by means of a referendum in 1946. A system of parliamentary government has continued until the present, though large-scale corruption scandals have led to changes in the party system and the electoral system (see the treatment of this in the appendix). These changes have now been almost sufficiently extensive to justify a claim that a new, reformed republic is in the process of being born in Italy.

The failure of a brief liberal republic in Spain in 1873–74 meant that monarchical rule and a dominating role of the military characterised the Spanish political order until 1931, when the monarchy was abolished and the Second Republic established. This was challenged by a military uprising in 1936, which led to the Spanish Civil War (1936–39) and the establishment of the long-lived autocratic regime of General Franco. On Franco's death in 1975 the monarchy was restored, in compliance with Franco's wishes. The new king, Juan Carlos, set about the construction of a liberal democratic regime, with his own role being that of a constitutional monarch. Despite threats to that regime from the right and the military, as well as from Basque and Catalan forces demanding autonomy for their regions, the Spanish democracy has established itself firmly and has thrived.

One could chronicle in similar fashion the development of democratic politics in every other country in Europe. Each would have its own points of interest, its special, often unique, features, its particular pattern of external influences and internal conflicts. The case of Ireland would illustrate how British democratic practice left its impression – positively and negatively – and how a contractual provision for national independence for all but the six counties of Northern Ireland led to civil war and different kinds of democratic political structures in the North and in the Irish Republic. Switzerland's version of democratic politics, with emphasis on the linked features of strong federal devolution of powers to the cantons and frequent use of referenda, together with a need to balance the linguistic, regional and religious elements in Swiss politics, is certainly without parallel elsewhere in western Europe. It does, though, by its contrast, illuminate what is significant about different styles of democratic politics. The Scandinavian countries also possess interesting forms of democratic politics, with each of the countries sharing some elements of similarity but each also differing from the others in important ways. Among those elements of similarity could be included the development of agrarian political parties to represent rural interests, strong institutional links between the government and economic interest groups, and acceptance of a major role for the state in the provision of welfare.

It is vital to avoid the error of assuming that liberal democracy (in whatever variant it exists in western European states) is the inevitable end-product of western European political history. No doubt idealists thought so after the First World War, when so many states became democracies for the first time. Yet civil wars, military dictatorships, fascist regimes and other non-democratic forms of rule replaced many of these democratic regimes before and after the Second World War. They did so because democracies were perceived to be ineffectual in the face of crisis: whether social, economic or political in origin. They did so because democracies sometimes lacked sufficient 'friends', whose interests were linked to the success of democratic politics, and who supported democratic regimes. They did so because democracies – precisely because they are open, tolerant forms of regime – can be especially vulnerable to determined attacks by less scrupulous and more determined opponents. Italy and Weimar Germany, Austria, republican Spain, Greece in 1967 are examples of the downfall of democracies. To these one can add East Germany, which, being delivered by the wartime conferences of the Allies to occupation by the Soviet Union, became absorbed as a communist-run republic in the Soviet Union's system of satellite states.

Nor should it be supposed that all that belongs now to the past. It is certainly not beyond the bounds of feasibility that social or economic crisis or external dangers could lead to some attenuation of liberal democracy, or even its abandonment, in one or more countries of western Europe. Democracy always has enemies, and always has critics. If democratic states become too tolerant, they leave themselves open to attack and overthrow (like Weimar Germany). If, on the other hand, they become too self-protecting, too anxious to suppress anti-democratic threats, they may run the risk of losing their democratic 'essence' by adopting censorship, repression of opposition, and internal espionage systems: in the name of 'combative democracy'.[2]

Changes in the contexts of western European liberal democracies

The story of the development of liberal democracy in western Europe is not only a history of constitution-making, of transfers of power from monarchs or dictators or aristocratic elites to 'the masses' by extensions of the franchise or by incremental restrictions on absolutist rule. These political changes were important and necessary. But there were accompanying changes in the economies, social arrangements and cultures of these societies which were in part themselves causes of democratic change and in part accompaniments to it. From a long and heterogeneous list of such changes, a small number of examples will be discussed here.

The relationship between economic development and the evolution of democratic politics has been much studied by political scientists. Where such a relationship has been posited, arguments exist concerning its causal direction: a kind of 'chicken and egg' problem – do democratic political arrangements foster economic growth, or is a certain level of economic development first necessary for the establishment of a democratic political system? There seems to be evidence of a symbiotic effect: that the two trends reinforce each other. Whatever the answer, the establishment of democratic politics in western Europe certainly tended to accompany rapid economic growth associated with the industrial revolutions of the nineteenth and early twentieth centuries. This economic growth produced a middle class which both demanded a role in the political process and had the wealth to enable it to carry out that role. The factory-owners of early nineteenth-century Britain, the professional classes in Germany in the middle of the nineteenth century, the shopkeepers and owners of small local businesses in provincial France: these were the motivating forces behind political reform and were the first beneficiaries of the extension of political power from the elites of absolutist regimes. Industrialisation and the growth of trade unions, coupled with the elaboration of socialist ideologies and the oratory of working-class leaders, produced, in stages and not without resistance from the incumbent political elites, inclusion of the proletariat in the democratic political process. Eventually, and at different times in different countries (see Table 1.1), women were granted equal political rights with men.

But it is important not to fall into the trap of 'economic determinism': of supposing that levels of economic development entirely and solely account for the development of democratic forms of politics. Other factors were also relevant in the case of western European countries. Three which are related, and which have obvious political relevance, are: the growth of education provided by, or regulated by, the state; the concomitant spread of literacy; and the availability of relatively cheap forms of mass communication and transport. These enabled the newly enfranchised sections of the population to read about political issues and political campaigns, and to discuss them with their neighbours. They enabled politicians to communicate with their electors and supporters. They enabled political leaders to travel swiftly (e.g. Gladstone's 'Midlothian Campaign' in 1879, or Hitler's campaign using air travel in the presidential election of 1932). They enabled those who shared some political 'interest' or concern to communicate with each other, to organise and to exert pressure on politicians, whether seeking votes for women or better working conditions for employees in some trade, whether concerned about the prohibition of the sale of alcohol or Irish home rule. Cheap rail travel, cheap postage, cheap newspapers and pamphlets, later cheap radio receivers, together with the ability of people to read and the willingness of people to take an informed interest in political issues, contributed much to the development of democratic politics in western European countries.

The other factor which should be mentioned is that of ever-increasing international contacts and interdependence. These have affected the growth of democratic politics in various ways.

Imitative effects can be observed: consider the swift spread of revolutionary ideas and actions in Europe in 1848–49, the more gradual but longer-lasting spread of socialist ideas in the second half of the nineteenth century and of communist ideas after the Russian revolutions of 1917, or the uprisings associated with the 'student movement' in 1968. The collapse of communist regimes and the associated rapid decline of western European communist parties in 1989–91 (with some of them – as in Italy – transforming themselves into 'parties of democratic socialism') is a similar phenomenon. The attainment of voting rights by women or by the working class, the lowering of the voting age to eighteen years, controls over corruption or possible corruption through disclosure rules concerning financial interests, laws governing data protection or personal privacy, rules requiring equal treatment of political parties by the broadcasting media, institutions for receiving and acting upon complaints against the administration by aggrieved citizens: these, too, have spread from one country to another by imitation.

International interdependence has also meant that international institutions have required certain forms or standards of political behaviour. The EU is the most obvious case. Not only must member states be established democracies; they must participate in the institutional life of the EU – in elections to the European Parliament (EP), in meetings of the Council of Ministers, and so on, institutions which have their own forms of politics but which require that common democratic standards exist in member states.

It thus becomes less and less imaginable that any country in western Europe – especially, but not only, those which are members of the EU – could replace its democratic political system and institutions with those of, say, a military dictatorship or some other form of authoritarian regime. Such a country would find itself isolated in Europe, suffering certainly from economic sanctions, and subject to continual pressures to restore a democratic regime. But there is no inevitability about this. A country *may* decide that its interests are best served by cutting itself adrift from Europe, especially if continued attachment to such a Europe may appear to involve loss of sovereignty over crucial policy areas such as taxation and immigration. The decision in 1982 of Greenland, a self-governing territory of Denmark, to leave the EC (which took effect in 1985) is an example.

Patterns of politics in western Europe

By examining a series of indicators, it becomes clear that the countries of western Europe share several important political characteristics, but that there are also various significant differences in their political arrangements and in the background factors which affect the politics and political structures of these countries. In later chapters, the more important similarities and differences will be analysed in more detail, and key features of each country are described in the appendix.

First, geographic and demographic differences provide a useful starting-point in surveying western European states. They differ as to their *size of territory*: France, Spain, Germany, Italy, Sweden and Norway are countries with extensive territories; the Benelux countries (Belgium, Netherlands and Luxembourg), Denmark and Switzerland are countries with small territories.[3] *Size of population* does not always correspond to relative size of territory. Germany, France, the UK and Italy are the states with the largest populations; Iceland, Luxembourg and Ireland have the smallest populations. There are differences in degree of urbanisation: Portugal, Ireland, Greece and Austria have the smallest share of their populations living in urban areas; Belgium, Iceland and the Netherlands have the largest. Size of territory and population size and distribution are factors basic to the problem of effective government. Government of a state with the territorial extent and population of Luxembourg or even Denmark or Switzerland is an undertaking of a different order than, say, the government of Germany, within which Bavaria is a *Land* (province) as large as Belgium and the Netherlands combined, and where Denmark or Switzerland are each matched in area by Lower Saxony, Baden-Württemberg or North Rhine-Westphalia. In France the city of Paris alone poses greater political problems, relating to size of territory and population, than does the state of Luxembourg. So the government of large, populous states will be an enterprise of a different order of complexity than the government of small or thinly populated areas.

The importance of *location*, mentioned earlier in this chapter, can be perceived in various ways. Western Europe is an extensive geographic area: from Finland and Norway to Spain and Italy, from Ireland to Austria (and Greece: a non-contiguous, but unarguably in all but physical position a west European, state). This means that location has political significance in absolute terms. The cold climate of Finland and Norway, for example, has different significance for the economy and politics of those states than does the proximity to Africa of parts of Spain. It has political significance in relative terms. For example, the peripheral location of Ireland, Finland, Portugal and Greece in relation to the densely populated, commercial and industrialised cultural and administrative 'core areas' of western Europe – the Benelux countries, northern France, much of Germany, Switzerland and northern Italy – has important political consequences, especially in the context of the policies of the EU (see Chapter 11).

Associated with territorial and locational characteristics is the issue of *boundaries*. In the past, boundary issues in western Europe have caused wars, motivated royal marriages, provoked nationalist uprisings, and informed long-running political conflicts. Since the Second World War, the question of the 'proper' extent of metropolitan France in relation to Algeria, the division of Germany into two states, and the status of parts of pre-war Germany placed under French, Polish and Soviet Union administration,[4] were of great significance for the politics of France,

Germany and their neighbours and allies. Even today, several such boundary issues remain matters of controversy, for at least some substantial minority of inhabitants of affected areas. The claims of Irish nationalists that Northern Ireland should be joined with the Irish Republic rather than remain part of the UK is perhaps the most significant and notorious of these present-day issues. Many lives have been lost, much public money spent on security measures, and considerable parliamentary and ministerial time and media attention devoted to the problem. But occasionally other such issues make the headlines: violence in support of claims by Corsicans to independence from French rule; the arrest of a leader of a South Tyrolean movement demanding unification with Austrian Tyrol; agitation by some Scots for dissolution of the Union with England; claims by Spain to the recovery of Gibraltar; concern among Greeks that the former province of Yugoslavia that they call Skopje (but which others accept under its own chosen name of Macedonia) might make territorial claims on Greek areas – all these are recent examples.

States differ as to their *wealth and resources* – and these matters constitute both an important context for politics (e.g. the relationship referred to earlier in this chapter between economic development and liberal democracy) and a significant part of the day-to-day, year-to-year political agenda (e.g. policies to encourage economic growth; issues of wealth distribution and taxation; international trade and exchange-rate policies; indeed, the controversial issue of a common European currency for member states of the EU). The coal and iron resources of nineteenth-century Britain, Germany and France; the discovery of North Sea oil by coastal states such as Norway, the Netherlands and Britain; the structures and skills of the banking sectors in Luxembourg and Switzerland; hydroelectric provision in Sweden: these are some examples of resources which can affect politics in the countries concerned. The relative poverty of certain countries or regions in the EU is the reason for the attention paid by the EC to regional and social policies, and the provision of not inconsiderable sums to finance those policies, since crass differences in living standards between different countries or regions in the EU are not conducive to either the economic development or the integration of the EU.

Several characteristics relating to the regime which each country possesses, characteristics which can be considered as an interrelated cluster, provide other categories for comparing political systems of western Europe.

The *constitutional basis* of the regime is one such factor. For example, there are in-built differences which arise from the contrast between the 'unwritten' and flexible constitution of the UK compared to the codified constitutions of other western European countries, and perhaps between constitutions legitimated by referenda compared to those instituted through other procedures. It is linked to (but does not entirely account for) the *form of regime*: presidential or parliamentary government; federal or unitary state form; the degree of plebiscitary decision-making permitted in the political system, and so on. The extent to which *liberal democracy and the rule of law* exist is another factor linked to the constitution, but influenced by other characteristics of the system. By and large, all western European states are now of the same general standard in respect of the centrality of these two principles in relation to political life. However, this has not always been so in the past (Mussolini's Italy; Hitler's Germany; Portugal and Spain before their transitions to liberal democracy; Greece under military rule; eastern Germany under communist rule) and is not a situation absolutely guaranteed for the future. Furthermore states bordering western Europe, and which may hope to become members of the EU, have only recently established the structures – and have not perhaps as yet consolidated the processes – of liberal democracy and the rule of law.

Political stability (a notoriously difficult concept to define satisfactorily) is another variable related to a country's constitution and form of regime. If political stability is defined by the persistence of particular regimes, then most western European countries appear to be stable in the medium term. If a longer time-span is taken, then since the end of the First World War

France has experienced three different republics and a period of German occupation (not counting the short-lived and rather artificial Vichy regime in the southern part of France in the Second World War). In that period, Germany has had two republics, the Third Reich and post-war occupation by the Allies, plus the communist regime in the former GDR. Italy, Spain, Portugal, Austria and Greece have similarly been governed under several different regimes over the past eighty years. The more northerly constitutional monarchies, on the other hand, – omitting the German occupation regimes in the Second World War – together with Switzerland and Ireland, can be regarded as having been politically very stable in that period, measured by the yardstick of regime persistence.

Political stability does not depend solely on the rules of the political game as provided in a constitution and operated by the regime which that constitution imposes. The *political culture* and the particular *'style' of the regime* also contribute to regime stability or volatility, as well as supplying reasons for other differences observable in the patterns of political life in different countries (such as the penchant for violent street protests in French politics, the locally oriented attitudes to politics in Switzerland, the trust in legalistic settlements of political conflicts in German public life, or the significance of tradition in British politics). Political culture consists, very broadly, of the shared knowledge, attitudes and values which a people or some subgroup of a people have in common, and which identify them as a separate political community. Language is often an important agent for conveying political culture, and sometimes has symbolic political significance for that reason, as in Belgium, to some extent also in Wales, Ireland, and Catalonia in Spain (but this is not always the case: the USA and UK share what is, in the main, a common language, but they have very distinct political cultures, while linguistic distinctions in Switzerland do not contribute to equally distinctive political cultures within the country). Individuals come to learn about the political cultures of their society through political socialisation, a process involving parental influence, schooling, social interaction in the workplace and in clubs and organisations such as churches, shared experiences in peer groups and information from the mass media. Immigrants are sometimes provided with special opportunities for intensive learning, covering the basics of the political system among other things.

So what differentiates citizens of the UK from, say, citizens of Germany or Austria, or what divides Protestant citizens of Northern Ireland and Catholic citizens of the Irish Republic, or what makes citizens of Sweden react differently to a political issue than citizens of Portugal, is not just that in each case they are ruled under different constitutional arrangements and by somewhat different regimes. They also have grown up in different political cultures, have different – and sometimes unconscious – assumptions about politics, have experienced different recent national histories and are part of different political traditions. The most obvious example, of course, is the cultural gap – which extends very much into the political realm – separating those German citizens brought up in the west, and those who had lived their lives and learned about politics in the former GDR.

Political stability and political culture relate also to the pattern of fundamental political *cleavages* which exist in a society (a topic further explored in Chapter 3), which will likely include divisions of social class, possibly of religion, language, region or urban–rural location. These cleavages, in turn, influence the pattern of *party politics*. Why one country possesses a Christian democratic party but another does not, why (prior to 1989) some countries had substantial communist parties while in others that party was politically irrelevant, or why regionalist or nationalist parties gain in strength in particular political systems may all be questions to be answered by reference to cleavage patterns. However, the party system can also be affected by the *electoral system*. Putting the relationship between the two in its crudest form, a proportional representation system may encourage (or at least do nothing to discourage) the development of a multi-party system, while versions of the 'first-past-the-post' majoritarian system, as used in Britain, tend to buttress the continuing existence of two, and only two, parties with realistic chances of forming the government.

In conclusion, it is obvious that significant differences exist among various political systems, differences which relate to the historical, geographic or economic contexts of those systems, to their more fundamental constitutional or regime-related characteristics, as well as to more detailed aspects of their structures and procedures.

But important similarities also exist. These may likewise be of utility in the understanding of western European political systems. These similarities exist:

- because of the shared heritage which the states of western Europe possess (for example, the spread of Christianity; the effects of the Napoleonic era; two world wars in the twentieth century);
- because of the increasingly similar contexts within which those states conduct their politics (for example, the move towards European integration; the legacy of the cold war; the influences of international financial and economic activities);
- because of the copying of the political institutions or procedures of one country by another (for example, the ombudsman system of dealing with grievances; systems of parliamentary committees; aspects of electoral systems);
- and because of the similar problems which confront decision-makers in those countries (for example, increased migration of peoples; the crisis of the welfare state; environmental protection and conservation).

Since comparative analysis is an indispensable method for identifying what is significant with regard to a country's political structures or procedures, comparison which relies on the identification of important differences and significant similarities, the chapters in this book will emphasise comparison in describing and discussing the various themes which constitute the political systems of western European countries.

Notes

1 Willy Brandt, on becoming chancellor of the Federal Republic of Germany in 1969, implemented a policy involving the negotiation of agreements with the Union of Soviet Socialist Republics (USSR), Poland, the German Democratic Republic (GDR) and other states of the Soviet bloc, replacing the rejectionist policy towards those states which his predecessors had adopted.

2 The term (*streitbare Demokratie* in German) is used to refer to the protective measures provided for in the Basic Law of the Federal Republic of Germany (such as the provisions for the prohibition of anti-democratic parties or political groups), in legislation (such as criminalisation of the act of denying that the concentration camps were used to kill Jews), and in administrative practice (such as the investigations by, and reports of, Federal and *Land* Offices for the Protection of the Constitution concerning extremist groups and parties).

3 This excludes principalities such as Monaco and Liechtenstein, which are tiny.

4 The Saarland area was entrusted to France (but returned to the Federal Republic in 1957); areas of what used to be German territory east of the Oder and Neisse rivers were administered as part of Poland, and since German reunification have been accepted by Germany as belonging to Poland; and a part of East Prussia on the Baltic Sea including the port of Königsberg (named by the Russians as Kaliningrad) was to be administered by the USSR pending a peace treaty, but was incorporated unilaterally into the USSR in 1946.

Further reading

Urwin, D. (1989) *Western Europe since 1945*, London, Longman, 4th edn.

2

The democratic political process

Liberal democracy

Today, all western European states share the same basic type of regime: all are liberal democracies. Of course significant variations exist. For example, the political power of the head of state, the extent to which direct participation of the public by means of referenda is allowed for, the type of electoral system in use, the role of the second legislative chamber, all vary from country to country. But the fundamental characteristics of liberal democracy are to be found in each state of western Europe. What are these 'fundamental characteristics'?

One is the principle of *representative government*. This means that governments both represent, and are responsive to, the wishes of the people. Elections are held to choose representatives of the citizenry, and these elections normally have an effect on the composition of government (though of course in many countries elections do not necessarily *determine* the composition of the government). Such elections are held periodically, are genuinely competitive (unlike those held in communist states in eastern Europe before 1990), and are conducted under rules which ensure the secrecy of the ballot and – to some degree, at least – the equality of each vote (see Chapter 4). This right to choose and change governments, a right exercised regularly independent of the whim of government itself, is protected in a liberal democracy by the constitution and by legal provision.

A second principle concerns the *separation of powers*. Depending on the provisions of the constitution and the conventions of the political process, some system of checks and balances exists whereby the authority to decide on legislation (the legislative power), the ability to administer and implement such legislation (the executive power), and the right to adjudicate on breaches of the law (the judiciary power), belong to distinct institutions. In this way, the government is not, even for the limited period of its term of office, absolute master of all things political. Generally it will require some form of approval by the legislature to take office in the first place and will have to confront periodic votes in the legislature in order to introduce new laws or pass an annual budget, and will answer to a constitutional court (or some equivalent institution) whenever its actions are challenged as breaches of the constitution. Checks and balances may go further: relations between the two chambers of the legislature, for instance, may be such as to limit the powers of each and indeed restrict the ability of a government with a parliamentary majority to fulfil its legislative programme (see Chapter 8).

Third, liberal democracy involves the principle of *freedom of opinion* and of the expression of that opinion. Periodic competitive elections, the idea of representative government, the separation of powers and a system of constitutional checks and balances: all these lose their significance if there is censorship, control of expression of opinion, punishment for voicing criticism of the government or the political system. Problems may arise concerning the extent to which expression of opinion should enjoy absolute protection. The propagation of anti-democratic doctrines, stirring up of religious or racial hatred, publication of libellous statements about politicians: all may be prohibited even in the most liberal of democratic systems. But such limitations should be adopted only after careful and serious consideration, should be subjected to testing in the courts, and should be universally, not selectively, applicable.

The fourth principle of liberal democracy is that of the *rule of law*. Governmental decisions are made according to procedures laid down in the constitution, in laws based upon the constitution, and in rules of procedure developed by parliaments and governments. Such procedures ensure that government cannot wilfully or viciously penalise individuals or groups simply by making decrees. Laws that are made apply to everyone (or to everyone in a particular category, such as members of the armed forces, those beyond the age of retirement, lawyers or motorists), and, equally, everyone is subject to the law, so politicians or their supporters cannot claim improper privilege by virtue of their position and the power of their office. In contrast to dictatorships (of individuals or of parties), governmental decisions made other than through the proper procedures can be successfully challenged in the courts; judgment will be pronounced by judges (independent of the government) who decide on such cases according to the law, rather than on the basis of ideological correctness or the need to please political patrons. The rule of law also requires that retrospective legislation (laws which apply to situations existing before the law was actually passed) should generally be avoided. The rule of law depends on the existence of a constitution which is given proper regard: again, in contrast to authoritarian systems where a constitution may exist but is disregarded.

Constitutions: the 'rules of the political game'

Liberal democracies therefore depend on their constitutions to provide the framework for their political systems. Constitutions may fulfil several purposes. They may give expression to the goals or purposes of the state, make reference to the conditions under which the regime was founded, elaborate claims to eventual union with some territory not yet within the boundaries of the state. In a federal state, constitutions will identify the functions which belong to the constituent provinces and those which belong to the federal government (see Chapter 10). They describe the institutions of government, their structures and powers, and they also indicate how such powers are limited (by the checks and balances of other parts of the political structure, for instance). They may also include a menu of civic rights, enabling the citizen to appeal to the constitution before a court of law, if that is necessary to assert those rights against other persons, against the government, or against some non-governmental institution.

Constitutions need to be superior to other laws if they are to be effective; otherwise, a government could change the constitution (extending, for instance, the period between elections and thus its own term of office) by use of its parliamentary majority in the same way that it can change rates of taxation or safety regulations for motor-cars. One consequence of this requirement is that the amendment of the constitution should be a more difficult process than amending other laws. So there may be unamendable sections of constitutions (the federal principle in the Basic Law of the Federal Republic of Germany is an example), and where the constitution can be amended, special legislative majorities (normally two-thirds in each chamber) or the approval of the electorate through the mechanism of referenda (as in Ireland, Italy or Switzerland) are required for such amendment.

Constitutions normally take the form of a single written document, adopted at some specific date. Because the idea of liberal democracy based on written constitutions is relatively new, the current constitutions of West European countries tend to be fairly recent (see Table 1.1).

The UK is very much an exception, since it has no single document that can be identified as its constitution. Many documents which are regarded as contributory ingredients of the constitution (such as the Bill of Rights of 1689, the Act of Settlement of 1701, the Parliament Act of 1911 which limited the power of the House of Lords) are relatively ancient, compared to the post-Second World War origins of many western European constitutions. Other elements of the British constitution are 'unwritten', consisting of custom, practice and certain legal precedents, conventions which guide politicians, and the opinions of experts.

Some commentators argue that there is no such thing as 'the British constitution'. This argument rests on four claims. First, the British constitution is not in fact 'superior law' which can supersede, declare invalid or override other law. Second, there is no constitutional court which will prohibit the government from doing something on the grounds that such actions conflict with the constitution. Third, provisions of the British constitution (such as the Parliament Act, or provisions governing the maximum life-span of a parliament) can be amended by the same process as the amendment of other laws. Finally, no two experts would agree about what precisely is included in the 'constitution' and what is not. Indeed, some 'received wisdom' concerning prescriptions of the constitution (such as the unconstitutionality of having the Secretary of State for Foreign Affairs sitting in the House of Lords rather than the House of Commons, or limits on the power of the House of Lords to reject certain types of legislation) turns out to have been mistaken, when such prescriptions are disregarded and no serious constitutional or political consequences follow. The doctrine of 'supremacy of Parliament' implies that there never can be a written constitution which is superior to laws passed in proper form by the British Parliament.

Even the cleverest and most prescient of constitutional draughtsmen could not anticipate in the wording of a constitution all the innovations and changes which can come about in a society: the effects of computers on personal privacy; the possibility of televising parliamentary proceedings; the creation of the EU, for instance. Nor can wordings be found which eliminate all ambiguity in a constitution. Indeed, ambiguity is sometimes deliberately included, so as to increase the acceptability of the constitution to all sectors of society, or to avoid the need at the time to settle some contentious dispute. So some authoritative institution is required to interpret the constitution, to apply its prescriptions to new situations, and to adjudicate among competing claims under the constitution. In many western European countries constitutional courts or similar bodies exist for just these interpretative and adjudicatory purposes. These are discussed in Chapter 9.

The political process

Important though constitutions are in aiding an understanding of politics in any country, they can no more convey a sense of what really happens in politics than a dictionary and a grammar manual can convey what poetry is, or than the rule book of soccer can offer the spectator an understanding of the tactics and skills displayed in a match. Constitutions describe a framework of rules within which the *political process* takes place. This political process in a democracy is the way in which the political demands of the inhabitants are communicated to the government, the ways in which the government acts upon those demands, and the changes which occur in society as a consequence.

This political process differs from one country to another, and differs even within the same country over periods of time. These differences are due in part, but only in part, to differences in the constitutions of those countries, or in constitutions of the same country at different times (the French Fourth and Fifth Republics are an example). Differences are also due to differences in political culture (see Chapter 1), to changes in the ways in which people behave in political situations, to different contextual circumstances (such as economic depression, pressures of would-be immigrants, the downfall of communist regimes in 1990), and so on.

Nevertheless, despite the variability of the political process from one country to another or across time-spans, it is possible and useful to identify the fundamental features of the political process in democracies. This provides the basis for understanding how the political process works, and offers a means of comparing different political systems in terms of the ways in which the political process operates.

There are numerous theories and models of the democratic political process, ranging from Aristotle to Rousseau and John Stuart Mill, to Huntington and Lijphart in our own time. Each of these theories or models offers useful insights into the way democratic politics operates. An American political scientist, David Easton, developed a model of the political process which provides a highly simplified 'map' of the democratic political process, but which, because it *is* so simplified, can be utilised to compare and analyse the democratic political process in different political systems (see, for example, Easton 1965). Easton regarded the political system as essentially a process by which demands from the public are converted by the political authorities into outputs. A two-way process of communication links government to the people. This process is presented diagrammatically in Figure 2.1.

Political systems, at least those that are democratic, are concerned with *demands* from the public. These provide *input* into the political process. Of course, people may want the government to do all sorts of things: ban the live export of animals, increase spending on education or hospitals, introduce a common currency for the EU (or oppose such a common currency), reduce crime, eliminate environmental pollution of various kinds, build more roads, subsidise public transport, boycott Chinese goods – the list is endless. People differ on the desirability of certain policies, but even when they agree on their desirability, they will differ about the degree of priority that certain policies should receive. For instance, parents of young children will presumably be more concerned about education and levels of family allowances than will childless couples; those with an aged,

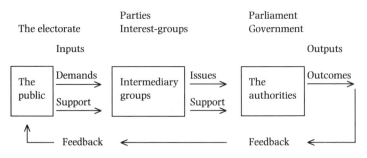

Figure 2.1 The political process

invalid parent will be more concerned about nursing-home provision and levels of old age pension than will other people; rural inhabitants, dependent upon public transport to get to work, lacking a railway service and with only infrequent bus services, will have different priorities for transport policy than will those living in the suburbs of a city, who enjoy frequent public transport services.

The direct and individual communication to the government of these multiple and changing demands from the public is impossible in any political system larger than a village. So some means of filtering these numerous and often contradictory demands is required, so that they can be aggregated into coherent alternatives which governments can consider and act upon. This filtering and aggregating function is largely carried out by *intermediary groups*: political parties and pressure groups (see Chapters 5 and 6). In various ways, these intermediary groups pay attention to the views expressed by their members and supporters and by the general public, they discuss these views, and – within the general limits of their own principles, interests and programmes – they then produce coherent policy proposals (which can be termed *issues*) and press governments to act upon them. An example of this aggregating and filtering process is the way in which political parties will at their party congresses debate motions from party branches, but in a 'composite' form, where several related propositions will be aggregated into a coherent single proposition for debate and decision. Left-wing parties (whether in government or not) will tend to be sensitive to demands for greater protection in the workplace, for defending and extending trade union rights, for increased social welfare provision. Environmental pressure groups or parties will pay special attention to demands for improved standards of environmental protection. Proposals for the routeing of new roads may engender opposition from local people whose amenities will be affected by particular routeing proposals, and parties and pressure groups may decide to help those local people by campaigning for changed routes or the total abandonment of such schemes.

Of course, in reality neither parties nor pressure groups are merely responsive institutions, waiting around until they can find causes to promote or cases to defend. Their members and leaders will themselves have agendas of proposals which they wish to press, because they see these as being in the public interest (or in the interests of that part of the general public identifiable as their clientele), and, in the case of parties, because they anticipate that such proposals will be sufficiently popular as to enhance the electoral prospects of the party in future. The British Labour party's attacks on imposition of value-added tax (VAT) on fuel, the strategy of the east German Party of Democratic Socialism (PDS) to act as the advocate of the interests of especially those east Germans disadvantaged by reunification and its consequences, or the positions of parties in Sweden, Norway and Finland regarding membership of the EU in the early 1990s: these all illustrate the linkage between identification of demands and attitudes among the electorate on particular issues, and the desire of parties for electoral success.

Similarly, governments often act upon demands which emanate from within their own ranks: from discussions and bargaining among the coalition partners in government, from the need to react swiftly to some sudden development in domestic or international affairs (severe flooding; a strike among public employees; a threat of war as in the case of the Falkland Islands in 1982 or Kuwait in 1990), or derived from some scheme developed within one of the ministerial bureaucracies, for instance. These inputs can be called *withinputs*, since they originate within government itself. Generally speaking, one could say that most of the business agenda of a government in any one year is some mix of such withinputs and responses to inputs from the public mediated through intermediary groups. The evidence for this can be found in, for example, the Queen's speech each year at the official opening of the British Parliament, outlining the principal features of the government's legislative programme for the forthcoming year, or the Government Declaration presented to the German Bundestag at the start of each new four-year legislative period which serves a similar purpose. Party manifestos at general elections, specific policy proposals which parties or pressure groups may issue from time to time, or the submissions of pressure groups representing particular businesses or social groups in advance of the annual budget in many countries are other instances of this mix of withinputs and public or group demands.

In response to demands, governments produce *outputs*. However, this responsiveness is subject to two major constraints. First, governments cannot do everything at once. They act within the constraints of time (since legislation is a time-consuming business even when it is straightforward and the government has a safe parliamentary majority, and is even more so when legislation involves complicated issues or when a government majority is not assured). Nor can governments afford to do everything they wish to at once. Available resources constitute another constraint (since new legislation always costs some extra money, if only in terms of administrative expenditures, and often large amounts of money, since demands are usually concerned with the desire for extra funds to be spent on roads, schools, old-age pensioners, agricultural or industrial subsidies, policing, and so on).

Outputs may take any of several forms. Parliamentary legislation is the most obvious of these, including the annual budget which governments produce. But sometimes ministers have powers to act without the passage of new legislation, so can issue decrees or regulations (which sometimes, but not always, have to be approved by the legislature). An output may even take the form of desisting from some existing proposed course of action: the abandonment by the Conservative government in Britain in 1994 of the imposition of an already scheduled second tranche of VAT on fuel is an example.

Outputs are one thing; *outcomes* are another. An outcome is what actually changes as the result of an output. This is not always what either the public and intermediary groups on the one hand, or the governmental authorities on the other hand, anticipated or intended. For example, a tax on some item may be increased in anticipation of producing additional revenue for the government, but the additional tax may result in such a decline in sales that the total tax product is less than before, not more: so the government loses revenue because of the tax increase. Speed restrictions on roads to reduce accidents or lessen harmful car-exhaust emissions, new forms of local government taxation to encourage thrift by councillors and their greater responsiveness to the electorate (the 'poll tax' in Britain, for example), new forms of administration in the health service, new systems of weapons procurement for the armed forces: these are other examples where changes made by governments have not always produced the desired effects, where outputs have not been matched by outcomes.[1]

But outcomes are what matter to the public, who are not concerned with the fine print of an act of parliament or the legalistic language of a ministerial regulation. They come to know what has changed as a result of the political process through various forms of *feedback*. This can be as obvious as increased income-tax bills, or higher taxes on cigarettes or petrol, or new regulations about driving or reductions in grants for daughters and sons going to university. They may have changes brought to their attention by the mass media: headlines in a tabloid newspaper, announcements in a radio news broadcast, a discussion in a current affairs programme on television. Certainly pressure groups and political parties (especially parties in opposition when things seemed to have gone wrong, or parties in government when they are going right!) will, by various means, seek to inform the public of what has happened, and why. As a result of feedback, the public will express new demands (repeal of legislation, reinforcement of some changed policy, extension of some change to new categories of people, and so on). And so the cycle of demands, intermediary group action, outputs by the authorities, outcomes and feedback begins all over again.

As well as demands, there is another category of 'input' from the public which is important in the political process. This is the input of *support*. The viability of the political process depends upon the public accepting, or at the very least not rejecting, the structure and functioning of the political system. This acceptance is related to three types of support.

First, there is support for the *authorities*, the term Easton employs to refer to the government in office for the time being. Governments with parliamentary majorities can do more or less anything if they are determined, until the next election comes round at least. However, their decision to act in a certain way, or to act at all, is in fact often constrained by various considerations. These include: the desire to be re-elected next time round;[2] in the case of coalition governments, the need to hold the coalition together and perhaps ensure that it can be re-created after the next election (and therefore not to force through legislation which one coalition partner strongly opposes); the wish to be seen to act democratically as well as responsibly, so that new policies or ministerial decisions are not totally rejected by the electorate, even if some decisions are unpopular; and the requirement that ministerial decrees or new laws have to be implemented, which may well involve persuasion of those responsible for their implementation that there is reasonable popular acceptance of those laws or decisions. In the medium term, low levels of support for the authorities do not damage the viability of the system, provided that fairly frequent opportunities are available to change the government through elections or, possibly, through changes in coalition partnerships, as in the Federal Republic of Germany in 1982.

More significant is the level of support for the *regime*: that is, for the format and procedures of the political process itself, outlined in greater or lesser detail in the constitution. Failure to create such support (for example, the Weimar Republic after the First World War) or its rapid decline (for example, the Fourth Republic in France after the Second World War) almost inevitably results in a change of regime, perhaps accompanied by revolution or its threat. The operation of the political process depends on the acceptability of the 'rules of the game' to the population (see Chapter 12). Even if a minority is opposed to the regime, provided there is sufficiently strong support from the majority, it will probably survive. The lack of such widespread support for the regime was a major factor contributing to the collapse of the communist regime in the GDR in 1989.[3]

A different type of support needed to preserve the cohesion of the political process is support for the *political community*. This is support not directed at the 'rules of the game' but rather concerning the composition of the 'nation'. In some cases, people who are the subject of one political system may wish to belong to another (the nationalist minority in Northern Ireland, for example; and, in the past, the French in Alsace-Lorraine, the Germans in the Saarland before and after the Second World War, or in the Sudetenland in the 1930s, and the German-speaking inhabitants of South Tyrol in Italy, could be mentioned as examples). In other cases, some section of the 'nation' may wish to constitute its own political system, separating from the existing system: nationalists in Scotland or Corsica are examples, though also relevant are the linguistic communities in Belgium, the Basques in Spain, and the Northern League in Italy, where the issue of support involves demands for at least large-scale changes in the regime to accommodate regionalist ambitions and a more autonomous regional identity.[4] Such challenges to the existing political community do not necessarily involve disputes about the *form* of government: the regime. A regional minority might desire to govern itself, but might well be content to do so by using in its own separate state the same parliamentary *procedures* of government employed by the state within which that minority is currently ruled.

The measurement of support is not always a straightforward matter. Support for the government of the day is ultimately indicated by the voting patterns at the next general election, but in the interim can be assessed through voting patterns in other elections (local council elections, elections for regional legislatures, for the EP, perhaps by-elections) and through opinion poll results. Opposition expressed by pressure-group activity and by communications to members of the legislature or to the mass media are other ways by which declining support for the authorities might be indicated. Declining support for the regime or for the political community is more difficult to identify, unless it reaches such proportions that it finds expression through civil disobedience, riots, large-scale emigration, terrorist activities, or even revolution.

The democratic political process, to operate successfully, presupposes the existence of conflict over demands combined with consensus concerning the authorities, the regime and the political community. Without conflict, there is no need for a political process; without consensus, without at least minimum levels of support for the political system, the operation of the political process will break down. This duality of conflict and consensus is discussed further in Chapter 12 in relation to some of the more significant contemporary political developments and problems in western Europe.

The political process in western Europe: some examples

In most states in western Europe, the general patterning of the political process takes very similar forms. Parties and pressure groups aggregate, filter and channel the demands of the public (especially of course those members of the public who are members or active supporters of those parties or pressure groups). They then transmit those processed demands to the authorities (a government dependent upon and responsible to a democratically elected parliament). The authorities deal with such demands, including those demands which (as withinputs) have emerged from within the governmental sphere itself, and produce legislation or regulations and decrees as their responses to them. The feedback process (including the involvement of the mass media) then communicates to the public the changes (outcomes) which have resulted from governmental action.

So in Britain, for instance, the political process is very much concerned with the legislative programme of the government (based largely on its election manifesto), but is also affected by demands transmitted by the parties and by pressure groups to the government and the House of Commons, by day-to-day events and by what other countries are doing. Members of Parliament (MPs) are in communication with constituents and their representative organisations, with local firms and pressure groups, and make known to ministers the most pressing concerns and demands which they, as MPs, have identified. They also communicate these demands to their party organisations; party conference motions, for instance, also reflect such concerns.

The same procedure applies in France and Germany, though with important variations in each case. In France the most important variation is the existence, in addition to the prime minister and cabinet of ministers, of a directly elected president, a president with significant political power. Especially when president and prime minister are from opposing political camps (as has happened during two periods of *cohabitation* in recent years) it becomes more difficult to target demands effectively or identify responsibility for political decisions and outcomes. In Germany, the existence of a federal state structure means that there are strong political subsystems, with their own legislatures and governments, and with their own areas of responsibility, at regional level, so demands have to be directed to the appropriate level of government. In addition, the need for the federal and *Land* levels of government to act in a coordinated manner on certain issues adds a further complication to the political process.

In Sweden and Norway the institutionalised role of interest-groups, their cooperation with government in the development of policy, and the important part played by expert advisers in shaping policy, are important features of the political process.

There is a supranational political process in existence: that of the EU (described in detail in Chapter 11). This differs from national political systems in several important ways. The relative lack of power of the EP, the continuing key role of national governments via the Council of Ministers and the European Council, the still limited range of policies which are matters for European-level decision-making are among the more obvious differences. Demands in the political system of the EU do not derive directly from members of the public, to be then mediated through political parties and pressure groups (though these do have a role). Rather, they are expressed by governments of member states and negotiated among their representatives or between those governments and the Commission. Withinputs play an important role, since many proposals originate from the Commission itself. Feedback is somewhat neglected, because issues dealt with by the EU seem to be of little interest to the mass media or the public (except for the more eccentric or unusual items concerning, for example, regulations for harmonisation of certain foodstuffs or challenges to the authority of the international football federation (FIFA) to regulate the numbers of foreign players in club teams). In any case, they are often complex and technical matters, not easily explicable to the readerships of tabloid newspapers or the viewers of television news programmes.

Political behaviour and the political process

The political process cannot be comprehended solely in terms of constitutional rules and institutional activity. The ways in which individuals behave in political situations – as members of the electorate, as supporters of political movements, as members of parties, as aggrieved citizens, as councillors or elected representatives in the national legislature – may have an effect on the political process. The provisions of the constitution and the rules and procedures which circumscribe the operation of electoral systems, of parliamentary business, of local government activities and so on, act as frameworks for political behaviour, but what actually goes on in politics depends on the decisions individuals make and the ways in which they act.

Political behaviour is affected by the political culture of a country or a community (the concept of political culture was discussed in Chapter 1). Individuals learn about their political culture, about the opportunities and constraints regulating political action, about the structures and rules affecting political institutions, through a process called *political socialisation*. Such political socialisation (involving indirect as well as direct learning about politics) occurs from a very early age, through family influences, the education system, peer-group influences, then later through the mass media, influences in the workplace and in voluntary associations (membership of a church, a sports club, a trade union, a charitable organisation), and of course through participation in politics.[5] People form attitudes, acquire knowledge, and develop judgments about politicians, political issues and political institutions; and their political behaviour is then influenced very much by such socialisation. Theories of electoral behaviour, for example, emphasise the potential importance of the influences of the home (e.g. how a person's parents voted, and what attitude the parents took towards politicians, parties or political issues), of education, of membership of a church or a trade union, of regional location, and so on. These features are assumed to be relevant in explaining how – and why – people voted in elections, or, indeed, whether they bothered to vote at all!

Participation in politics shows significant variations from one country to another, and indeed there can be marked variations within one country at different periods of time (Germany during the Weimar Republic and the Federal Republic; Italy before and after the dramatic changes in the party and electoral systems in the 1990s; Spain in the period of the Franco dictatorship and today, for example).

What might be termed 'orthodox' modes of political participation include participating in elections by voting, but also, for a minority, by campaigning for a candidate or a party, or attending election campaign events; becoming a member or active supporter of a political party or pressure group; taking an active role in some political organisation (perhaps even holding local office as a district party chairman or the secretary of a branch of some national pressure group); or even seeking to be a candidate for local or national public office. In addition, there are 'unorthodox' modes of political participation: taking part in demonstrations, participating in acts of civil disobedience (such as 'sit-ins' or blockades), or joining secret organisations planning illegal actions (as some animal rights protestors have done, as well as members of xenophobic radical right-wing groups or left-wing terrorist organisations).

The greater the frequency or intensity of the mode of political participation, the fewer the numbers who will be involved. Thus while in national elections in most western European countries 70–80 per cent of the electorate turn out to vote, the numbers attending campaign events are normally small; the membership of political parties is usually even smaller (a few hundred thousand for each of the main parties in France, Germany and the UK, and much smaller numbers for smaller parties in those countries, or for parties in small countries such as Ireland, the Netherlands or Portugal), but the percentage of the membership taking an active role in political parties by attending meetings, assisting in election campaigning, or taking the responsibility of local office-holding is extremely low. The same applies to most interest-groups.

Levels of political participation vary among social groups. For example, in most cases fewer women than men participate in politics, at least beyond the basic act of voting in elections. Many reasons have been suggested as accounting for this gender difference: the persistence of traditional attitudes against female participation in politics; the greater difficulty which married women with children have in finding time to attend political events, which often take place at inconvenient times and locations; the prejudice of candidate selection committees against women candidates (or – if the members of these committees claim themselves not to be so prejudiced – their anticipation of potential voter prejudice against women candidates); gender stereotypes which mean that women, if they do participate as active members of political parties, are often allocated what some regard as suitably 'female' responsibilities, as secretaries, or organisers of social events, for instance. There is evidence of change in recent years; though still low, the numbers of women in many national parliaments are increasing, and more women are assuming senior positions in parties and in governments than was the case twenty years ago.[6] This increase in female participation has been aided in some cases by two factors. First, proportional representation electoral systems based on party lists seem more conducive to both the selection and then the election of women than electoral systems based on single-member constituencies, where selection committees have to put forward just one candidate as their nominee. Indeed, selections for a party list which did not now include a significant proportion of women would be so obviously gender-biased as to be a handicap to the party concerned.[7] Second, some parties are imitating the Green party in Germany, and instituting gender quotas for candidate selection for public or party offices.[8]

Gender is not the only social factor that has been identified as having 'skewed' rates of political participation. Ethnic minority groups in some countries have suffered from low levels of political participation (Catholics in Northern Ireland, the offspring of former Commonwealth immigrants in Britain, and non-whites in the Netherlands and France, for example). Prejudice, lack of opportunities for participation and alienation from the dominant political culture are among the reasons for such low levels of participation. Age is another factor. In many of the 'establishment' parties, for instance, there are very few younger members and office-holders under forty years of age are rare indeed. National parliaments have few elected representatives under thirty (partly explicable by the need for aspirants to contest elections unsuccessfully once or twice before being given more favourable opportunities). In part, this is a reflection of growing lack of interest in, or even outright rejection of, orthodox politics by younger generations. 'New politics' parties (such as ecological parties) and extremist parties seem to be more attractive to younger voters, but many younger people seek to participate in politics through association with movements (movements concerned with the environment, peace or anti-militarism, animal rights and anti-racism are among the more popular of these) or pressure-group activities.

Political communication

Finally, the significance of political communication in the political process must be given recognition. The development of the mass media (and especially, since the end of the Second World War, of television) has had significant effects on the political process. Politicians, parties, governments and pressure groups have all had to adapt their behaviour to the knowledge that the press and broadcasting media now closely scrutinise and report upon their statements, decisions and actions. The opportunities and risks presented by the mass media to politicians for communicating with the public in election campaigns and on other occasions have also changed the context within which politics is carried on. Consequently, governments, political parties and the more wealthy or significant pressure groups now employ 'public relations' experts to enable them to exploit these opportunities and avoid, if possible, the risks that a 'bad press' or negative television or radio broadcast can incur.

Political communication includes all forms of communication which have political content (television current affairs programmes, radio news broadcasts, electoral campaign leaflets and posters, letters to legislators from constituents, speeches at party conferences, banners carried in demonstrations, and so on). Without political communication there would be no political process and no politics. It is the means by which demands are transmitted to intermediary groups. It is the way in which those groups convey to the authorities the demands which the groups have discussed and decided are important. The authorities use political communication in their debates and meetings, and in conveying to the public the results of those debates and meetings (outputs). Finally, it is the method by which feedback of outcomes to the public can occur.

Therefore in liberal democracies the ways in which political communication takes place are of central importance. First, there must be freedom of communication (of speech and of other means of expression). The corollary of this is that there must be no censorship. As stated earlier in this chapter, these fundamental requirements are frequently incorporated explicitly in the constitution.[9] Second, the structure of ownership and control of the media of communication constitute an issue highly relevant to the state of democracy. If the state, or some business enterprise or wealthy individual, is able to control the content of all, or a substantial part, of what is published in newspapers and magazines, or broadcast on television and the radio, then the plurality and openness of the media of mass communication are negated or unduly limited, and the democratic political process will suffer in consequence. Some countries therefore have laws or procedures which can be used to restrict the creation of a position of monopoly or dominance in ownership of newspapers or broadcasting companies. In countries where the state has a significant position of dominance or control in broadcasting this is increasingly challenged by those wanting a more diverse and open mass media market.[10] There are numerous developments relevant to this question of democratic access to, and control of, political communication. These include, for example, new broadcasting technologies; the extension of commercially operated broadcasting channels; new computer-related publishing technologies; the Dutch system of allocation of broadcasting time proportionally to the main politico-religious interests in the state; and the emphasis placed on broadcasting by regional interests (for example, in Belgium, Spain and Wales, as well as the constitutional allocation of broadcasting as one of the responsibilities of the *Länder* in Germany under its federal system).

Political communication is significant in another respect also. It is the means by which political culture is transmitted, and indeed itself reflects that political culture. The decentralised structure of the German press, compared to the centralised structure of the French and British press (where almost all the daily and Sunday newspapers of any considerable circulation are published from Paris and London), reflects more than simply differences between the federal structure of the German state and the unitary structure of the French and British states. It also indicates the strength of regional identity in the former case. The bilingual organisation of the Belgian press and broadcasting networks is another example of the linkages between the mass media and political culture.

Comparing political systems and political processes

This chapter has endeavoured to identify the significant similarities which western European states possess as democracies, and to offer a schema within which the differences in the political arrangements of those states can be compared and better understood. Western European democracies share with other democracies a range of features, but the common historical heritage of western Europe (see Chapter 1) has resulted in the political systems which have emerged over the years sharing characteristics which non-European (or, now, the emerging eastern European) democracies do not necessarily possess, or at least do not possess in the same way.

But differences among western European political systems remain, and are often important. The federal systems of Germany, Switzerland, Austria and now Belgium mean that many of the characteristics of those systems and the political processes within them are markedly different from those in more centralised states, such as the UK, France or the Netherlands (see Chapter 10). The powers of the president in France make executive government, and executive–legislative relationships, in that country more complex than they are in, say, Italy or Ireland, or in constitutional monarchies such as the Netherlands or the UK. Switzerland and Norway, having chosen, by decision of the people through referenda, not to be linked to the EU, lack the dimension of political relationships with the EU which member states possess (such as involvement in the policy-making process via the Council of Ministers, participation in elections for the EP, or constraints on policy imposed via the EU), but have instead separate political problems accommodating their political systems to a western Europe otherwise consisting of member states of the EU. The UK's lack of a codified written constitution, the almost unique electoral system employed in Ireland, the establishment of the Green party in Germany's party system, the powers of the regions in Spain: these are other examples of features of western European states which make the political process in each of them in some way 'special'.

The chapters which follow, dealing with political institutions in western Europe, will identify what is common to the political systems and political processes of western European states, but will also reveal the existence of significant differences, and discuss what effects those differences have on the political processes in those states.

Notes

1 An excellent example, though not a European one, was the constitutional amendment (the Eighteenth Amendment, in force from 1920 to its repeal in 1933) prohibiting the sale or consumption of alcoholic beverages in the USA. Though average levels of consumption fell slightly as a consequence of prohibition, drinking habits switched to spirits rather than beer or wine (so leading to greater likelihood of intoxication), and evasion of prohibition led to increases in crime, health problems from consumption of contaminated drinks, hypocrisy and corruption among those charged with enforcement of the law, and other unintended and undesirable effects.

2 In countries which hold by-elections, such as the UK and Ireland, it is possible also that, to remain in office, a government needs to avoid losing seats between general elections, if its overall majority is small (as was the case with the Labour government in 1978–79, and the Conservative government in 1995–96, for instance). Defections of supporters in the legislature also need to be avoided; the SPD–FDP government in the Federal Republic of Germany (1970–72) and the Fine Gael–Labour government in Ireland (1986–87) are examples of coalitions losing their majorities by defections, and thus facing great difficulties in passing any legislation.

3 One interpretation in these terms could be that until about September 1989 there was decline in support for the authorities (the Socialist Unity Party (SED) dictatorship); then came a period of decline in support for the regime itself (communist rule); and this was fol-

lowed by decline in support for the political community, with the very existence of the GDR as a separate state being challenged by pressures for reunification. Of course, even in the first of these periods, there were those who rejected both the regime and the political community.

4 The developments in the early 1990s in what used to be Yugoslavia provide an extreme example of what happens when acceptance of a defined political community disappears. Going outside Europe, the situation in Sri Lanka (where Tamils demand independent status), in Kashmir, and of the Kurds in Turkey and Iraq are other examples of problems concerning support for the political community.

5 For immigrants into a country, political socialisation into the culture of the host country may have to be a more overt and intensive process, possibly involving language learning as well. The efforts made to convey information about politics and opportunities for political participation which are made in countries with high levels of immigration, such as the USA and Australia, and, in western Europe, Switzerland, Sweden and Germany, illustrate the importance of political socialisation as an instrument of political integration.

6 Recent examples include Margaret Thatcher (Conservative party leader and British prime minister); Edith Cresson (prime minister of France); Mary Robinson (president of Ireland); Vigdís Finnbogadóttir (president of Iceland); Gro Harlem Brundtland (prime minister of Norway); Heidi Simonis (prime minister of the German *Land* of Schleswig-Holstein); Margaret Beckett (deputy leader of the British Labour party); and there are numerous examples of female ministers, including even one in Switzerland, a country that has been slow to encourage female participation in politics.

7 The Irish electoral system, though not properly classifiable as a party-list-based proportional representation system, also favours female candidates more than the British or French single-member constituency system, since it does involve parties selecting several candidates for each constituency. Interestingly, the German system uses both single-member constituencies *and* party lists, and it is clear that women have significantly greater chances of being selected for (and then elected from) party lists than constituency seats. For details of these electoral systems, see Chapter 4.

8 The German Greens have a rule that there should be equal numbers
   of women and men on party lists for local, regional and national
   elections, for instance, and try to ensure through gender quotas
   that party offices are shared equally between women and men. The
   German Social Democratic Party (SPD) has adopted a somewhat
   less rigorous minimum restriction, and the Christian Democratic
   Union (CDU) more recently has also taken steps to ensure that
   greater numbers of women are nominated for party offices. The
   British Labour Party began experimenting with controversial
   'women-only' shortlists for candidate selection in some constituencies after the 1992 general election, and has introduced rules for the
   Parliamentary Labour Party regarding the election of the shadow
   cabinet designed to ensure that more women are elected to that
   committee.

9 Of course, even in the most democratic of states there are limits
   placed by the law on freedom of speech and other forms of expression. Libel and slander laws, laws against stirring up racial hatred,
   blasphemy laws and limits on election campaign expenditures are
   examples. However, these laws restricting freedom of expression
   can be justified on the grounds that one right (that of freedom of
   expression) conflicts with other rights (such as protection of freedom of religious belief, or protection of fair competition in elections),
   and that therefore some compromise has to be made. But these
   limits do not amount normally to 'censorship', which means the
   prohibition before publication of communications deemed damaging on political or ideological grounds, the banning of publications
   on grounds of political incorrectness, or the imposition of penalties
   after publication because of the political content of some article or
   broadcast.

10 The French state's control of broadcasting in the period before the
   Law on Audiovisual Communication of 1982, the dominance
   of the Springer publishing 'empire' in the Federal Republic of
   Germany, the British (1988–94) and Irish (1972–94) government
   bans on broadcasts by those associated with terrorism (directed
   especially at Sinn Fein and the Irish Republican Army (IRA)), and
   the controversy concerning the former Italian prime minister
   Berlusconi's utilisation of his own broadcasting and publishing
   businesses for party political purposes are some of the issues in the
   past twenty years which have been matters of public debate relating
   to democratic freedoms of political communication.

Reference

Easton, D. (1965) *A Systems Analysis of Political Life*, Wiley, New York.

Further reading

Allum, P. (1995) *State and Society in Western Europe*, Cambridge, Polity.
Schwarzmantel, J. (1994) *The State in Contemporary Society. An Introduction*, London, Harvester-Wheatsheaf.

3

Sources of political conflict

Pluralism and liberal democracy

As liberal democracies, the countries of western Europe are committed to the pursuit of social and political pluralism. Within a pluralist perspective, political differences are seen as inevitable. They are a result of people's differing social values, individual beliefs and material circumstances. The diversity of political ideas is not only recognised but also highly valued. It follows that freedom of opinion and expression are considered fundamental rights in liberal democratic states. Some state forms have displayed little tolerance of political conflict and have attempted to overcome or at least by-pass such conflict by imposing a single state ideology. In contrast, liberal democracies are committed to open political competition, reflecting the diversity of political opinion within civil society. Political power is dispersed through institutional checks and balances and not controlled by a single institution or political leader.

In western Europe, commitment to political pluralism is not simply a matter of principle. It was considerably strengthened through the inter-war experience of German nazism and Italian fascism. Each was an attempt to unify a nation through a monolithic state ideology and state repression of 'undesirable' political and social activity. Each proved untenable within its own country and the virulent nationalism it engendered led to a world war. For western Europe, the value of pluralism has been further underlined by the failure of the communist experiment undertaken by the Soviet Union during the cold war years.

Given that pluralism is a guiding principle for modern western European society, the problem remains that if political differences are allowed to escalate, they can lead to conflict expressed in divided communities, social instability or even civil war. How can the fragmentation of society be avoided under a pluralist system? Liberal democracies work on the basis that, properly channelled, different views can be contained and resolved and that the resulting consensus helps to promote a vital, peaceful and stable society. Chapter 2 of this book has described how, in a liberal democracy, the resolution of conflicts depends on the acceptance of 'ground rules' as expressed in accepted political procedure (often laid down in a written constitution), in effective institutions of government and in competing political parties and pressure groups. Later chapters investigate in more detail the way in which democratic principles are put into practice through the institutions of government. This chapter explores some of the common social and political conflicts that have affected the countries of western Europe and the attempt to 'tame' them by channelling them into the democratic process.

Social and ideological bases of political conflict

In political science, the term 'cleavages' refers to social divisions which are sufficiently serious to form the basis of opposing collective identities and to give rise to organisations to promote or protect these collective interests. Some of the most significant, or 'salient', cleavages for western European countries have been class, religion and region. All of these have inspired strong loyalties and have been expressed through politically active interest-groups and political parties. Through political parties in government, they have helped to shape the political life of western European countries. Why should these particular divisions (rather than, for example, age or gender) have become the definitive ones? Also, the cleavages we have noted are not equally salient in all the countries of western Europe. Why are regional differences, for example, politically more significant in Spain than in Germany? According to the political theorists Lipset and Rokkan, the answer to these questions lies in the timing of some key historical developments in each of the European countries.

Lipset and Rokkan (1967) argued that the extension of voting rights to mass publics was crucial for the consolidation of political 'cleavages' between sections of western European populations. Prior to mass enfranchisement, political parties had represented a small, wealthy and educated electorate. There were no great differences in social or material circumstances within the European voting publics. In Britain, for example, prior to the first moves to extend the franchise in 1832, the electorate for the House of Commons comprised less than 5 per cent of the adult male population (Kavanagh 1985:4). At this time, then, parties did not represent competing social cleavages, but were the means used by a small, cohesive elite to exert political influence.

With the extension of the franchise, new political parties emerged, alongside the existing ones, to channel the interests of citizens who had previously had no voice in parliaments. These parties represented new, radical ideologies. Moreover, they linked these ideologies to demands based on differing sectional interests within the population. For example, socialist ideals were linked to the interests of the industrial working class. The creation of new parties as formal channels of representation raised public awareness of collective identities and helped to strengthen them. Workers became aware that their personal interests and problems over wages, working conditions and housing were shared by other workers. As collective identities became stronger, they in turn provided a stable pool of voters (or 'electoral clientele') for political parties. In each country, these developments 'froze' the new party systems into a pattern which reflected social differences at the time of mass enfranchisement.

Several factors determined which cleavages were most salient at the time of mass enfranchisement. Lipset and Rokkan suggested that the timing of two 'revolutions' was particularly important in each country's development. The first was the national revolution: the consolidation of state authority throughout its territory. The second was the industrial revolution which triggered industrialisation and urbanisation. Eventually, these two revolutions were to take place throughout western Europe. However, mass enfranchisement occurred at different stages in the development of these two major social upheavals, resulting in the formation of different cleavage patterns from country to country. Lipset and Rokkan identified four basic sources of conflict with the potential to mobilise mass publics: the cleavage between subject and dominant cultures (now usually referred to as the centre–periphery cleavage); the church–state cleavage; the cleavage between the primary and secondary economy (the urban–rural cleavage); and the class cleavage. The first two were the direct product of national revolutions in western European countries; the third and fourth were prompted by industrial revolutions. The common experience of the national and industrial revolutions created the potential for the development of any of the four basic cleavages in the countries of western Europe. However, depending on each country's special circumstances, some conflicts were never to become salient enough to channel political competition, some were resolved, and some, although salient, were marginalised by more pressing conflicts.

The centre–periphery cleavage
Prior to the national revolution, a state's control of areas at the periphery of its territory was often no more than nominal. Peripheral areas often had distinctive local cultures or even a separate language, and had developed their own ways of regulating the life of their community. States sought to centralise control, consolidating their political authority within their territorial boundaries by enforcing standard laws, markets and a common state culture. Inevitably, there was a backlash from communities in outlying areas, where people wanted to keep their independence from the emerging central authority. In some

countries, the battle between the dominant (centre) and subject (peripheral) cultures became bitter and entrenched. In Spain, for example, distinctive groups such as the Basques and the Catalans fought to preserve their language and culture from eradication by the Castilian state.

The countries of western Europe achieved at least a temporary resolution of the centre–periphery dispute, which was reflected in each country's state structure. Britain and France, for example, became centralised unitary states, whereas Germany and Switzerland each adopted a form of federalism, leaving the component regions a measure of autonomy in relation to the centre. The importance of the national revolution and its settlement is reflected in each country's constitution and sometimes even in its name. The French constitution proclaims France to be an 'indivisible' republic; the UK's full title is the United Kingdom of Great Britain and Northern Ireland; and Germany is a Federal Republic.

The church–state cleavage

The efforts of the state to consolidate its position inevitably brought it into conflict with the existing authority of the church. In France, the struggle between church and state was intense. Here, the centralising state aimed to create a progressive and explicitly secular society. In particular, it was determined to establish universal state education, free from the control of the church. The church–state conflict became entangled with that between the centre and periphery, as the inhabitants of reactionary outlying areas fought to retain their Catholic identity. In other countries, religious conflict focused on denominational differences. In Germany, the main religious divide fell between Protestant and Catholic sectors of society. Here, as in the Netherlands, Catholics were considered second-class citizens and Catholicism became a focus of identity for these minorities. In the Scandinavian countries, where the state Lutheran church was liberal in outlook, moralist-evangelist parties developed to represent the more fundamentalist religious stance of a substantial sector of the population.

The urban–rural cleavage

The cleavage between the interests of urban and rural populations was evident even in medieval times in the form of differences between the peasants (often led by the landed nobility) and the merchants and tradesmen of the towns. It intensified with the European industrial revolutions and growth in world trade. In many countries, this conflict was expressed through the opposition of conservative-agrarian and liberal-radical parties. In Britain, this conflict had been submerged by the class conflict by the late nineteenth century. However, urban–rural divisions continued as a primary determinant of political competition in many western European countries well into the twentieth century. Urban–rural conflicts developed as the emerging cities came to control the country's wealth, cultural norms and political decision-making, often at the expense of the rural areas. The more ruthless the control exercised by the cities, the more likely it was that the potential for urban–rural conflict would be realised. In the Scandinavian countries, where the cities controlled national political life, the peasants rebelled against political marginalisation and economic exploitation. The legacy of this struggle could be found in the distinctive agrarian parties which formed in the Scandinavian countries to promote the interests of rural communities. In recent years, these agrarian parties have lost their distinctive 'rural' identity and have transformed into 'centre' parties, competing within the predominant socio-economic (class) cleavage. Since the Second World War, there has been a considerable expansion and standardisation of public services throughout western European countries. This has helped to reduce tensions between urban and rural areas, leaving the urban–rural cleavage less significant for contemporary political competition.

The class cleavage

Class conflict developed in every western European country as a result of the industrial revolution. Large numbers of people were recruited to work the new heavy industries and the expanding farming and forestry industries. Everywhere, workers protested against their harsh working conditions and short-term contracts. They formed labour unions and then socialist political parties to fight their cause. In Britain and the Scandinavian countries, the established parties and classes resisted the demands of the working class, but did not tend to engage in active repression. In these countries, broad-based, pragmatic centre-left parties formed to represent the needs of the working class through parliamentary channels. In some other countries, such as Austria, France, Germany, Italy and Spain, the established classes took repressive action against working-class activism, with the result that socialist parties in these countries developed a more radical stance. These socialist parties were uncompromising over questions of ideology and strongly bound to their clientele group of industrial workers.

Ideological 'families' in western European party systems

Given the number and complexity of those factors which could and did influence that first consolidation of the party system in each country, it is perhaps surprising how similar western European party systems turned out to be. In particular, a number of ideological 'families' of parties evolved in all manner of different settings in response to the social cleavages noted above. These included liberals, conservatives, Christian democrats, social democrats and communists. In each country, the relevant party of each ideological family developed its own priorities according to the specific needs of its electoral clientele. Nevertheless, shared ideological positions bound each family across the national boundaries of western Europe.

Liberals were a powerful force from the mid-nineteenth century onwards. Their aims at this time included resistance to the idea of absolute monarchy, the promotion of constitutional government, the defence of individual liberties and property, and the extension of the franchise. Liberals were trenchant secularists, particularly where faced with a reactionary church as in France or Italy. Today, it is difficult to appreciate the radicalism of these claims, as they are all now firmly established principles of liberal democratic government. In fact, liberals have been more successful than any other ideological family in influencing the philosophy and political institutions of western Europe.

In contemporary politics they are victims of their own success. Their ideas are so widely accepted within the constitutional order and by other parties that they no longer have an independent profile. Moreover, many liberal parties have been unable to sustain a distinct electoral clientele. While liberals agree on the importance of defending both individual liberties and property, factional divisions occur over which should be given priority when these two principles come into conflict with one another. While this key argument has proved damaging to many liberal parties, it has established them as parties of the centre, placed between the more polarised positions of socialist and conservative parties. This central position has made liberal parties quite flexible when it comes to participating in government coalitions. The ability to work with moderate parties of the left or right has helped to keep them actively involved in parliamentary politics in spite of their rather vague profile.

Conservatives were identifiable from the start of the nineteenth century through their opposition to the ideals of the French Revolution and liberal radicalism. The conservative ideology is strongly linked to its country of origin, as each conservative party aims to defend the traditions and established interests of its own nation. While attachment to the nation is shared by conservatives, conservatism finds a different expression from country to country. This makes the essence of conservatism rather elusive. However, in addition to their nationalism, there are some common factors which help to unite conservatives as an ideological family. One is the defence of private property and private enterprise. In the post-war years, this stance has prompted a rejection of state intervention in the economy. While conservatives have become reconciled to the principle of a welfare net, more radical factions and parties are committed to 'rolling back the state'. A profound pessimism about human nature leads conservatives to uphold principles of authority and law and order.

Since the Second World War, Christian democratic parties have played a major role in many western European party systems. Perhaps the most distinctive characteristics of Christian democracy have been its integrative nature and its commitment to pluralism. These are reflected in its electoral appeal, its ideology and its policies. Christian democracy began largely as a working-class movement but extended its appeal to the middle classes. Except in the Netherlands, Christian democracy was essentially a Catholic movement until the 1880s, when, starting in Germany, Switzerland and France, it also became a vehicle for Protestants. In many countries, Christian democratic parties have been able to bridge the class and denominational divisions which marked the pre-war electorate.

In terms of ideology, Christian democracy has incorporated many of the views held by liberals, conservatives and socialists within a wider framework of moral and Christian principles. In common with liberals, Christian democrats uphold human rights (including property rights) and value individual initiative. However, Christian democrats criticise liberal secularism and are less 'individualist' than liberals in that they value the individual as part of a social and religious community. Christian democrats share a common outlook with conservatives in their view of the evolutionary development of society, but they are not necessarily 'traditionalist' in the sense of being opposed to change. With conservatives, they strongly oppose communism. In common with socialists, Christian democrats are committed to social solidarity, but on behalf of society as a whole rather than any particular sector of society. They believe that the state should take responsibility for the weakest in society and should guide the economy, but do not advocate excessive state intervention. Certainly in the early post-war period, their ideas on social solidarity and social welfare were based on their belief that the spiritual welfare of the community took priority over the material interests of private individuals or any class.

The experience of the Second World War gave a boost to these values and saw a surge of popular support for Christian democratic parties. These parties were closely involved in post-war reconciliation through European supranational organisations such as the European Coal and Steel Community (ECSC) and European Economic Community (EEC), and they remain firm advocates of the EU. During the course of the post-war period, the Christian identity of these parties has been eroded, leaving them as representatives of a broad centre-right or centre-left electorate. However, certain issues still reveal their roots. While Christian democrats have gradually come to accept that questions of contraception, abortion or divorce should be left to the private individual, they still adopt a 'pro-family' stance. Also, they can be firm advocates of church schools in the perennial conflict between the church and state over the control of education.

The rise of the socialists at the turn of the twentieth century displaced the liberals and radicals as the main opposition to establishment groups and values. Socialist parties were formed exclusively to represent the interests of the working class against those of the propertied and entrepreneurial classes. From the start, the socialist movement was torn by conflicting ideological views. The key split concerning party formation was provoked by Marx's 1848 Communist Manifesto and the 1917 Russian Revolution. Marxism-Leninism, the official ideology of the Soviet Union and later of the countries of eastern Europe, was to divide western European socialists into two main groups: socialist reformists who were willing to work within the liberal democratic framework; and communists who were committed to the destruction of bourgeois democracy.

Socialists have attempted to secure public ownership of the means of production, often through the nationalisation of key industries. After the Second World War, they were often instrumental in the expansion of the welfare state to cover areas such as education, health, unemployment and pensions. Since these early achievements, they have tended to become more moderate and pragmatic 'social democratic' groups, largely in order to secure a greater share of electoral support. There is little public support in contemporary western Europe for a break from capitalism, or even for the large-scale nationalisation of industry. This has left socialists and social democrats to campaign for a more equitable distribution of resources within the framework of a capitalist, free-market economy.

The anti-system communist parties gained in respectability in western Europe through their work in resistance movements during the Second World War. They promised to make radical changes to government, which secured them a large following in some countries, particularly in France and Italy. However, their ties with the Soviet Union hampered their integration into the post-war party systems and their reluctance to modernise increasingly restricted their electorate to the industrial working class and a few intellectuals. In the 1970s, the communists in France, Italy and Spain tried to become more independent of the Soviet Union, experimenting with a new style of 'Eurocommunism'. However, this made no lasting impact on western European voters. The collapse of the Soviet Union following the 1989 eastern European revolutions has robbed the western European communist parties of much of their rationale. They are currently revising their programmes to try to present a more modern image to their electorates, in most cases as radicals with a leaning towards environmentalism.

Other sources of political competition

Lipset and Rokkan's work has been enormously influential in the work of those political scientists who compare sources of political conflict in western European societies and the way in which such conflicts are expressed and represented.[1] Certainly, the period of consolidation of the party systems following the primary mobilisation of the western European electorates proved remarkably long-lasting, beginning in the 1920s and lasting well into the 1960s. During this time, much of the European electorates' voting behaviour could be accounted for by the cleavages identified by Lipset and Rokkan. From the 1970s onwards, voting behaviour began to change as old sources of political conflict either lost or gained in relevance, or were supplemented by new concerns.

Before looking at explanations for these developments in western European party systems, it is important to point out that the four basic cleavages identified by Lipset and Rokkan cannot account for all of the political conflicts represented in European parliaments since the 1920s. Some electorally significant parties have campaigned on an ideological platform which is not derived exclusively from centre–periphery, religious, urban–rural or class conflicts. During the 1930s many countries, including Austria, Germany and Italy, had experienced a wave of support for parties of the extreme right. Since the Second World War some new parties, such as the Poujadists in France, have been unique to their own country. Green or alternative parties have emerged throughout Europe, and can be seen as members of a new ideological family which crosses national boundaries.

Lipset and Rokkan's analysis assumed that party representation is based on identifiable social cleavages within a plural society. However, some parties have not attempted to represent the interests of a particular section of society against those of other sections. Instead, they have tried to unite a whole society behind them, employing a populist approach. In the late 1950s and early 1960s, the French Gaullist party was little more than a personal vehicle for de Gaulle. Party activists and supporters were motivated by loyalty to de Gaulle rather than to his party. The General saw himself as above politics, and did not operate within the traditional 'tendencies' (cleavages) of French partisan competition. Instead, he appealed to 'the nation' to endorse his leadership. The nation obliged, and de Gaulle's varied electorate included farmers, workers and business people. The contemporary 'Gaullist' Rally for the Republic (RPR) has retained some of the ideological values of the earlier party, but has shed the early populist approach and now campaigns on a more conventional basis for the vote of a centre-right electorate. A more extreme populist approach can be found in the new parties of the extreme right which have gained prominence since the 1980s.

Lipset and Rokkan's analysis assumed that voters choose on the basis of their social background and on the ideological views derived from these. These assumptions have proved more appropriate for some countries than for others. In Britain and West Germany there was a fairly clear pattern of sectional voting during the early post-war years. Taking the example of West Germany, many workers tended to hold left-of-centre views and to vote for the SPD. In France, however, the link between social indicators and voting choice has been comparatively weak. Ideological views were strongly held in France, but were not necessarily consistent with a voter's social background, making it difficult to tell whether a French voter's choice was motivated more by social background or by ideological stance. Also, until the development of presidential election campaigns beginning in the mid-1960s, French parties had not fought elections on the basis of a clearly defined policy programme. Instead, they had tried to convey to the electorate the particular set of ideals they represented. While parties are now expected to define their policy aims, abstract ideals still play an important part in French elections. For example, the Socialist Party (PS) has stood for an egalitarian society, often expressed as 'social progress'. Overall then, French voting motivations are relatively difficult to assess. A vote for the PS might have been cast primarily because the voter was working class, because he or she identified socialists with a progressive or even anti-clerical stance, or (at least during the 1970s and early 1980s) because the PS advocated socialist solutions in government policy.

Cleavage change and its implications for party competition

Since the late 1960s, there has been evidence of change in the 'frozen' party systems of western Europe. The traditional parties are becoming less successful in channelling the vote as many voters opt to vote for 'new' parties, to vote for different parties from election to election, or not to vote at all. This raises a number of questions. Given recent developments, do social cleavages still act as sources of political conflict? Do they still define political competition? Or is there another explanation for political conflict and political competition in contemporary western European countries? There is as yet no clear answer to these questions: the following sections can only note some possible explanations.

While the western European party systems consolidated (and stagnated), the social cleavages which underpinned them were changing continuously. Some authors have identified the Second World War as a crucial turning point for European societies (see Kirchheimer 1966). The turbulent inter-war period and the experience of the Second World War destroyed the rigid class structures which had been typical of the western European democracies. As a result of the war, many of the propertied classes had lost their savings and assets, women had joined the workforce in areas previously reserved for men, and there was a new sense of social equality which meant that the old pre-war hierarchies could not be re-established. In the years which followed, the expansion of the welfare state was fundamentally to change the nature of social and political conflict. A massive expansion in secondary education produced literate and numerate populations. This had implications both for the workforce, as employees became socially mobile, and for the electorate's attitude towards their government. The western European countries began to reach the limits of industrialisation, leading to long-term mass unemployment and new patterns of work and leisure. Writing about France, Mendras and Cole (1991) have characterised the changes in society over the last thirty-five years as nothing short of a 'Second French Revolution'. Throughout western Europe, profound social change has altered the way in which the major cleavages based on class and religion are translated into party competition in western Europe.

Economic change and changes in the class vote
Over a number of decades, a pattern has emerged in the development of the workforce in the countries of western Europe. The primary sector (agriculture), in decline since industrialisation, has continued to shrink. The economy has moved through a phase in which the secondary sector (manufacturing industries such as steel, ship-building and car manufacturing) has dominated. This is in turn being replaced by an increasing reliance on the tertiary sector based on new, light industries and services such as electronics and banking. While all countries appear to be

following this pattern, some have developed at a leisurely pace, whereas others have accelerated over recent years to catch up with their more advanced neighbours (see Table 3.1). Britain and (West) Germany have taken a comparatively slow route from an agricultural economy though one based on manufacturing to a service-based one. In France, Italy and Spain, modernisation of the economy began later, but has proceeded more rapidly. Between the 1960s, when Franco first permitted a relaxation of his principle of autarky, and the mid-1980s, Spain has seen a complete overhaul in the economy. In Greece, the process of modernisation began very late, but the recent pace of development has been nothing short of precipitous.

Where an accelerated development has taken place, it appears that the phase of industrialisation (where the emphasis is on the manufacturing sector) has been truncated, often peaking at a lower level than in those countries characterised by slower development. Since 1960, there has been a universal rise in the percentage of people working in the tertiary sector. Given these developments, it is likely that socio-economic differences which used to be expressed in a simple class cleavage between workers and entrepreneurs might shift to conflicts more relevant to a workforce dominated by the tertiary sector. Contemporary socio-economic cleavages might develop, for example, between public sector and private sector employees; or between people dependent on welfare payments and those in a position to pay for private sector services. Relevant indicators of a 'modernised' socio-economic cleavage might be expected to include a person's education, earnings, security of employment and tax status.

Currently, western European party politics is still dominated by the class cleavage established during the phase of industrialisation. In the longer term, though, these profound changes in society and in the workforce are certain to influence political competition. One early casualty of the ageing of the class conflict has been the ideological family of communist parties. The communists, who saw their vote decline irretrievably in the post-war period, had relied for support on a shrinking pool of blue-collar workers based in the manufacturing industries. In time, unless they are able to adapt their appeal, other parties also might find

Table 3.1 Percentage of total labour force engaged in agricultural, manufacturing and service sectors in selected countries, 1960–90

	1960	*1970*	*1980*	*1990*
United Kingdom				
agriculture	4.7	3.2	2.6	2.1
manufacturing	47.7	44.7	37.7	29.0
services	47.6	52.0	59.7	68.9
West Germany				
agriculture	14.0	8.6	5.3	3.4
manufacturing	47.0	48.5	43.7	39.8
services	39.1	42.9	51.0	56.8
France				
agriculture	23.2	13.5	8.7	6.1
manufacturing	38.4	39.2	35.9	29.9
services	38.5	47.2	55.4	64.0
Italy				
agriculture	32.6	20.2	14.3	9.0
manufacturing	33.9	39.5	37.9	32.4
services	33.5	40.3	47.8	58.6
Spain				
agriculture	38.7	27.1	19.3	11.8
manufacturing	30.3	35.5	36.1	33.4
services	31.0	37.4	44.6	54.8
Greece				
agriculture	57.1	40.8	30.3	24.5
manufacturing	17.4	25.0	30.2	27.4
services	25.5	34.2	39.5	48.2

Source: Organisation for Economic Cooperation and Development (1985; 1992).

themselves at a disadvantage as their traditional voting clientele is eroded through social change.

The impact of secularisation on the religious vote
While there is still evidence of a religious cleavage in European society, religious life has changed considerably during the post-

war period. Contemporary western European populations can be described as 'unchurched' in the sense that many people retain broadly Christian beliefs and a nominal attachment to the Catholic or Protestant church, but do not regularly attend mass or church services (Davie 1992:223–5). In surveys carried out in ten European countries in 1981, only 12 per cent of respondents had no religious denomination (see Table 3.2).[2] The Netherlands is unusual in that the sector of society with no religious affiliation is, at 35 per cent, larger than either of the Protestant and Catholic sectors.

In spite of generally high levels of religious affiliation, there has been a dramatic decline in religious practice (religiosity) in western Europe during the post-war period. In general, religiosity remains higher in the Catholic countries of southern Europe than the Protestant north. The Irish Republic is a special case: its overwhelmingly Catholic population displays by far the highest levels of religiosity in western Europe. This is explained by the fact that religious identity is bound up with the conflict over the Irish state and national identity, so that territorial and religious identities reinforce one another. Religiosity is also high in Catholic Italy and Spain. France corresponds to 'northern' behaviour in this respect: even though it is a Catholic country, church attendance is as low as in Protestant Denmark. Belgium is starkly polarised in religious belief and practice. It has a higher than average share of people without denomination, yet those who are affiliated tend to be regular churchgoers.

What is not yet clear is whether the trend toward secularisation will continue, eventually eroding religious values as well as religious practice. This seems likely, as younger people in Europe are less attached to traditional beliefs than older people, are less likely to have ties with the church and are less regular churchgoers. These appear to be 'generational' rather than 'life-cycle' differences. That is, younger Europeans are likely to retain a secular orientation rather than become more religious as they grow older. Certainly, in France, the decline in religious practice began with young people and was noticeable from 1965. It was not until 1970 that a real drop in the level of religiosity was

Table 3.2 Religious affiliation in selected countries (percentage of respondents)

	Catholic	Protes-tant	Non conf.[a]	Other	None	N/A[b]
Catholic countries:						
Belgium	72	2	–	2	15	9
Eire	96	2	–	2	–	–
France	71	1	–	28	–	–
Italy	93	–	–	1	6	–
Spain	90	–	–	1	9	–
Protestant countries:						
Britain	11	67	7	6	9	–
Denmark	1	91	–	3	5	–
'Mixed' countries:						
Germany	41	48	–	1	9	1
Netherlands	32	18	8	4	35	3
N. Ireland	25	29	41	5	–	–

Source: adapted from Giorgi (1992:644, Table 1).
[a] Non conf. = Non conformist, i.e. non-mainstream Protestants, including Protestants outside the Anglican church in Britain and Northern Ireland and neo-Calvinists in the Netherlands.
[b] N/A = no answer.

recorded for the population in general (Mendras and Cole 1991: 65).

How have these changes in religious life affected the translation of social cleavages into political competition? For many countries, there was in past years a clear connection between religious affiliation and party choice. Now, a prominent denominational vote is found only in Northern Ireland, where the majority of practising and non-practising voters alike cast their vote according to their denomination, Catholic or Protestant.[3] Again, this special case is explained by the overlap between religious identity and the constitutional conflict over the border between Northern Ireland and the Irish Republic.

Elsewhere, it appears that denomination is in itself no longer the best indicator of how religion affects the vote. A voter's religiosity now has more impact on voting choice than his or her denomination. That is, for example, the vote of those who are only nominal Catholics is more likely to be determined by factors other than their religion. However, religion is likely to be decisive in the vote of those Catholics who attend mass regularly. Evidence for a link between religiosity and party choice can be found in countries with very different religious backgrounds, including Catholic Italy, Protestant Norway and countries with a 'mixed' denominational background such as the Netherlands and (West) Germany. In all countries, the non-religious tend to vote disproportionately for parties of the left, including the social democrats, socialists, communists and greens. Religious voters tend to vote for the centre-right, particularly for Christian democratic parties. This means that the widespread decline in religiosity has the potential to undermine the traditional electoral strongholds of the centre-right in western European countries. In France, for example, Catholics had traditionally voted for parties of the centre-right. Now this tendency is only valid for practising Catholics. The number of practising Catholics in France fell from 25 per cent of the electorate in 1967 to 14 per cent in 1986 (Frears 1991:132–3, Table 11.2).

Changes in voting behaviour

The widespread social changes noted above have prompted a response from political parties. In order to increase their share of the vote, political parties have tried to adapt to social change and to extend their appeal to voters beyond their 'natural' clientele established with the freezing of party systems. During the postwar expansion of the welfare state, parties vied with one another in their promises of better public services if they were elected to office. The focus of electoral campaigning shifted from the representation of sectional interests to the provision of government services for public consumption. Party organisation has changed too, giving less priority to local branch organisations and public meetings and more to links with government bodies and the media (see Chapter 5).

There are also signs that voters are changing. One significant development is a decline in voters' 'partisanship', or loyalty to a particular party. New generations of voters are less likely to identify so strongly with a party that their vote can be predicted with confidence from election to election. For example, in West Germany, the percentage of non-identifiers – those who had no attachment to any particular party – rose from 13.3 per cent in the federal election of 1980 to 25.2 per cent in 1987, the last federal election before German unification (Schultze 1987).

It seems likely that a decline in partisanship is related to changes in political socialisation. During the period of party system consolidation between the 1920s and 1960s, young voters entered the electorate having been nurtured within a particular voting tradition. Family voting loyalties tended to be reinforced through social contacts and at work. This was particularly marked where opposing subcultures lived quite separate lives, as in Belgium and the Netherlands. The expansion of educational opportunities and the increasing tendency to move to a different region to find work have changed this monolithic pattern of political socialisation. Voters are more likely to come into contact with conflicting political ideas, and are forced to decide their own position for themselves.

Partisan voting appears to be giving way to issue voting. Rather than voting automatically for 'their' party, voters are increasingly likely to compare the policies advocated by the competing political parties and to vote for the party whose policies are most likely to benefit their personal interests over the years until the next election. The particular issues of the day are likely to have a much greater impact on this pragmatic style of voting than on the traditional partisan vote. Particularly those parties competing over socio-economic differences must expect to work harder for their votes than in the days of relatively straightforward class competition. The rise in public sector employment has produced a sizeable 'new' middle class of salaried workers who are well educated and socially mobile. These voters tend to display less party loyalty and to cast their vote more independently than those who can be placed in a traditional class category.

Since the 1970s, many European countries have experienced periods of increased voter volatility. One concern is that the tendency for people to change their vote from election to election could destabilise the party systems of western Europe. While voter volatility can certainly be unsettling, it need not destabilise the system if votes are swapped between mainstream parties rather than given to peripheral or anti-system parties. Since the 1980s, voting support for the usual parties of government has in many countries been noticeably eroded by gains made by 'challenger' parties (Mackie 1995:182), but it is not yet clear whether this trend will continue. Perhaps a more serious problem in the longer term is the tendency for more people to abstain from voting. Since the 1960s, most countries in western Europe have experienced falling turnouts at national elections (see Table 3.3). This trend would seem to indicate a decline in confidence in party government itself, rather than disaffection with a particular party.

New sources of political conflict

From the 1970s onwards, new conflicts began to find representation in western European elections and party systems. In some cases, these concerned familiar cleavages and ideologies, given a new lease of life by changing social and economic circumstances.

In many countries, the uneasy peace between the centre and periphery was broken in the 1970s when there was a resurgence of regional (or peripheral) nationalism. Regionalist groups emerged to claim recognition of their nationalist identities, demanding greater concessions to self-rule or even advocating separation from their host states. Particularly affected were Belgium, Britain, France, Italy and Spain. A common cause of conflict between the centre and periphery was the internal distribution of resources: peripheral areas believed that they were bearing the brunt of the economic recession of the early 1970s.

Table 3.3   Turnout in national elections in western Europe since the 1960s[a]

	1960s	1970s	1980s	*Most recent election (to 1995)*
Austria	92.7	91.4	87.9	83.7
Belgium[b]	85.4	85.7	86.9	86.2
Denmark	87.1	87.0	84.8	82.2
Finland	84.7	80.8	76.1	71.4
France	74.8	80.6	68.9	65.6
Germany	84.7	90.2	84.1	76.9
Greece	81.7	79.4	81.5	81.5
Iceland	89.6	88.8	87.7	87.6
Ireland	73.5	75.7	71.5	67.5
Italy[b]	89.7	89.2	83.8	82.7
Luxembourg[b]	84.2	84.0	85.0	82.5
Netherlands[c]	92.5	83.0	83.2	80.0
Norway	82.5	81.5	83.0	76.4
Portugal	–	83.4	72.1	67.4
Spain	–	71.3	72.7	76.3
Sweden	85.9	90.8	87.5	85.3
Switzerland	63.0	51.9	46.5	45.3
United Kingdom	76.5	74.9	75.2	77.7
Average (unweighted)	83.1	81.6	78.8	76.4

Source: reproduced from Mackie (1995:175, Table 6.3).

[a] Valid votes as a percentage of the electorate.

[b] Compulsory voting.

[c] Compulsory voting in the 1960s.

Also, the integration of international markets was leading to the faster development of areas which were already relatively wealthy and the stagnation of underdeveloped regions. The well-placed regions which comprised Europe's 'golden triangle' (including the south east of England, most of West Germany and parts of France and northern Italy) were benefiting disproportionately from trade generated within the EC at the expense of the peripheral areas geographically farthest away. This development coincided with a cultural revival in the 1960s and 1970s in the peripheries of Europe.

Together, these factors repoliticised the centre–periphery cleavage. While most of the affected countries experienced surges of extremist activity connected with these demands, militant, fundamentalist movements became entrenched in Northern Ireland, the Basque country and Corsica. Other groups organised as political parties to contest elections and to lobby by legal means. Regionalism has sometimes been identified with a reactionary stance, sometimes with a progressive cause. Only in exceptional cases (the Basque country, for example) has the centre–periphery cleavage helped to define political competition in the post-war period. Elsewhere, the regionalist parties have competed within the context of the more conventional socioeconomic divide.

A familiar ideology re-emerged in the 1980s as new parties of the extreme right began to gain ground in some countries. Discredited after the Second World War, neo-fascist parties had virtually disappeared from parliamentary politics in most countries. (An exception was the Italian Social Movement (MSI), which attracted a consistent if low level of support throughout the post-war period, but was shunned by the mainstream parties.) The new 'populist' parties of the extreme right take pains to distance themselves both from the anti-democratic elements of ideology which in the past led to authoritarian dictatorship and from their thuggish fringe supporters. Nevertheless, their re-emergence has been a cause for concern throughout western Europe and they tend to be kept at arm's length by the mainstream parties. Contemporary parties of the extreme right denigrate mainstream parties as ineffectual and promise strong (if often simplistic) solutions to combat problems typical of modern society. They are extreme nationalists and xenophobes. Typically, parties of the extreme right target immigrants as the cause of their country's moral decay, manifested in crime, unemployment and housing problems. They promise to restore law and order using strengthened police powers. At an ideological level, their aim is to restore their country and society to a mythical former state of glory. In line with their mistrust of foreigners, they reject international alliances such as the EU. The new populist parties support new right free-market economics rather than old-fashioned corporatist autarky. They may also argue for constitutional reform rather than adopting an anti-democratic stance.

Prior to the 1994 electoral upheaval in Italy (see below), the most successful party of the extreme right was the French National Front (FN), which by 1986 had established a consistent level of electoral support of around 10 per cent. More alarming was the prospect of a resurgence of nationalist extremist sentiment in Germany. Given the disillusionment felt following the initial euphoria of unification, it was feared that the 1994 German election would see an upsurge in support for parties of the radical right.[4] These fears failed to materialise and the radical right did not gain a single seat in the national parliament.

During the 1980s, a new family of parties gained a place in western European party systems – the alternative or green parties. These share a number of common aims. As ecologists, they challenge all other established parties with their claim that constant economic growth must be halted or even reversed in order to create a sustainable society. They argue for the reduction or closure of civil nuclear plant. Greens are strong advocates of equal rights, particularly for minority groups in society. They have a global understanding of equality which encompasses solidarity with the Third World. They believe in wealth-sharing between rich and poor nations and aid to develop self-sufficient economies. Greens prefer alternative life-styles characterised by more individualism, self-realisation and self-determination; less materialism; and, sometimes, less emphasis on the family unit. They uphold the principle of participatory democracy rather than representative democracy, which, they believe, tends to lead to the formation of political elites.[5] Many of the green parties of western Europe are divided into two factions: one radical or fundamentalist and the other more moderate and pragmatic. Where green parties have won seats in elections, the more moderate faction has usually come to dominate the parliamentary or council party group.

While ideological aims of the greens are global, their appeal seems to be sectional. Green parties can be associated with a distinct social base within the new middle class, consisting of younger voters with a university education, who, if employed, tend to work in the public sector. It can be argued that the green parties and their distinctive voting clientele have added a new cleavage to those identified by Lipset and Rokkan, namely a cleavage dividing materialists and postmaterialists (see Inglehart 1977). Not everyone agrees that materialism versus postmaterialism constitutes a true cleavage in the technical sense. Some critics doubt that the green parties, the organisational expression of postmaterialism, are fundamentally different from other new left parties and that they therefore do not amount to a new cross-cutting cleavage in western European party systems. Also, green parties remain a very marginal electoral force.

The future of political competition in western Europe

For political scientists, the debate on the future of party politics continues. One argument suggests that the changes we have noted are evidence of 'dealignment' – a general weakening of the electorate's attachment to political parties. Continuing dealignment would imply a decline in cleavage politics, with parties becoming less significant in channelling political conflict. Alternatively, dealignment might be a preliminary stage in a process of 'realignment' – a weakening of old party loyalties prior to a reorientation of the electorate in support of a new party alignment (Dalton *et al.* 1984). If this is the case, realignment would appear to be supplementing the old divides rather than replacing them completely.

The institutional hurdles to realignment are greater in some countries than in others. For example, the electoral success of the greens and the far right has been partly determined by the electoral system in use in each country (see Chapter 4). They have been effectively locked out by plurality electoral systems, such as those in use in Britain and France. This was demonstrated by the experience of the extreme right FN in France, which in 1986 won 30 seats in the one-off use of proportional representation. When the two-ballot system has been used, the FN has at best secured a single seat.

In all countries, though, new parties face difficulties in establishing themselves. New parties are often small parties. Unless they are breakaway groups from established parties, they will not have had the opportunity to build up a loyal electoral clientele. They must somehow win voters away from the parties they have supported in the past, or, alternatively, appeal to a sector of the electorate which has previously abstained from voting. In 1994, Italy was the exception to the rule when public confidence in the traditional parties collapsed and allowed two new parties of the right, Forza Italia and the National Alliance, to form the backbone of the new government (see the appendix). Elsewhere, though, the old cleavages and the parties which have channelled them are proving remarkably resilient. The class cleavage, while undergoing a transformation from one between workers and entrepreneurs into a more contemporary socio-economic divide, is still represented by parties of the right and left, and continues to dominate political competition in western European party systems. Religion also remains a strong influence on the vote, with religiosity now the key explanatory factor rather than denomination. Society is changing, but for the time being, the party systems of western Europe seem to be keeping pace.

Notes

1 Lipset and Rokkan's hypothesis of the 'freezing' of party systems is the subject of ongoing debate between theorists of parties and party systems. In their attempts to prove or disprove this hypothesis, much depends on how theorists interpret the key concepts of Lipset and Rokkan's original argument and on the methods they employ to test the hypothesis. A good introduction to this debate, together with excerpts from some of the major works, is provided in Mair (1990).

2 The surveys were carried out by the European Values Systems Study Group (EVSSG) as part of a general study on European values. The

countries covered were Belgium, Britain, Denmark, Eire, France, Italy, Netherlands, Northern Ireland, Spain and West Germany. A follow-up study is currently in progress. The results of the 1981 survey are published in Harding *et al.* (1986). In addition to the 12 per cent of Europeans claiming no denomination, 57 per cent were Catholics, 28 per cent Protestant (including 2 per cent Nonconformist) and 2 per cent 'others', mainly from non-Christian denominations (Harding *et al.* 1986:34–5).

3 Fifty-eight per cent of practising Catholics support the Social Democratic and Labour Party (SDLP), favouring union with the Irish Republic, and 62 per cent of churchgoing Protestants supported the Democratic Unionists or the Official Ulster Unionists. The relationship was similar for non-practising Catholics and Protestants, suggesting that denominational identity rather than religiosity is the key factor in channelling the religious vote (Heath *et al.* 1993:63).

4 Germany distinguishes between right-wing extremist groups, which are kept under official surveillance, and right-wing radical groups, which are considered legitimate.

5 Thomas Poguntke (in Müller-Rommel 1989:175–94) classifies parties which combine these characteristics as 'new politics parties'. He describes them as 'left-wing, emancipatory political parties which are concerned with a broader set of issues than merely ecology' (176), and argues that they are a completely new type of party. He maintains that green parties which do not combine all of these features are simply conservative 'green' formations. He identifies two green parties as conservative green formations: the Austrian VGÖ and the Swiss GPS. Interestingly, in each of those countries which maintains an ecologist green group there has also been a radical 'new politics' green party: the ALÖ in Austria and the GBS in Switzerland.

References

Dalton, R., S. Flanagan and P. Beck (1984) *Electoral Change in Advanced Industrial Democracies. Realignment or Dealignment?*, Princeton, NJ, Princeton University Press.

Davie, G. (1992) 'God and Caesar: religion in a rapidly changing Europe', in J. Bailey (ed.) *Social Europe*, London, Longman.

Frears, J. (1991) *Parties and Voters in France*, London, St Martin's Press.

Giorgi, L. (1992) 'Religious involvement in a secularized society: an empirical confirmation of Martin's general theory of secularization', *British Journal of Sociology*, 43:4, 640–56.

Harding, S. and D. Phillips, with M. Fogarty (1986) *Contrasting Values in Western Europe. Unity, Diversity and Change*, London, Macmillan.

Heath, A., B. Taylor and G. Toka (1993) 'Religion, morality and politics', in R. Jowell, L. Brook and L. Dowds, with D. Ahrendt (eds) *International Social Attitudes. The 10th BSA Report*, Aldershot, Dartmouth.

Inglehart, R. (1977) *The Silent Revolution. Changing Values and Political Styles among Western Mass Publics*, Princeton, NJ, Princeton University Press.

Kavanagh, D. (1985) *British Politics. Continuities and Change*, Oxford, Oxford University Press.

Kirchheimer, O. (1966) 'The transformation of the Western European party systems', in J. Lapalombara and M. Weiner (eds) *Political Parties and Political Development*, Princeton, NJ, Princeton University Press.

Lipset, S. and S. Rokkan (eds) (1967) *Party Systems and Voter Alignments*, New York, Free Press.

Mackie, T. (1995), 'Parties and elections', in J. Hayward and E. Page (eds) *Governing the New Europe*, Cambridge, Polity Press.

Mair, P. (ed.) (1990) *The West European Party System*, Oxford, Oxford University Press.

Mendras, H. and A. Cole (1991) *Social Change in Modern France. Towards a Cultural Anthropology of the Fifth Republic*, Cambridge, Cambridge University Press.

Müller-Rommel, F. (ed.) (1989) *New Politics in Western Europe*, London, Westview Press.

OECD (1985) *Labour Force Statistics 1963–1983*, Paris, Organisation for Economic Co-operation and Development.

OECD (1992) *Labour Force Statistics 1970–1990*, Paris, Organisation for Economic Co-operation and Development.

Schultze, R.-O. (1987) 'Die Bundeswahl 1987 – eine Bestätigung des Wandels', *Aus Politik und Zeitgeschichte*, B12/87: 3–17.

Further reading

Gallagher, M., M. Laver and P. Mair (1995) *Representative Government in Modern Europe*, New York, McGraw-Hill, 2nd edn.

Mackie, T. (1995) 'Parties and elections', in J. Hayward and E. Page (eds) *Governing the New Europe*, Cambridge, Polity Press.

Mair, P. (ed.) (1990) *The West European Party System*, Oxford, Oxford University Press.

4

Electoral systems

What are elections?

Elections have a long history, going back certainly to the city-states of ancient Greece and periods in the history of ancient Rome. They are used in a wide variety of contexts. The pope is elected by the college of cardinals, and the secretary-general of the United Nations Organisation is elected by members of the General Assembly. Local authorities, trade unions, political parties, student unions, and voluntary organisations of various kinds use elections to select their representatives and officers.

Elections are by no means the only way in which incumbents of public offices are selected. Jurors in court cases are chosen by lot, from those eligible on the electoral register. The positions of chairman of the National Executive Committee of the Labour party, president of the German second chamber (the Bundesrat), and president of the Council of Ministers of the EU are examples of posts filled by some sort of rotation. Judges are usually appointed on the basis of professional qualifications (though in the USA some are elected by the voters, and in Germany judges of the Constitutional Court are elected by the two chambers of the legislature). Ministers and ambassadors are usually appointed in effect by the prime minister or other head of government. Succession to the throne in the UK, the Netherlands, Belgium and other constitutional monarchies in Europe is determined by heredity, as is succession to hereditary peerages for members of the House of Lords.

Yet none of these alternative methods of selection – randomness, rotation, appointment or heredity – is considered suitable for determining the composition of a representative legislature or the choice of party (and sometimes, as with the president in France, the person) to lead the government. Why not? Because elections are seen as a necessary and prominent characteristic of representative democracy. The electoral process is the way in which the wishes of voters are communicated concerning the choice of who should serve as their representatives. That process, to greater or lesser degree, provides transparency in that everyone can see how the choices made by the people become translated into a particular set of representatives, and those representatives and governments derived from them can claim legitimacy on the basis of such elections. These reasons are all associated with the democratic nature of *representative* government. Elections are the way in which the political preferences of the electorate can make a direct input into the political process, and affect the political choices which governments and legislatures make in a democracy. No professional qualifications can substitute for such election by the people. Random choice or rotation would not reflect the balance of opinion among the electorate, nor signal changes in that balance.

What do elections do?

In the political systems of western Europe, elections are used for three main purposes: to select representatives of the electorate; to confirm governments in office, or change them; and to give legitimacy to the government. As will be seen, these purposes are not always mutually compatible. Because some types of electoral system emphasise representation, while others seem primarily designed to select governments and support them through provision of stable legislative majorities, the choice of electoral system itself is often the subject of contention, as will be discussed later in this chapter.

Elections to parliaments or local councils are primarily concerned with selecting representatives of the people, who will then debate and decide upon matters of political concern on behalf of the people. In communist states, such as the former USSR or China, elections are usually non-competitive: only one candidate per seat is nominated, having been selected by the party. The electoral process still goes ahead (the voter usually having the formal right to reject that candidate), because elections serve as a form of acclamation for the ruling party and a useful opportunity to mobilise the population. In such regimes, elected assemblies usually have no significant political powers anyway. Even in western Europe it is not unknown for a candidate to be elected unopposed (for example in the UK and Ireland it is usual for the Speaker of the parliament seeking re-election to be elected unopposed). Competition is regarded as an essential component of elections in representative democracies, since such competition encourages the airing of different points of view, criticism of the policies of those in power, and responsiveness of candidates and parties to the electorate. In national elections, at least, it is therefore normal for an election to be competitive, with candidates nominated by different parties, though in local elections in some countries candidates may more frequently be unopposed because of the lesser importance at local level of party affiliation and the greater significance of the candidate's personality and past political record.

An important issue may be the number of levels of government in a society for which elected representatives should be provided. All western democracies now have at least two levels – national and local – while federal systems have at least three (see Chapter 10). The introduction of elected regional councils in Italy, France and Spain demonstrates that this issue is not confined to federal states. Involved in this is the question of what should be represented through elections: in particular, what level of subcommunity should have its own elected council, and what that community should be in terms of identity. The devolution debate in Britain, for example, poses the question of whether Scotland and Wales should have their own elected assemblies, and, if so, whether it would then be proper or equitable to deny to the regions of England the same right.

Although political parties in their modern form are not much more than a hundred years old, they are now an integral part of the electoral process. They select candidates, and present the electorate with programmes to guide them in their choice. They coordinate teams of successful candidates, in government or in opposition to government, once the election is over. A modern election is unthinkable without parties: so much so, that party competition in free elections has become one of the defining characteristics of liberal democracy.

So an election determines the party composition of the House of Commons, the German Bundestag, the French National Assembly, the Danish Folketing, the Luxembourg Chamber of Deputies and other national legislatures in western Europe, as well as the EP, regional assemblies such as those of Bavaria, Catalonia and Sicily, and local councils in Lyons, Oslo, Shropshire, Glasgow, Dresden and elsewhere throughout western Europe. Each successful candidate owes his or her seat to the choices made by voters.

Although parties are the institutions through which representation via elections is effected, the basis of representation can have many dimensions. Populations of particular areas are the most obvious of these dimensions: the local or regional constituency. But interests can be said to be represented (see below, Chapter 6), as can social categories of various kinds: ethnic groups, gender groups, social classes, religious groups, etc. So a representative is rarely only the representative of his or her party supporters, or even of all the electors in a locality. Party factions (e.g. pro- and anti-Maastricht Treaty MPs in the Conservative party in the UK in the 1990s, or the various groupings within the French Socialist party), gender, interest-based ties (e.g. Labour MPs sponsored by trade unions in Britain, farmers in the French Gaullist party), regional loyalties (e.g. east German members of the German Bundestag, Scottish and Welsh MPs in the House of Commons, representatives of Italian-speaking districts in the Swiss Nationalrat) and various other characteristics of the populace can be considered to be 'represented'. Of course, several of these dimensions of representation may exist simultaneously;

an elected representative usually has to balance party, local, sectional and interest-group considerations both when acting as a legislator and when seeking re-election. What is regarded as an appropriate 'mix' of these dimensions of representation varies from country to country. In Britain, France and Ireland, for instance, local constituency interests are regarded as a priority alongside party; in Belgium, the language community is regarded as paramount; and so on.

Elections also change governments, or confirm governments in office. Governments consist chiefly, if not always solely, of members of political parties, whether government is of one party or a coalition of parties, and such governments depend on the support of party majorities in the legislature. So the electorate, when it chooses representatives, simultaneously gives its verdict on the choice of government, or at least may influence the outcome of coalition negotiations by its votes for various parties. It may decide to confirm a government in office, as it did in the Federal Republic of Germany in October 1994, or it may decide to put a new government in place of the old, as it did in the UK in the general election of 1979, in France in 1981 through the presidential and legislative elections, and again in France in 1993 through legislative elections and in 1995 through presidential elections. It may even leave the choice apparently unclear, as it did in the Federal Republic of Germany in 1969, in the UK in 1974 and in France in 1986.

Election campaigns focus on this choice of governments, often minimising the role of individual candidates in so doing. The voter is exhorted to vote primarily for a party, and the candidate will usually ask for votes on the basis of party affiliation rather than personal qualities. Indeed, some electoral systems confine the voter to a choice among pre-selected party lists, and the voter has little or no say in determining the personal composition of the legislature. Elections are thus a way of allowing the electorate to deliver a verdict on the policies of competing parties and on the past record of the government. There is a tendency for the successful party to claim that its victory provides it with a *mandate* – that is, it claims that the electorate, by its decision, has given the government a licence to proceed to implement the policy proposals in its platform, based on its electoral manifesto (though the implementation of new policies unanticipated in that manifesto may be controversial precisely because no mandate can be claimed for them). John Major in 1992, Helmut Kohl in 1994, Jacques Chirac in 1995, could all claim after their victories that they could now introduce or continue the policies and governmental strategies that they had offered to the voters during the campaign.

Governments do not only change as a result of elections, though. Government coalitions may change between elections, as happened in the Federal Republic of Germany in 1966 and 1982, and as used to occur frequently in Italy and in the French Fourth Republic (see Chapter 7). But such changes will be undertaken in the knowledge that the electorate will deliver its verdict on the new government at the next election.

Elections give legitimacy to governments and to the legislatures which support them. They enable a government to claim to exercise 'government by the people', a claim that is essential if the political system purports to be democratic. In western democracies, to accentuate the legitimacy of the electoral process, emphasis is placed on turning out to vote, even in 'safe' seats.

Of course, elections fulfil certain other functions in the political system as well: functions which are incidental, rather than central, but which nevertheless are of significance.

First, they offer a high-profile opportunity for public participation. Other than perhaps a few religious feast days, such as Christmas and Easter – and, in Germany and the UK, some televised lottery draws when prizes are particularly large – it is impossible to imagine in western Europe any other occasion when an activity is shared by two-thirds or three-quarters of the adult population, except for national elections. Elections are often the only form of political participation in which many adults engage.

Second, elections are one of the methods by which activists are recruited for political careers. They allow aspirants to compete for selection as party candidates (since to stand as a non-party candidate is to renounce any real possibility of a political career in all western European countries). They provide victorious party candidates with the qualification for later selection as members of the government. Behind the scenes, agents or party managers, by organising successful campaigns for their candidates, can perhaps extend their careers to regional or national level.

Third, elections contribute to the political education of the public. Parties often spend vast amounts of money on publicity, which is in fact noticed by more of the electorate than cynics might suppose. Such publicity may not persuade many of the electorate to vote differently than they would have done without that publicity, but it can have an effect on the information and expectations which voters bring with them to the polling station. The press and broadcasting commentaries and news reports supplement the leaflets, poster slogans and election broadcasts of the parties themselves. Issues such as the level of public sector borrowing, environmental pollution, social services provision, law and order, privatisation of state-owned industries or utilities, or problems of education may be brought prominently to public attention during election campaigns in a manner which informs a receptive public more effectively than at any other time.

Types of electoral system

Electoral systems vary from country to country and over time, even within the same country. Indeed, there seems to be no end to the imaginative invention of new – actual or potential – electoral systems, of those used in the past, employed in the present, or proposed for the future.[1] Electoral systems are usually set out in the form of legislation, perhaps based on general prescriptions stated in the constitution. Such electoral laws provide rules relating to two different aspects of electoral systems.

The first is the organisational aspect: who is qualified to vote, and to stand for election; when elections may, or may not, be held (in the UK elections must be on a working day – though not necessarily on the customary Thursday; in Germany, on the other hand, elections must be held on a Sunday or a public holiday); times when the polling stations shall be open; procedures for counting votes and declaring the results; regulations governing the financial aspects of campaigning. These organisational rules may vary considerably, without in themselves affecting the outcome of elections. Only major organisational changes, such as the enfranchisement of women, tend to have any significant bearing on electoral outcomes.

It is the second aspect – procedures for translating votes into allocations of seats, including the stipulation and revision of constituency boundaries – which really matters with regard to the outcomes of elections, and it is in terms of such procedures that typologies of electoral systems can usefully be developed.

In Europe, three different types of translation process (which, for convenience, will be termed the 'electoral system') can be distinguished (see Table 4.1).

The *simple majority* or 'first-past-the-post' type of electoral system elects members to the legislature in single-member constituencies.[2] The candidates with the largest numbers of votes win. Sometimes, as in France (see below), special conditions and even a second round of balloting may be required, but the essential feature of the system is that local representatives are chosen directly in territorially defined constituencies, without reference to votes cast in other constituencies.

The *proportional representation* (PR) system uses some sort of party list mechanism, by which votes are cast for a party, though some systems may provide for the voter being able to influence *which* candidates on a list are elected. Each party receives a share of seats in close proportion to the share of votes which its list has obtained.[3] Qualifying conditions may be imposed (such as specification of a minimum percentage of votes as necessary for a party to receive any list seats) True proportionality may be affected by other factors, such as the size of constituencies in which separate party lists are presented and seats allocated: the fewer the constituencies, the closer the proportionality, and a single national constituency offers the closest degree of proportionality. The principle depends on votes being given for parties, and such

Table 4.1 The electoral systems of western European countries[a]

State	Maximum legislative term	Total number of seats in lower house[b]
'First-past-the post' systems:		
France	5 years	577
United Kingdom	5 years	651
Proportional representation systems:		
Austria	4 years	183
Belgium	4 years	150
Denmark	4 years	179
Finland	4 years	200
Germany	4 years	656
Greece	4 years	300
Iceland	4 years	63
Italy	5 years	630
Luxembourg	5 years	60
Netherlands	4 years	150
Norway	4 years	165
Portugal	4 years	230
Spain	4 years	350
Sweden	4 years	349
Switzerland	4 years	200
Preferential systems:		
Ireland	5 years	166
Malta	5 years	65

[a] This table refers to systems for national elections only. Detailed aspects of electoral systems can be found in the appendix.
[b] Normal size; some legislatures may vary in size from election to election.

votes then being translated into seats for parties. Most western European countries use some version of this type of system.

The third type is the *preferential* system of voting, which is not designed to give accurate proportional reflections of party votes in terms of seats, and indeed may not necessarily do so, but instead gives the voter the opportunity of ensuring that her or his vote has the maximum chance of making a difference as to which candidates are elected. Ireland and Malta use this system.

To illustrate the way in which these systems operate, and to emphasise their differences, the electoral systems of the UK and France, the Netherlands and Germany, and the Irish Republic will be described.

The United Kingdom

The electoral system of the UK has developed, without any major discontinuity, over many centuries. A degree of uniformity in what was previously a set of disparate constituencies, franchise qualifications and technical arrangements, was first introduced by the Reform Acts of 1832, 1867, 1884 and 1885, which together also gradually extended the right to vote so that most of the male adult population was enfranchised by the end of the nineteenth century; the principle of universal male suffrage was adopted in 1918. The secret ballot, which did much to eliminate electoral corruption, was introduced by the Ballot Act of 1872. Women received the right to vote in two stages, by legislation in 1918 and 1928, after the suffragette campaign had brought the matter very forcibly to public attention before the First World War. The Representation of the People Act (1948) abolished several anomalies, such as the university seats in the House of Commons, which had given graduates in effect a second vote, as well as the remaining few constituencies which elected two MPs.

The voting system itself is very straightforward. Each constituency elects one MP. That MP is the candidate who obtained the largest number of valid votes in the constituency. There is no requirement that the candidate should obtain an absolute majority of votes cast (i.e. more than 50 per cent). With a few exceptions, all citizens over the age of eighteen who are entered on the current electoral register may vote. Elections must occur within five years of the previous election: they usually occur earlier, because the prime minister has the right to select the date of the election within the five-year limit, and of course in doing so will seek to secure advantage to the governing party. If the government has only a small overall majority of seats, an election may even take place within a year or two of the previous election (for instance in 1950 and 1951; 1964 and 1966; and twice in 1974). Seats which become vacant for whatever reason between general elections are filled at by-elections. Candidates usually represent one of the political parties, but independents can and do present themselves for election. There are few restrictions on the right to stand for election: members of the peerage and prisoners serving sentences of one year or longer are among those disqualified from nomination.

The advantages and disadvantages of the UK electoral system are explored in more detail in the section on electoral reform, later in this chapter. Advantages include the close identification of the elected MP with the local constituency, and the high probability that one party will emerge from the election with an overall majority of seats, and thus be able to form a government which usually can be confident of remaining in office for four to five years. This comes about because of the vagaries of the single-member constituency arrangement, and the fact that constituencies vary so much in the size of their electorates (even soon after a periodic boundary revision). Disadvantages include the disproportionate representation of large and of small parties, enabling a party to govern with well under 50 per cent of the vote, and alloting to small parties far fewer seats than their vote share would suggest they should have.

The French Fifth Republic
In contrast to the uninterrupted development of the British electoral system, that of France has been revised radically on several occasions. These revisions have usually accompanied the several changes of constitution which have occurred in France since the introduction of universal male suffrage in 1848. The right to vote was extended to women only after the Second World War. The use of a system of proportional representation, using party lists in constituencies based on the departments, was held to be at least partly responsible for the weaknesses of the political system of the Fourth Republic. When de Gaulle came to power in 1958 and founded the Fifth Republic, the voting system

for National Assembly elections reverted to a pre-war method: the two-ballot simple majority system. This system, with slight variations, has also been used since 1962 for electing the president of the Republic.

For legislative elections, with the sole exception of those held in 1986, constituencies each elect one member to the national Assembly. There are now 577 constituencies: 555 for mainland France and 22 for the overseas departments and territories. Except for the practice of holding elections on a Sunday, the procedures are very similar to those in the UK. However, to be elected on the first ballot, a candidate has to secure more votes than all other candidates together: in other words, obtain an absolute majority of valid votes. Relatively few seats are filled after the first ballot. Where that provision of an absolute majority has not applied, a second ballot is held one week later. To stand in the second round, a candidate must have obtained votes at least equal to 12.5 per cent of the electorate (so will need a share of the *vote* well in excess of 12.5 per cent because turnout will be less than 100 per cent). In fact a process of inter-party bargaining on the left and on the right will take place in the days following the first round, and usually only one candidate from the left and one from the right will stand for the run-off election, even if more than one from each wing would be qualified to stand in the second round. This is in order to avoid 'splitting' the right-wing or left-wing vote, and thus losing the seat. Very occasionally, a candidate may also be qualified to stand in the second round from the Greens or the National Front, for example. The winner on the second round is the candidate with the most votes, whether that is in fact an absolute majority or not.

Legislative elections are held every five years, though the National Assembly may be dissolved earlier and new elections held (but not sooner than twelve months after the previous elections) should the president so desire. François Mitterrand called early elections in 1981 and 1988 following his election, then re-election, as president. Vacancies between elections are filled by substitutes, who are elected at the same time as members of the

National Assembly, but by-elections occur if no substitute is available for whatever reason.

The president is elected every seven years (or earlier if a vacancy occurs), by a procedure similar to that used to elect the National Assembly. An absolute majority of votes is required for election. Should no candidate obtain this on the first round of balloting, the two candidates with the highest numbers of votes on the first round go forward to a second round of voting two weeks later. The fact that only two candidates compete in the second round has encouraged the development of two party 'blocs' in the Fifth Republic: one on the left and one on the right. This system of direct election of the president raises fundamental questions about the relationship between the executive and legislative branches of government, the role of the National Assembly, and the 'balance of power', especially in periods of 'cohabitation', between the president and the prime minister (see Chapters 7 and 8).

Advantages of the French system are that it preserves links between legislators and local constituents, and, by exaggerating the vote share of large parties into disproportionate shares of seats, encourages – as in the UK – the formation of overall majorities for single-party or for bloc-based governments. The two-ballot arrangement ensures that voters on the first round can express their 'true' party preference, allowing them on the second round to vote more 'tactically'. A disadvantage is the disproportionality which penalises small parties or declining parties (like the Communist Party in recent years). It is difficult to identify clear advantages or disadvantages which attach to the direct election of the president under this system, since the legitimacy and authority which derive from that election really provide the basis for the 'dual-executive' arrangement of the Fifth Republic. However, it has meant that occasions may arise (and had twice arisen by 1995) when the president and prime minister are of different party blocs, compelling the tensions of 'cohabitation' to emerge (see Chapter 7), and that there has been a process of concentration of parties into two blocs because of the requirements imposed by the two-ballot system for electing the president.

The Netherlands

Since 1918, when it abandoned the French-style two-ballot electoral system which had been in use until that date, the Netherlands has employed a very straightforward system of proportional representation based on party lists. The country is divided into nineteen electoral districts. A party may present lists in any or all of these districts (and the list in each district may contain the same, or different, names of candidates compared to those on that party's list elsewhere). Voters cast their vote by selecting one name on any one party list in their district. Theoretically, that choice of name can affect who, for that party, is elected, but only very rarely does a candidate obtain sufficient votes in this way to alter the ordering of candidates decided upon by the party.

Parties are then allocated seats according to their share of the total number of votes cast. The country is treated as one constituency, combining all the district lists, for purposes of calculating the number of seats to which each party is entitled. There is no special qualifying percentage necessary (other than the arithmetic share needed to qualify for a seat, the so-called 'electoral quotient'). This means that nowadays a party will obtain one seat for every 60,000 votes (approximately) it receives (this quotient will vary slightly, depending on the size of the electorate and the level of turnout). So a party which, nationally, obtains 20 per cent of votes cast will receive very close to 20 per cent of the seats. Voting was compulsory until 1970, but since the abolition of compulsion turnout has remained relatively high, by western European standards: it has been between 80 and 90 per cent in recent elections.

Advantages of the Dutch electoral system include its simplicity of operation (despite the fact that voters vote for named candidates rather than for parties as such), and the very close degree of proportionality between votes and seats which it produces.

Disadvantages include the large number of parties which obtain seats. However, even under the system used before the First World War many parties obtained seats, so it cannot be said that proportional representation has caused the proliferation of parties; and since 1945, although between seven and fourteen parties have been represented in the legislature, the main parties usually have won 70–90 per cent of votes and over three-quarters of seats, so the party system is reasonably 'structured' and stable.

The Federal Republic of Germany

When the Federal Republic of Germany was created in 1949, its choice of electoral system was greatly influenced by the idea that unrestrained proportional representation in the Weimar Republic had contributed to the conditions that led to the downfall of democracy and its replacement by the Nazi regime. Post-war West Germany had also had experience of local and provincial elections in the zones of occupation, experience which guided its choice of system to elect the first Bundestag. After modification of that 1949 electoral system, what emerged in the Electoral Law of 1956 (which has remained substantially unaltered up to the present) is an electoral system that allows the voter two separate votes: one for a local constituency candidate (as in the UK), and one for a regional party list. Unlike the French two-ballot system, the two votes in the German electoral system are cast at the same time. The overall composition of the Bundestag is proportional to the votes parties receive for their regional lists.

There are now normally 656 seats to be filled at a federal election.[4] With the first vote an elector chooses a named candidate in one of the 328 constituencies. Whichever candidate secures the largest number of votes is declared elected. The remaining 328 seats are allocated by reference to the second vote, which an elector gives to a party list in the *Land* in which the local constituency is located: for Bayreuth, the Bavarian list; for Freiburg, the Baden-Württemberg list; and so on. There is no requirement that the party list which a voter selects is that of the party to which the constituency candidate chosen with the first vote belongs. Indeed, 15–20 per cent of voters decide to split their votes, by selecting a constituency candidate of a party different from that for whose list they have voted. The crucial point about the two-vote system is that it is the second (party list) vote that is decisive. Each party that qualifies for an allocation of list seats obtains that number of seats which (when the number of constituency seats won has been also taken into account) will give it a total representation in the Bundestag proportional to its share of party list votes. Given the same share of party-list votes, a party with more constituency seats will obtain fewer additional list seats; if it obtains fewer constituency seats, it will get more list seats. So the system is one of overall proportional representation, in which the constituency seats are merely an unusual element.

To qualify for an allocation of list seats, a party must fulfil one of two conditions: it must either win at least three constituency seats (though if it wins two or one, it keeps those seats, of course), or it must obtain at least 5 per cent of the national total of votes cast for party lists. Because the votes for lists of small parties who do not meet these conditions are 'wasted', those parties who do qualify for list seat allocations generally obtain slightly larger shares than their percentage share of votes would indicate. This is illustrated by the result of the 1994 federal election (see Table 4.2).

Elections are held on a Sunday, at four-year intervals. Very exceptionally, the Bundestag can be dissolved ahead of time by permission of the president of the Republic. This has so far happened twice: in 1972 (because the governing coalition had lost its majority, but the opposition did not possess a majority either) and 1983, after the CDU-CSU/FDP government engineered its own defeat on a vote of confidence, in order to obtain legitimation from the electorate for the mid-term change of coalition which had occurred in the previous October. There are no by-elections; a vacancy is filled by the next available candidate from the relevant party list taking the vacant seat. Thus party strengths remain unchanged during the legislative period, unless an elected member changes party during the period.

Table 4.2 Federal Republic of Germany: Bundestag election of October 1994

Party	Percentage of list (2nd) votes	Total seats allocated	Percentage of total seats	Constituency seats won	List seats allocated
CDU	34.2	244	36.3	177	67
CSU	7.3	50	7.4	44	6
FDP	6.9	47	7.0	–	47
SPD	36.4	252	37.5	103	149
Greens	7.3	49	7.3	–	49
PDS	4.4	30	4.5	4	26

Note that:

(i) the Greens and FDP obtained all their seats from the list allocation (and indeed were not in second place in any constituency);

(ii) exceptionally, a party (the PDS) qualified for a distribution of list seats by winning at least three constituency seats, rather than by obtaining 5 per cent of list votes;

(iii) there was an unusually large number of 'surplus' seats (16 in all: 12 for the Christian Democrats and 4 for the Social Democrats), and that this increased the majority of the government by eight seats;

(iv) the total number of seats allocated to each party was very nearly proportional to its share of list votes.

The advantages of the German system are that it combines reasonably exact overall proportional representation of parties with constituency representation (as in the UK), though in fact few electors seem to be aware of the name of their constituency representative, and discourages (by means of the 5 per cent qualification for list seats) representation of small parties, thus encouraging stable government based on a coalition usually of only two parties. The lack of by-elections means that a government with even a small overall majority can govern for its full term, provided the coalition holds together. Disadvantages are the key role which it has given in government to the small Free Democratic Party (FDP), which normally has determined which other party it will join with in government, and the possibility of five or six parties obtaining seats in the Bundestag, which could make formation of stable coalitions difficult.

Ireland

Arthur Griffith, founder of the Sinn Fein party, called the single transferable vote (STV) system 'the one just system of election in democratic governments' (quoted by O'Leary 1975:155). It is an electoral system which in fact generally produces a more proportional representation of parties than do the UK and French electoral systems, but proportional representation of parties is a by-product of the system, not its goal. The system is designed to ensure that each successful candidate elected in a constituency is ultimately selected by more voters than is any non-elected candidate. It is intended to maximise the power of the voter in selection of winning candidates.

As used in Ireland, the system involves multi-member constituencies, each electing three, four or five members. Each voter has one vote, but that vote is 'transferable', because it is given not as an unconditional, unalterable indication of a single selection (by means of a cross, in the UK, for example), but by ordering candidates preferentially, using the numbers 1, 2, 3, etc. for as many candidates as the voter wishes to discriminate among. To be elected, a candidate must obtain a quota of the votes cast. This quota is set, such that it represents the smallest number of votes that will just elect the number of candidates required, but no more. As a formula, it is:

$$Q = \frac{V}{S+1} + 1$$

Where Q is the quota of votes needed for election, V the total number of valid votes cast and S the number of seats to be filled. Thus, in a four-member constituency in which exactly 52,000 valid votes had been cast, the quota needed for election would be 10,401 (i.e. 52,000/5 + 1). Only four candidates can obtain 10,401 votes, not five ($5 \times 10{,}401 = 52{,}005$, which is greater than the number of votes available).

The first count adds up the numbers of first-preference votes (i.e. those where a 1 has been placed by a candidate's name). Any candidate whose votes then reach or exceed the quota is declared elected. If insufficient candidates are elected on the first round, any 'surplus' votes – i.e. votes in excess of the quota – given to elected candidates are redistributed, to candidates who have been given the 'second preference' (i.e. have 2 by their names), in proportion to all the second preferences on votes for the successful candidate. Unless that redistribution fills all the remaining seats, a further round of redistribution occurs: all the votes for the candidate who, at that stage, has the fewest votes, are redistributed to the next preferences on those voting papers. This process of reallocation continues, redistributing surplus votes and those of the least popular candidates, until all the seats are filled (an example is shown in Table 4.3). Voters need not, of course, vote 'loyally' for all the candidates of one party: they may use as their basis for placing candidates in order of preference the previous legislative record of the candidates, where they reside, what policies they promote, their personal characteristics, or any other criteria which the voters think appropriate.

Elections are held on weekdays, with maximum periods between elections of five years (though earlier dissolutions and general elections are common). Vacancies between elections are filled through by-elections, using the same procedure as at general elections.

Advantages of this STV system are the relatively great amount of choice which it gives to the voter, who can select an order of preference with reference to any criteria desired (not just party sympathy), and can select among different candidates of the same party without 'splitting the vote' for that party; and the greater degree of proportionality which it generally provides for parties (without being designed to produce accurate party proportionality). Disadvantages are held to be the opaque procedure by which votes are translated into seats, involving sometimes long counts and complicated processes of vote transfer, and the limits on representation of smaller parties because of the small number of members elected from each constituency.[5]

Table 4.3 An example of an election by single transferable vote[a]

Candidate	Round 1		Round 2	Round 3		Round 4
Arnold	7,001	(+500)	7,501	elected		elected
Booth	9,001[b]		elected	elected		elected
Curtis	2,000		2,000	2,000[d]		eliminated
Davies	2,200	(+500)	2,700	2,700	(+200)	2,900
Evans	4,298	(+500)	4,798 (+1,000)	5,798	(+1,800)	7,598 (elected)
Fitzroy	4,500		4,500	4,500		4,500
Gale	1,000		1,000[c]	eliminated		eliminated

[a] Thirty thousand votes have been cast, and three persons are to be elected. Thus the quota is 7,501 votes.

[b] Booth has obtained the quota and is elected; her 1,500 surplus votes (9,001–7,501) are allocated in proportion to all the second preferences on all her 9,001 votes. It is assumed here that they are shared equally among Arnold, Davies and Evans, who thus obtain 500 extra votes each. This allocation gives Arnold 7,501 votes, so Arnold is elected, but has no surplus votes to reallocate.

[c] On the next round, all the votes of the candidate with the lowest number of votes are allocated to the second preferences shown on the voting papers. It is assumed here that all go to Evans, who now has 5,798 votes. Still no other candidate has the necessary quota for election, so the candidate with the lowest number of votes of those remaining is eliminated.

[d] Curtis's 2,000 votes are given to the second-preference candidates on his ballot papers: 1,800 to Evans, 200 to Davies. Evans now has the quota and is elected.

Note that on different patterns of second-choice redistributions, once Booth is elected any of the other candidates could still be elected, and that it is conceivable that third or later preferences could be used in order to decide which candidates are elected (for instance, had Evans not quite obtained the quota on round 4, then Davies's 2,900 votes (including 200 second-preference votes) would have had to be redistributed in order to decide whether Evans or Fitzroy was elected).

Electoral reform

In few countries is there complete or lasting satisfaction with the electoral system in use at the time. No system is, or can be, perfect, if only because people disagree as to what would constitute 'perfection'; they want electoral systems to do different things. The long debate concerning the electoral system to be used uniformly for future elections for the EP has given further stimulus to discussion about the different properties which characterise different electoral systems, about what electoral systems do and about how well they do it.

Though there are many controversial issues regarding details of electoral systems, the main debate concerning electoral reform relates to two questions. First, what should be represented through the electoral process: local or regional constituencies? social categories (such as ethnic or religious minorities)? voters' party preferences? Second, should an electoral system give priority to the function of reflecting reasonably accurately the party preferences of voters, or should it seek to translate votes into seats in such a way as to ensure (or at least make probable) that a government can be formed with a stable legislative majority? Of course, these alternative criteria are often advocated or criticised for reasons of party or sectional advantage.

In countries where party preferences are not divided conveniently between two, and only two, alternative parties, accurate representation of party preferences may prevent the formation of governments based on single-party majorities, which can count on a safe majority of parliamentary seats sufficient to keep them in power until the next scheduled election. The problem is linked to the dominant role played by parties in western European democracies. Governments are formed by a party or parties, which claim authority on the basis of their parliamentary majority. Proportional representation of parties tends to require, more often than not, the creation of a coalition government, simply because one party alone will rarely command a majority of seats. Coalitions are necessarily compromises and are at the mercy of one party or another threatening to leave the coalition, thus depriving it of its legislative majority and ability to continue in office. Even when only two parties are involved, as has usually been the case with coalition governments in the Federal Republic of Germany, one party can attempt to 'blackmail' the other in order to obtain concessions. The small FDP tried to do this in 1966, for example, to get its own way on financial policy, but instead of making concessions the larger Christian Democratic party formed a 'grand coalition' with the SPD. This 'grand coalition' gave serious consideration to reforming the electoral system, to prevent such 'blackmail' happening again. An expert report recommending adoption of a system rather like that of the

UK, based on single-member constitutencies, was presented to the government, but the Social Democrats calculated that this would harm their chances of ever leading the government, so refused to support the change. No serious proposal for substantial reform of the German system has been made since.

In Ireland, there have been two referenda to try to replace the STV system by the system used in the UK, the most recent of which was in 1968. On both occasions, the electorate voted to retain STV. In France, the parties of the left had felt unfairly disadvantaged by the two-ballot electoral system introduced for the Fifth Republic. So they introduced a list-based system of proportional representation based on the departments for the 1986 National Assembly elections. This electoral system, as intended, did penalise the right by restricting the number of seats which the Gaullist and Republican parties won, compared to what they could have expected to secure under the two-ballot system (and also, incidentally, siphoned off votes which they might otherwise have obtained, votes which helped to elect candidates from the extremist National Front). Even so, the Gaullists and Republicans obtained sufficient seats to be able to form a government, and that government then reverted to the two-ballot system for future elections. In Italy, revelations of corruption affecting all the established parties, and discontent with the instability of coalition governments and the inability of those governments to improve the economic and social conditions of the Italian people, contributed to the success of a referendum in 1993 on the system of election for the Senate. This led to legislation in 1993 which introduced a substantial modification of the list-based proportional representation system for future elections for both chambers of the legislature, with only a minority of seats in each chamber to be allocated proportionally from party lists.

It is in the UK, however, that electoral reform has been most thoroughly and frequently debated, even though that debate has not produced any radical amendment to the 'first-past-the-post' electoral system. The reason for this persistent debate is that the electoral system developed piecemeal over several centuries. It pre-dates the invention of poltical parties or the introduction of universal suffrage. The UK has never experienced either political revolution or occupation by a foreign power, so there has never been the occasion for a complete redesign of a system in which anomalies and inequities have accumulated over many years. True, alternative systems have been considered and recommended. Indeed, an all-party conference in 1917 unanimously condemned the existing system, but its members could not agree upon any one alternative to it. In 1929, the Labour government succeeded in passing a bill to replace the existing system with a variation called the 'alternative vote', but failed to get the proposal through the House of Lords. The two general elections of 1974, with their inability to provide any party with a secure majority of seats and their gross inequity to the Liberal Party, revived the issue of electoral reform. The Hansard Society produced an influential report in 1976, analysing the faults of the system and recommending the adoption of either STV or an 'additional member system' very similar to that used by the Federal Republic of Germany. The Liberal Democratic party wants to introduce STV. The Labour Party created the Plant committee to investigate the merits and disadvantages of alternative electoral systems; after four successive elections in which the Conservatives were able to form a government with a share of the vote well under 50 per cent, and in 1992 with only 43 per cent of the vote, a substantial minority in the Labour Party wishes to see a change of electoral system.[6]

The 'first-past-the-post' system in the UK is defended on four grounds. First, it tends to produce safe majorities of seats for a single party. This party can then form a government in the knowledge that it can govern until it wishes to call another general election, and can introduce the policies in its manifesto and take responsibility for these without the complication of negotiation with a coalition partner. Second, it tends to provide a second party with a substantial number of seats, which can then be identified as the main opposition party and as the alternative government at the next election. Third, it is simple to understand and operate: the voter has only one mark to make on the ballot paper, and the candidate with the most votes wins the seat.

Finally, it provides personal identification for the voter with a local MP, and provides the MP with a local base.

It is criticised on five grounds. First, it greatly exaggerates relatively small changes in electoral opinion at elections, so that unduly large changes in party strengths result. Indeed, because of the prevalance of 'safe' seats, where even large changes of opinion do not affect the outcome, changes of government can result from small alterations in the opinions of a minority of the electorate in a few 'marginal' constituencies. Second, it is generally unfair to parties other than the 'big two', unless those other parties have regional concentrations of strength, like the Scottish Nationalist Party. Third, it can leave large areas of the country represented by MPs from only one party, despite substantial electoral support in those areas for other parties.[7] Fourth, it does not in fact *guarantee* a working majority for one party (and a government which receives a majority at an election can see it disappear through by-elections or because MPs of the government party cross to the opposition – both of which factors reduced the majority of the Major government to almost nothing by 1996). Nor does it even guarantee a 'fair' outcome, in the sense that (as in 1951 and February 1974) the party with the most seats may not be the party with the most votes. Finally, because of the infrequency of revision of constituency boundaries, votes in some constituencies can be worth 'less' than votes in other constituencies.

Consider the following facts. Since the Second World War, no party has won 50 per cent of votes, yet only one election has produced a government with fewer than 50 per cent of seats in the House of Commons. Second, in 1983 the Conservative government won more seats than it had in 1979, yet had a smaller percentage of the votes cast than in 1979. In the same election the SPD–Liberal Alliance won 26 per cent of the vote but only 3.5 per cent of seats, compared to Labour's 28.3 per cent of votes and 37.8 per cent of seats. Third, in 1992, the prime minister's constituency, Huntingdon, had an electorate of nearly 93,000, and the Isle of Wight nearly 100,000, but Newham North-West had only 46,471 registered electors and Surbiton 42,421. This meant that just under 89,000 voters in Newham North-West and Surbiton have two MPs, but larger numbers in Huntingdon (or the Isle of Wight) have only one MP. Further such anomalies affect, or have in recent times affected, Wales, Scotland and Northern Ireland, as a result of special legislation.

Certainly, were some form of proportional representation, or even STV, to be adopted for parliamentary elections in the UK, coalition government would be inevitable. Experience in other countries does not suggest that this would therefore necessarily be weak government or unstable government. It would rob the Conservative and Labour parties of any expectation that they could govern alone, though, which is one reason why both parties have opposed electoral reform.

Aside from the arguments about fairness and government stability, some commentators have suggested that the British electoral system also produces inefficient government, because of the style of 'adversary politics' which it promotes (the idea that all issues have two, and only two, incompatible policy solutions). Thus the UK has had nationalisation, denationalisation and renationalisation of the steel industry since the Second World War, and similar violent swings of policy have been experienced concerning housing, education, industrial relations and public finance. Such critics argue that a different electoral system would encourage compromise, as it does in other European countries, by producing coalition governments which would have to seek a consensus, and would have to try to win the 'middle ground' of politics if they were to retain electoral support. The system in the UK, on the other hand (continue these critics), seems to reward extremism in the two main parties. Politicians who embrace the principles of the party most enthusiastically and uncompromisingly are adopted for safe seats and climb highest in the party hierarchy, eventually obtaining ministerial office. Moderation is seen as lack of commitment, as weakness. In other countries, such as the Federal Republic of Germany. Italy, the Netherlands and Austria, criticism is sometimes heard of the political compromises which proportional electoral systems produce. The voter, claim those critics, is unable to make a clear and decisive choice at elections, since only after post-election negotiations can a government be formed.[8] Compromise thus may be interpreted as misrepresentation of the voters' decision in the election. (On the actual situation concerning coalition government formation, see Chapter 7.)

Electoral reform is never undertaken for altruistic motives alone. Parties foresee advantages or disadvantages for themselves in any suggested change of the method of translating votes into seats, and sometimes (as in France ahead of the 1986 legislative election) attempt to manipulate the electoral system to their own benefit. However, such cases of actual or attempted manipulation through electoral reform do not always succeed, for three reasons: first, parties may make erroneous predictions about the likely outcome of an election held under the new system; second, electoral behaviour may change precisely because of the conditions of the new electoral system (e.g. if proportional representation is introduced, supporters of smaller parties may now vote for these, without fear of wasting their votes, a fear which in the past may have led them to vote for a second-choice larger party); and third, electoral systems are linked to so many other aspects of the political system (the party system, political culture, political communication, etc.) that it is difficult to predict just what changes would occur, and especially if a foreign electoral system is 'imported'. So electoral reform is an issue in which party advantage is necessarily involved, but it is also one in which manipulation to obtain party advantage is a risky and uncertain venture.[9]

Notes

1 Electoral systems used in fictional contexts can also be interesting. Two examples concerning Oxbridge colleges can be mentioned. In Colin Dexter's *The Riddle of the Third Mile* (an Inspector Morse mystery), to be elected master of an Oxford college, a candidate needed six of the eight available votes, and had to avoid having any vote cast against him (Dexter 1984:113). In C.P. Snow's book *The*

Masters, for a candidate to be elected master of the college, an absolute majority of the fellows must have voted in favour (Snow 1963:64).

2 Some multi-member constituencies do exist, or have existed in the past, in some systems using the simple majority system of election, but with usually no more than two or three members being elected per constituency. In some British local government elections, especially for parish councils where these still exist, several members may be elected, and each voter is then allowed to vote for as many candidates as there are seats to be filled.

3 A special case is where voters 'construct' a list by their votes for candidates, as in Baden-Württemberg for *Land* elections. In that *Land* some seats are filled by direct election of candidates in constituencies. The remaining seats are filled so as to produce an overall result that gives parties proportionality of representation, but the additional seats are filled by the candidates of the parties who, having failed to win constituency seats, have the best results as losing candidates for their party.

4 For many years there were normally 496 seats to be filled (plus West Berlin representatives, nominated by the West Berlin city council, with restricted rights). The enlargement to 656 followed the unification of Germany prior to the 1990 federal election and the incorporation of Berlin into the Federal Republic. Before and since unification, it has been possible for there to be more seats allocated at any election than the 'normal' number: if a party wins more constituency seats in a region than its total entitlement on the basis of its share of list votes, it keeps the additional seats, but other parties receive their full proportional allocation, thus increasing – temporarily – the total number of seats in that region. These temporary additional seats are called *Überhangmandate* (surplus seats).

5 In a four-member constituency, for instance, a party with less than one-fifth of the vote will not normally obtain a seat. If that were the case uniformly throughout the country, there would be in effect a 20 per cent threshold for representation. This assumes that all voters vote for all the candidates of their most preferred party first, before selecting candidates from any other party, but only on the basis of that assumption can one even begin to assess what the 'vote' for any party has been, and thus what its 'proportional representation' should be in terms of seats.

6 As the likelihood of a Labour government with an overall majority became greater in 1995–96, so interest in and support for electoral reform diminished within the Labour party: see the special issue on 'Plant in retrospect', *Representation*, 33(2), Summer/Autum 1995.
7 A special instance of this is Scotland, where the Conservatives win relatively few seats; Scottish nationalist sypathisers therefore claim that the party has no 'mandate' to govern Scotland.
8 Though since the 1972 election in the Federal Republic of Germany there has always appeared to be a clear choice for the voter at general elections: to support the re-election of the governing coalition, or to vote for the opposition party or 'bloc' (in 1983–94, for instance, this bloc consisted of the SPD and the Greens).
9 A useful review of the complexities involved in reforming electoral systems is to be found in Bogdanor (1983).

References

Bogdanor, V. (1983) 'Conclusions: electoral systems and party systems', in V. Bogdanor and D. Butler (eds) *Democracy and Elections*, Cambridge, Cambridge University Press.
Dexter, C. (1984) *The Riddle of the Third Mile*, London, Pan.
O'Leary, C. (1975) 'Ireland: the North and the South', in S. Finer (ed.) *Adversary Politics and Electoral Reform*, London, Anthony Wigram.
Snow, C.P. (1963) *The Masters*, London, Macmillan.

Further reading

Blackburn, R. (1995) *The Electoral System in Britain*, Basingstoke, Macmillan.
Bogdanor, V. (1984) *What Is Proportional Representation?*, Oxford, Martin Robertson.
Bogdanor, V. and D. Butler (eds) (1983) *Democracy and Elections*, Cambridge, Cambridge University Press.
Broughton, D., D. Farrell, D. Denver and C. Rallings (eds) (1995) *British Elections and Party Yearbook 1994*, London, Frank Cass (and earlier volumes in this series since the 1991 Yearbook).
Butler, D. and D. Kavanagh (1992) *The British General Election of 1992*, Basingstoke, Macmillan (and earlier volumes in the Nuffield British General Election Series).

Conradt, D., G. Kleinfeld, G. Romoser and C. Soe (eds) (1995) *Germany's New Politics*, Providence, R.I. and Oxford, Berghahn.

Lijphart, A. (1994) *Electoral Systems and Party Systems*, Oxford, Oxford University Press.

Mackie, T. and R. Rose (1991) *International Almanac of Electoral History*, Basingstoke, Macmillan, 3rd edn.

Reeve, A. (1992) *Electoral Systems: a Comparative and Theoretical Introduction*, London, Routledge 3rd edn.

5

Linkage organisations: political parties

Party systems and democracy

In Chapter 2 the role of political parties and their competition with each other through elections were claimed to be among the essential features of a modern democracy. In Chapter 3, the way in which various ideological 'families' of parties have developed in western Europe was described. In Chapter 4, the relationships between parties and electoral systems were examined. Other chapters also refer to parties as relevant to various aspects of the political system, and as significant actors in the political structures and processes of the EU. So clearly parties interpenetrate numerous institutions and processes in modern democracies. All western European states, since they are classed as democracies, have competitive party systems, and it is hard to imagine how their political systems could function as democracies without parties.

Political parties are organisations which seek to participate in government as a consequence of the success of their candidates in elections; indeed, one of the few definitions of political parties enshrined in law (the German Party Law of 1967) emphasises regular participation in elections as a defining feature of a party. Whereas interest-groups are organisations which seek only to *influence* government (see Chapter 6), parties want to *become* the government, alone or with coalition partners.

Another defining feature of a political party is that it seeks to promote some ideology, programme or cause (which is a principal reason for a party to seek to participate in government, of course!). In many cases, the labels which parties adopt give an indication of this: socialist parties; conservative parties; Christian democratic parties; nationalist parties; green parties; and so forth. Some parties represent a very general tendency within the bounds of which substantially different sets of policies can be developed and promoted (for instance, the British Conservative party under Mrs Thatcher was very different in its programmatic aims to that under Mr Heath; the West German CDU originally had a strong collectivist element in its early post-war programme, but rapidly became an unambiguously centre-right party). Others represent a more defined programme. Socialist and social democratic parties have been instances of this. Other parties may stand for a single cause or issue as their main priority (some green parties emphasising ecological issues; nationalist parties seeking separation from the state; some right-wing extremist parties which are primarily anti-immigrant), and thus may be little different from pressure groups, except for their use of elections and direct representation in the legislature as means to promote their cause.

The term 'party system' denotes the several parties within a political system – usually that of the nation-state – and their interrelationships (see below). Party systems perform many functions. They structure political competition through elections, so that voters can make clear and meaningful choices when they cast their ballots. They allow politically significant groupings in society, such as social classes, regions, linguistic groupings and social and economic interests which are thought to be of especial political importance, to participate in politics in a coherent and transparent manner. In this way, the principal cleavages within a society can be represented by parties. Party systems provide competing 'teams', which can participate in government (alone or in coalition), or become challengers to the governing parties. They transmit the demands of citizens to the governing authorities – to presidents, ministers, parliaments, local councils – and constitute one of the 'feedback' channels by means of which citizens can be informed of what, if anything, has been done to satisfy those demands. In relation to Figure 2.1, parties are 'linkage organisations', intermediaries between the people and the powers that be, between 'them' and 'us'. (The parties individually have other functions also: these are described later in this chapter.)

This function of acting as a two-way 'linkage organisation' is what all competitive party systems have in common. Where only one party is permitted to exist, as happened in Nazi Germany, in the Soviet Union until 1989, and as is the case in Cuba, China and North Korea today, the single party tends to identify with the government, with the state authorities, with a single overriding ideology, and is not able or willing to concern itself with the wishes of all the people, or of all types of social grouping, and is certainly not able or willing to act as opposition to official policy. Because of this lack of opposition parties, reform movements in eastern European countries in the late 1980s had to express themselves through loose, unofficial (indeed, usually illegal) 'citizen movement' organisations. Only when their demands for reform were met, which was more or less simultaneous with the downfall of communist regimes in those countries, were democratic and truly competitive party systems permitted to form.

The composition and style of party systems

Though all western European party systems perform, by and large, the same functions, great differences obviously emerge when the composition and style of national party systems are more closely examined. Even in the same country drastic changes in party systems may occur. These changes may be caused by changes of circumstances, a new constitution or electoral system, changes in the social or economic context of politics, or the emergence of a new cleavage in political life, for instance. The party systems of Germany before the First World War, in the Weimar Republic, in the early years of the post-war West German state, in the years from 1961 to 1990, and since reunification, have all been markedly different in terms of the numbers and types of parties and the ideological positions represented by those parties. The French party system today is different from that of the Fourth Republic. The Italian party system has changed dramatically over the past few years. For a time, it seemed that the creation of the Social Democratic Party (SDP) in Britain in 1981 would change the Party system significantly, but its failure to establish itself and its merger with the Liberal party marked the end of that opportunity.

Four major differentiating characteristics allow distinctions among party systems to be identified. First, and most obviously, the *number* of parties which exist in a country can vary. However, as Sartori has demonstrated, determining the number of parties in a party system is not a straightforward matter. His scheme for classifying party systems (see later in this chapter) starts out from the concept of *relevant* parties: those whose representation in the legislature is relevant to the decision about which government takes office, or else who possess 'blackmail potential', in so far as they can affect decisions on some, if not all, legislation (Sartori 1976:122–3). The British Liberal Party during most of the post-second world war period (though not in 1974 or 1977–79) is an example of an 'irrelevant' party in Sartori's terms, yet it always had *local* relevance in some areas. The French Communist Party or the German radical right-wing Republican party at national level could be termed 'irrelevant' today, perhaps. Other possible criteria for counting parties of course exist: the number of parties which exceed some stated percentage of the vote at national elections and the number of parties with a certain percentage of seats in the lower house of the legislature would be other possibilities.[1] Leaving aside non-competitive one-party systems (of which there is now no case in western Europe), applying some rule for counting parties would allow the classification of party systems into two-party and multi-party systems; though this latter category may be too large and varied to be useful, and Sartori (see below) has developed an interesting scheme for differentiating between types of multi-party system.

Second, the *relative size* of parties will differ as between different party systems. This may occur even where the number and the ideological basis of parties are similar. The British party system, for instance, has the same three nation-wide parties in the 1990s as existed in the 1950s, but the Labour Party is smaller both in terms of membership and seats in Parliament than it was in the 1950s, when trade union membership was much larger, and the Liberal Party is stronger and has a firmer membership base than in the 1950s. The decline in strength of the French Communist Party means that the structure of the party system in France in the 1990s is different from the party system of the 1970s and 1980s. The SPD in eastern Germany is much smaller in terms of membership and voting support than the party in western Germany (even after allowing for the smaller population in eastern Germany), because of competition from the PDS in eastern Germany.

Third, the *cleavages* which form the context of party competition and the ideological basis of parties may vary. In some countries (Belgium, for instance) language differences may be represented in the party system. The importance (or indeed even the existence) of parties representing a particular religion or denomination may vary: the United Kingdom has no Christian democratic party, for instance. Regional parties exist in some countries: those defending regional interests in Corsica, Scotland, Catalonia and the Basque region in Spain, the Northern League in Italy, the PDS in eastern Germany, and even to some extent the Christian Social Union (CSU) in Bavaria, are instances. The Swedish People's Party in Finland represents the Swedish-speaking minority there. Agrarian parties exist in Scandinavia and Switzerland. Ecological parties now are active in many countries, though in only a few are they politically significant. Northern Irish party conflicts are concerned with the issue of retention of the union with Great Britain or pursuit of union with Ireland, conflicts which are reinforced by religious cleavages. Some observers have claimed to identify the replacement of the cleavage of social class in Britain by a cleavage between 'public sector' and 'private sector' interests, with the Labour

Party representing the former, the Conservatives the latter. Thus the 'menu' of parties offered to the voter differs from country to country, and may differ within a country over a period of time.

Finally, party systems vary in terms of the *ideological distance* between different parties. There are two indicators of ideological distance. One is whether parties are able, at least in principle, to consider forming coalitions with each other, when that becomes necessary to secure a legislative majority, or whether – a weaker test – one party will allow some other party to support it in government, without becoming part of that government (known as 'toleration'[2]). Two parties which cannot contemplate ever sharing membership of coalitions presumably have incompatible ideological positons. Where such incompatibility of parties exists, the party system may be said to be 'polarised', containing within it extremist or 'anti-system' parties. So a second indicator is whether some parties are 'anti-system parties' (another term used in Sartori's classificatory scheme): that is, whether they profess to seek to replace the existing regime, either by peaceful or violent means. Many communist parties in the past in western Europe regarded parliamentary democracy as a form of regime which serves the interests of capitalism, and wished instead to introduce a regime to serve the interests of socialism. In the case of some parties of the far right in Germany, France, Austria and Italy, for instance, as well as some parties of the far left (such as the PDS in Germany) doubts exist concerning the extent to which they genuinely accept the 'rules of the game', the parliamentary democratic regimes in which they undertake their activities. Nationalist or separatist parties may also be 'anti-system': not in terms necessarily of the regime form, but rather of the 'political community' (see Chapter 2). Such parties may wish to link their regions to some other state, or indeed wish to form a separate state. The nationalist Sinn Fein party in Northern Ireland and the Scottish Nationalist Party are examples.

Of course it is evident that there may be considerable ideological distance between factions within a single party: within the

British Labour Party (as illustrated by conflicts over Clause Four of the party's constitution, or disputes about the form and degree of trade union power within the party) or Conservative party (over Britain's position and role within the EU), within the SPD in Germany, within both the Gaullist and the Socialist parties in France, or, until recently at least, within the formerly powerful Christian Democratic Party in Italy. Usually, however, these differences do not go as far as hindering attempts by the party to join or form governments.

This review of the major dimensions according to which differences in party systems in western Europe can be identified and analysed raises the question of how a useful comparison and categorisation of party systems can be undertaken. After all, it would seem as though every country has a party system which is different from those of other countries in so many ways. One such attempt at a classificatory scheme which can be employed for comparative purposes is that of Giovanni Sartori, aspects of which have been described earlier in this chapter.

Sartori (1976) developed a typology of party systems, based on the number of relevant parties in a party system, and the kinds of party which the system included. Three of the categories which he identified are applicable to western European party systems.

The *two-party system* exists where two parties dominate and these normally govern in alternation, each able to count on a majority of seats in the legislature without needing any other party in order to construct a governing majority. Clearly, Britain since the end of the Second World War has been such a case. The Labour and Conservative parties have formed alternating governments, and only rarely has either party lacked an overall majority. No coalition has been necessary. This is very much a consequence of the British 'first-past-the-post' electoral system which almost invariably provides these parties with absolute majorities of seats in the House of Commons, even though they obtain considerably less than 50 per cent of the vote at general elections (see Chapter 4). The Liberal Democrats hope to be in a position one day to bargain with one of these larger parties, possibly even to the extent of entering a coalition, but unless some far-reaching reform of the electoral system is undertaken, that opportunity will depend as much on the chancy arithmetic of election results (producing a 'hung parliament' with no single-party majority of seats) as on the electoral successes of the Liberal Democrats.

It is arguable that France also falls into this two-party category, at least in terms of the presidency, where the electoral system sets up a 'run-off' between the top two candidates, usually candidates of the 'left' and 'right' party blocs (Jospin and Chirac in 1995, for instance). It is also possible to regard the 'government' and 'opposition' as associated with these two blocs (even when cohabitation becomes necessary, with the government and the president coming from opposite blocs). However, in terms of electoral support and representation at subnational level, there is much to be said for classifying France as a multi-party system, with at least six parties: the Communists and Socialists on the left; the Greens; the Republicans and Gaullists on the right; and the far-right National Front (Morris 1994:130–52). As with Britain, the French simple-majority electoral system (though modified by a two-ballot provision) contributes to this situation.

Ireland is a more doubtful case; in some periods, single-party majority governments have been formed, but in other periods coalitions of two parties have been required, so alternation of single-party governments cannot be regarded as the norm.

In many countries, the number of parties contesting elections, the electoral system and voting behaviour all contribute to a situation where a single party can rarely, if ever, secure an absolute majority of parliamentary seats. In such countries, two species of multi-party system exist.

One is the *moderate multi-party system*. In such a party system, there are usually between three and six parties, with governments being formed from no more than two or three; competition for votes is directed at the centre of the political spectrum. The Federal Republic of Germany is a good example of this type of party system. From 1961 only three parties obtained seats in the Bundestag (until the Greens won seats in 1983). Coalitions were necessary, since no single party could command a majority of seats alone; usually the small FDP joined with one of the two larger parties, the CDU-CSU or the SPD, though between 1966 and 1969 a 'grand coalition' of the CDU-CSU and SPD existed, with the FDP in opposition. Despite the entry of the Greens into the Bundestag, and the addition of the far-left PDS since reunification in 1990, this two-party coalition arrangement has not changed. This is because the two largest parties, the Social Democrats (1969–82) and the Christian Democrats (since 1982) have, together with the FDP, been able to form a government with a majority in the Bundestag, but neither major party has managed to secure a majority of Bundestag seats on its own. Opinion polls show that even many respondents who are supporters of these two parties prefer the idea of a coalition government to single-party rule, possible because of the memories of the Nazi period. To form a government, therefore, both the Christian Democrats and the Social Democrats know that they will almost certainly need the Free Democrats, and that knowledge, together with the necessity of attracting 'swing' voters from the other party (voters likely to be located on the left wing of the Christian Democrats or the right wing of the SPD), forces the parties to compete for the centre ground.[3] Austria, Denmark, Norway and the Netherlands (in recent years) are other examples of this category of party system.

The third type of party system sometimes found in post-war western Europe has been the *polarised multi-party system*. In such cases, rather more than five relevant parties exist; one or more of these may be an 'anti-system' party, seeking the replacement of the existing political regime by some other type of political system; coalition governments will tend to involve three or more parties as a rule; and political competition will tend to be polarised towards both the right and the left of the political spectrum, not concentrated on the 'centre ground'. Italy has been regarded as such a case: governing coalitions have usually consisted of four or five parties; a communist and a far-right party have had representation in the legislature; and party competition has been directed towards the right and left of the political spectrum. Whether the recent upheavals in the Italian party system will place Italy in the 'moderate' multi-party category remains to be seen. Finland and France have been suggested as other candidates for this category (Keman 1995:127–8). Before the war, the party system of Weimar Germany was an obvious example of such a party system. The party system of Fourth Republic France (1946–58) was another typical case.

However, it will not always be easy to categorise party systems as clearly belonging to one or other of these types. Party systems can be in the process of changing from one type to another, or they may exhibit some, but not all, of the qualifying characteristics. Sweden, which sometimes has coalition government and sometimes single-party government by the Social Democrats, is an example of a system which is hard to categorise in terms of Sartori's typology.

Why do party systems vary?

Party systems reflect the history of a society and its degree of homogeneity. If a society is deeply divided – by class, religion, ethnicity or language, for instance – its party system will doubtless reflect those divisions. Historical experience, such as occupation by an enemy in wartime and resistance to such occupation (Italy, France), civil war (Spain, Ireland), religious divisions and anti-clericalism (France), or the overthrow of dictatorship (Spain, Greece, Portugal) can be echoed in the format of the party system. But other factors may also shape the party system. The law may prohibit certain types of party (two parties were banned in the Federal Republic of Germany in 1952 and 1956 because they were judged as being anti-democratic and thus unconstitutional). The electoral system may make it extremely difficult for small parties to survive or new parties to establish themselves (Britain's 'first-past-the-post' system, or restrictions on proportional representation in Germany and some Scandinavian countries, for instance). National or international developments may influence the formation, success or survival of parties: the growth of environmental awareness and the rise of 'new politics' movements encouraged green parties to form. The end of the cold war made western European communist parties superfluous, or at least cut off funding upon which they had relied, and led to their rapid decline after 1988 (Bull and Heywood 1994).

Party systems are not static. Of course, they change in some degree all the time: no two elections, for instance, produce the same result except in the most general terms. Parties change, and sometimes that change is of such an extent that the party system itself changes (examples are the ideological positions of the Austrian Freedom Party, which moved to the right in recent years under its populist leader, Jörg Haider; the deradicalisation of the German Green party since 1990; and the modernisation of the British Labour Party under the leadership of Kinnock and Blair). Party system change is usually considered to be some very significant change in the number of relevant parties, in the cleavages which parties represent, in the size and ideological position of parties or in the addition or disappearance of anti-system parties. Examples of such party system change include:

- the 'explosion' in the number of parties in the Danish party system from 1973, when the 'format changed from a five-party system to a ten-party system' (Bille 1992:200);
- the rise and consolidation of the National Front in France since the mid-1980s;
- the changes in the Italian party system in the early 1990s involving the near-disappearance of the Christian Democratic and Socialist parties which had for so many years provided leadership of governing coalitions, and the rise of the Northern League, the increase in strength of extreme right-wing parties, and the surge in support for the PDS (Democratic Party of the Left – the reformed communist party);
- the addition of the Greens in the 1980s to the three-party system (CDU-CSU, SPD and FDP) which had for so long existed in the Federal Republic of Germany.

The formation of new cleavages in society, the attraction, especially to younger generations, of 'new politics' rather than the bread-and-butter issues of 'old politics', and increased electoral volatility all make changes in western European party systems more likely than in the past (Mair 1990).

The functions of political parties

Parties perform several important political functions which facilitate the democratic political process. It is possible to imagine some of these functions being performed by other organisations and institutions; for other functions, though, parties seem indispensable. Parties generally carry out a combination of functions in a reasonably effective way, though this does not mean that they cannot be criticised for the way in which some functions are performed, or sometimes neglected.

Parties perform five essential functions in democracies. First, they *represent* different interests and social groups within the political arena: at elections, in parliaments, in local government, in the EP and in other institutions.[4] They give expression to the demands or criticisms of their 'clientele': the working class in the case of socialist parties; farmers in the case of agrarian parties; the middle class and producer interests in the case of conservative parties; special cause groups in the case of ecology parties or nationalist parties. Parties will speak for these groups and interests through representatives elected to public office, in delegations to ministers, in the context of election campaigns, through interviews in the media, and so on. Without parties, such groups and interests would be confined to the activities of interest-groups, which would probably represent and express their interests less effectively, less coherently and certainly often less powerfully, because they would lack the opportunity to participate in government, and would not have the resources upon which at least the larger parties in western European democracies can rely. Interest-groups would also not be able to simplify the multiplicity of options which may exist in particular policy areas (such as social policy, or education) so that a coherent and restricted number of alternative programmes could be presented to the electorate.

Second, most parties endeavour to gain sufficient support at elections to enable them to *participate in government*, either alone, or in coalition. Those parties that fail in this endeavour have the opportunity to act as opposition to the government: criticising it, challenging its decisions, and trying to demonstrate that they could do the job better – given the opportunity! Government in most western European democracies is 'party government',[5] and parties, through their manifestos and programmes (and, in the case of coalitions, through the bargaining among the parties which occurs prior to the formation of coalitions), provide coherence and direction to government, and take responsibility for policy decisions when in government. This trend towards 'party government' has grown during the twentieth century. Not only is it rare for parliamentarians or ministers now to be without party affiliation, but also most issues are debated or decided in terms of party interests, and party affiliation has become a pervasive factor in appointments to government agencies and various other public offices.

Some small parties may never have any realistic chance of being included in a government, particularly if they are extremist or anti-system parties, and because of ideological distance (see above) are difficult or impossible for other parties to ally with. This may apply to parties concerned with some single, overriding issue: regional autonomy or separatism, for instance, or environmental protection. Yet even these parties may, generally or on particular issues, influence governments by their criticism, their representation of a particular clientele, or their status in the party system as a 'protest party' which could draw support away from a government at some future election. The wooing of small parties by the British Labour government in 1979, after it had lost its overall majority in the House of Commons and its pact with the Liberals had been terminated, showed how, in some circumstances, even very small parties can obtain concessions or patronage from a government. The German liberal party, the FDP, has been a member of governing coalitions in the Federal

Republic uninterruptedly since 1969, and has been a partner in governing coalitions for more years than either the Christian Democrats or Social Democrats, because its votes in the Bundestag have been needed to create governing majorities. Yet the vote share of the FDP has fluctuated between 5 and 13 per cent, being generally much lower than that of the British Liberals, for instance.

Parties want to be in power, or to influence those parties which are in power, in order to realise their policies. Governmental office is the prize in the political game because in that way parties can translate the wishes of their supporters, of those interests which the parties represent, into policy. Of course, being in office means more to a party than just the opportunity to put policy proposals into action. Office provides a party and its leaders with publicity, patronage, the chance to gain a reputation as an effective government (though carrying the risk also of being blamed when things go wrong!): and these advantages pay off at election time.

Third, parties act as *channels of recruitment* of political leaders. In western European democracies, it is rare indeed for the head of government or other ministers not to be long-serving members of political parties. This is not accidental: since democracy relies on party government, it is logical that party leaders and members of the party elite should also take leading roles in government, and their experience within the party is relevant to their role as heads of government or as ministers. Exceptionally, political leaders are imported from outside the normal parliamentary and party career structure: Silvio Berlusconi, who became prime minister of Italy following the founding in 1993 of Forza Italia, had made his fortune and reputation in business, not as a party politician; his successor, Lamberto Dini, was a banker who become finance minister in 1994, but was not a member of a political party at that time; Ernest Bevin, in the wartime coalition headed by Churchill, was a prominent trade union leader (though a member of the Labour Party, of course); Ludwig Erhard, economics minister in the Adenauer governments in West Germany, was a former professor, and became a member of the CDU only in 1963, the year he became chancellor of the Federal Republic; another German example is Klaus Kinkel, who joined the FDP only at the time of his appointment as justice minister, but then became foreign minister and leader of his party shortly afterwards; Raymond Barre became prime minister in France before joining his party.[6]

However, the overwhelming majority of prime ministers, chancellors, presidents, mayors, members of cabinets and leaders of local councils reach their positions of public importance only after many years of service to their party. First comes the hard work within the party organisation, and perhaps election to party office; then the struggle to secure election to the local council or the national legislature, followed by a period of loyal service in that position; only then comes the slow, often unsteady, climb up the ladder to ministerial office, followed perhaps by election as leader of the party. Even then, some party leaders find the step to becoming leader of the government can be delayed: Willy Brandt and François Mitterrand both lost several elections before they became federal chancellor in Germany and president of France respectively. Some party leaders, such as Hugh Gaitskell and Neil Kinnock in Britain, or Franz-Josef Strauss in West Germany, never do make it to the very top.

Fourth, parties offer the most important (though not the sole) channel of *political participation* for the public. Those members of the public who join political parties have opportunities to influence the selection of candidates for local and national elective office. Indeed, in a safe seat or for top places on a party list, such selection may be the equivalent of election to the legislature or to a local council. Party members can make inputs to the policy formation process; they can raise funds for the party; they can assist in the election campaigns of the party. In some parties, members participate directly in the election of the leader (the Labour and Liberal Democratic parties in Britain, and the SPD in Germany,[7] for instance). Members can also stand for party office or serve as delegates to party committees and congresses, and even seek nomination themselves for selection as the party's candidate for public office. The fact that so few people *do* become members of political parties, and even fewer of those wish to play any active role in the party, means that the influence of those who are active is so much greater. Despite complaints that membership participation is often obstructed by local elites, opportunities do exist for members to affect how their parties act and the decisions that are made. Increasingly, parties are trying to encourage people to become members, and, once members, to be active. The active participation of women, for example, is being encouraged in many parties, and gender quotas for office-holding, for candidate selection and for the choice of delegates to party congresses are in place in several parties: especially, but not exclusively, in parties that are left of centre.

Finally, parties provide two-way *channels of communication* between members of the public and the institutions of government. They transmit the demands and opinions of the public (especially, of course, their own members and supporters) to the legislature, to ministers, to councillors, to administrators. They also justify or criticise, and clarify the complexities of, government policy, which serves to inform the public about what is being done, or being planned, by the authorities. This occurs most intensively in election campaigns, but at other times as well the press, radio and television, public meetings, personal communication between the politician and a member of the public or a delegation (such as the 'surgeries' which many British MPs hold regularly in their constituencies at weekends) serve as channels of political communication. In any western European country, broadcast interviews or talk shows, party political broadcasts, newspaper reports, and many other forms of communication involving party representatives demonstrate how frequent and widespread party-related forms of political communication are.

The organisation of parties

Each party of course has its own pattern of organisation.[8] But similarities in party organisation do exist. Sometimes these similarities are identifiable because of legal requirements that certain structural features must exist: the Party Law of Germany (1967) and that of Austria (1975) are examples of explicit mandatory requirements. Sometimes experience and a shared desire to promote a democratic form of organisation indicate that certain organisational patterns are effective. Sometimes similarities exist because of a particular ideological attitude towards organisational and procedural issues (green parties place particular emphasis on organisational 'openness' and gender quotas, for instance, and many communist parties, at least in the past, have accepted organisational principles associated with 'democratic centralism'). Parties, like other organisations, also learn from each other, so many imitate particular organisational features.

Three distinct levels or locations of party organisation can be identified. The earliest of these, in terms of the history of party development, is that of *parliamentary party organisation*. It is true that, once a party system within the national legislature existed, other parties formed on an extra-parliamentary basis: the Labour Party in Britain, the Greens in West Germany, the National Front in France, Forza Italia in Italy are examples. But parties first developed in many European countries from the tendency of MPs who shared similar ideas and principles to associate together, to discuss problems and coordinate legislative strategies. This happened with the Whigs and Tories in the British House of Commons in the eighteenth century; in France with the groups of the National Assembly during the early stages of the French Revolution; in Germany in the 'Frankfurt Parliament' in 1848–49, then in regional assemblies and in the Reichstag of the unified German state in 1871. Today, the parliamentary party organisation exists to coordinate support for the government, or criticism of it, and to optimise the image of the party ahead of the next election. Except for very small parliamentary parties, organisational features usually include a leader (who may or may not also be the 'leader of the party') and a number of other officeholders, a system of committees dealing with policy sectors, and some paid staff. In a few parties, such as the British Conservative party, or Fianna Fáil and Fine Gael in Ireland, the parliamentary party chooses the party leader, and in some others (such as the British Labour Party) contributes to the election of the party leader. An important part of the parliamentary party organisation is the business manager (in Britain, the chief whip), responsible for communication between the parliamentary party leadership and backbenchers, for ensuring party unity in crucial votes in the legislature, and for arranging schedules of speakers for parliamentary debates.

Since members of the legislature wished to secure their own re-election and that of their party associates, they fostered the growth of party organisation at the level of the constituency. This second, 'grass-roots', level of organisation is the arena within which individual party members and supporters can participate, and where they and the candidate come into direct contact with the voter, especially at election time. In the nineteenth century (with the exception of working-class parties, such as the German Social Democrats) many local parties existed almost exclusively as organisations to prepare for and contest elections, and went into hibernation at other times. Today, local parties are no longer solely concerned with election campaigning; they are involved in fund-raising, membership recruitment, the selection of candidates for elections to local, national and (in countries which are members of the EU) European elected assemblies. They also act as channels of communication between the electorate and the authorities. They influence party policy directly (through discussion and then the transmission of recommendations to the national party organisation: by the submission of resolutions to the party conference, for example) or indirectly (through election of delegates to committees or conferences which decide on party policy, for instance).

Finally, local party organisations are linked together into a *national party organisation*. This will usually include a party headquarters, normally located in the same city as the parliament and government (unless it is a regionally confined party). This head office will be staffed by professional party managers and technical assistants of various kinds. Authority will be exercised by the party leader and some form of national party executive, responsible for day-to-day decisions and for the implementation of the resolutions of the national party conference, as well as the planning and organisation of election campaigns. However, the pattern and extent of authority within the national party organisations varies greatly, between countries and between parties within any one country. In Britain, the Conservative party conference has very little power compared to the conference of the Labour Party; the party chairman in the Conservative Party (an appointee of the party leader) has a more executive role than the – annually rotating – party chairman in the Labour Party. In France, the desire of local 'notables' to preserve their independence from encroachments by party headquarters is one cause of the relative weakness of national party organisations of some parties, especially of the right and centre. In federal states, the province may be an important level of party organisation: in the selection of candidates for party lists, for instance, as well as in the organisation of election campaigns for provincial legislatures.

Parties may possess auxiliary organisations, either linked formally to the party or ancillary to it, but with independent organisation. Most parties, for instance, have a youth organisation, which serves to link young people, especially those just reaching voting age, to the party but in an organisational structure more suited to youth than what may seem to be an over-bureaucratic parent organisation. Such youth organisations are often a radical influence within the party, and can act as 'nurseries' from which future leadership talent can be drawn. Some parties have separate women's organisations, though in these days of feminist consciousness and gender quotas within parties, such separate organisations are seen increasingly as patronising and redundant. Various interest-groups may have formal organisational links to parties. Trade union affiliation to the British and Irish Labour parties and the Danish Socialist Party are the most obvious examples, but most left-wing parties have close ties to trade unions, many of which make it an obligation of party membership that members also join appropriate trade unions.

Christian democratic parties similarly have links with the Catholic church. Farmers, the professions, pensioners and ethnic groups are other examples of interest-groups with organisational links to some western European parties.

In an ideal world, parties would utilise their organisational structures to perform the various functions discussed earlier in this chapter. But parties not only engage in national and subnational politics as single 'actors'; they also have their own internal political conflicts. The Labour Party in opposition in the 1980s and the Conservative party in government in the 1990s are recent British examples. The Green party in Germany until after the 1990 Bundestag election (when it lost its representation in the Bundestag) was split between factions, known as the 'fundamentalists' (*Fundis*) and the 'realists' (*Realos*), who were divided on policy and on strategy. The French Socialist Party has various factions within its ranks. Communist parties in western Europe in the 1980s were divided, usually between 'traditionalists' intent on preserving what they regarded as the untouchable ideological heritage of Marx and Lenin, and 'reformers' who wished to adapt and modernise, just as Gorbachev was hoping to make the Communist Party of the Soviet Union adapt. The radical right-wing Republican party in Germany seems to have gone into terminal decline because of internal quarrels over tactics and policy. In some cases, factionalism may tempt a group to leave the party and form a new party: the Independent Socialists (who later became the German Communist party in the Weimar Republic) in Germany during the First World War, the Social Democrats who broke away from the Labour Party in Britain in 1981, and the Austrian Liberal Forum which was formed from a breakaway group of the Freedom Party in 1993 are examples.

The future of political parties in western Europe

Political parties in western Europe are apparently under threat from several sources. One source of concern is the declining attractiveness of parties for their members, and their failure to attract new members. Levels of membership have been declining in many western European parties. Those members who remain in the party tend not to be as active as in past years. Recruitment, especially of younger members, is becoming more difficult (except for green parties and some parties of the far right), resulting in increases in the average age of the remaining membership. Other, more focused, forms of political participation are preferred by many who wish to engage in political activity: movements, pressure groups, single-cause political undertakings (to block a motorway route, to prevent the export of live animals from Britain to continental Europe, to obstruct the transportation of nuclear waste, for example). This tendency means that parties are losing resources: there are fewer activists to help in fund-raising and electoral campaigning, or to accept the responsibilities of party office-holding, and the income which members' subscriptions and donations might produce is in decline. Since membership tends to relate to voting support, the decline in membership causes some parties to be concerned about their electoral chances at future elections.

Another problem is a more rejective or hostile attitude towards parties in general on the part of the public. The Germans have invented the term *Parteiverdrossenheit* (alienation from parties or being 'fed-up' with political parties) to describe this trend in Germany. Its indicators include declining turnout at elections, declining respect for parties or party politicians, and unwillingness to join parties or be identified as supporting them, and such phenomena are by no means found only in Germany.

Several factors have been suggested as contributing to this tendency. These include the scandals that have hit some parties recently: the corruption associated with Italian party leaders; impropriety concerning party financing through donations from industry in Germany; allegations concerning bribery which have affected Belgian, French, Spanish and German politicians; a series of scandals in Britain concerning Conservative MPs (ranging from sexual improprieties to accepting money for asking parliamentary questions) and Labour councils at local government level.

Another factor is an almost contradictory complaint. On the one hand, claim critics, parties seek to intrude into every realm of public life (membership of broadcasting supervisory boards; representation on school governing bodies; appointments to the civil service or the judiciary based on party sympathies; regular presence in the mass media; and so on). Yet on the other hand parties are perceived as failing to govern effectively in an age when more and more complex problems challenge society: the issues raised by gene technology or the spread of computers; rising crime rates; the effects of longevity on social services, pension provision and health care; the proliferation of addictive drugs; threats to world peace caused by localised hostilities (Iraq and Bosnia are recent examples). These problems have encouraged new parties to form, often with claims to be different from the cold, established, and – in their view – 'tainted' parties. Such successes as recently enjoyed by small parties in Italy, by Political Spring (POLA, a breakaway party from New Democracy) in Greece in 1993, by the PDS in elections in eastern Germany in 1993–94, or by the STATT party in winning seats in the Hamburg *Land* legislature at the first attempt in 1993 are uncommon.[9] But the increasing willingness of voters to consider novel parties is symptomatic of the problems facing the established parties in western Europe.

The ambiguous status of parties in the political systems of western European democracies is also a problem. Few constitutions recognise formally the existence of political parties alongside the other institutions of the state (such as parliaments, courts or ministries).[10] A small number of countries have specific legislation concerning political parties in the form of a Party Law (Austria, Germany, Portugal and Spain). Yet, as this chapter has indicated, modern democracy depends on the functions carried out by parties. True, in many countries political parties receive some funding from public sources to enable them to carry out their functions – examples are Austria (since 1975), Belgium (1989), Denmark (1987), Finland (1967), Germany (1967),[11] and Norway (1970). However, the heavy costs of maintaining offices and staff, organising party congresses, employing experts and commissioning opinion surveys, as well as the periodic expenditures on election campaigning where these are becoming increasingly costly, mean that many parties face financial difficulties. Membership income remains static or is in decline; state subsidies – where these exist – remain limited; donations from wealthy individuals or business concerns, especially in times of economic recession, may not be as readily forthcoming as before; for left-wing parties, declining trade union membership may affect party finances through lower donations or affiliation fees.

So, despite their centrality in the democratic political process in western European states, political parties find that they lack resources (financial resources and active membership in particular) at the same time as their reputation among the public is falling. This combination of trends may have serious consequences for the operation of democracy in western Europe in the twenty-first century.

Notes

1 There may be some debate about whether to apply a uniform basis for counting parties in different countries, since the existence of different electoral systems – especially non-proportional electoral systems in the UK, in France and in Ireland – makes comparison of the number of parties difficult.

2 For example, in Saxony-Anhalt, one of the German *Länder*, a coalition of the Social Democrats and the Greens lacked a majority after the 1994 *Land* election, so relied upon votes of the representatives in the *Land* parliament of the extreme left Party of Democratic Socialism to elect the prime minister of the *Land* and to pass legislation. This was controversial, since many politicians, in the SPD and in other parties, regard the PDS as too extreme to be considered as a potential governing partner, thus well illustrating the 'ideological distance' indicator. The Swedish Social Democrats have often governed with the support of the Communists (called, since 1989, the Left party). The support by the Liberals for Callaghan's Labour government, after that government had lost its majority in 1977–78, is another example of 'toleration'.

3 This of course applies only for as long as the FDP can retain its representation in the Bundestag; in 1994, it came uncomfortably close to elimination. With or without the FDP, there may be circumstances where either a grand coalition or a coalition of the SPD and the Greens becomes feasible or necessary.

4 The German Basic Law imposes on political parties the responsibility of participating in 'forming the political will of the people' (Art. 21(1)), which is very much associated with this function of representation.

5 The concept of party government is explored by Katz (1987:4–8). He also investigates alternatives to 'party government', suggesting that perhaps Switzerland's emphasis on decision-making by referenda and an almost permanent system of power-sharing by parties leaves it outside the category of 'party government' systems (Katz 1987:20).

6 France, because of its semi-presidential system and the rule that ministers must not retain membership of the National Assembly, offers a number of examples of ministers who have not progressed to office through a party career. Several of the other examples cited here occured in times of crisis, or because some special expertise was demanded, which could best be provided by a minister despite the lack of party affiliation (or at least lack of orthodox party political career) of the person concerned.

7 In the SPD this was unofficial. According to party rules, the party congress elects the chairman, but in 1993 it was decided to consult the membership as to which of the three candidates they preferred. The victory of Rudolf Scharping in that ballot was then confirmed by the party congress. Because of the circumstances (an unanticipated challenge to Scharping at the 1995 party congress), his successor, Oskar Lafontaine, was elected in the orthodox manner, by votes of delegates at the party congress, and not by consultation of the membership.

8 These organisational patterns are set out in diagrammatic form for most western European countries in the relevant country sections in Katz and Mair (1992).

9 'STATT' means 'instead of', and the party (formed by disaffected Christian Democrats in Hamburg) claimed to be 'instead of' the other parties, their procedures and policies. A similar new party (Action for Bremen, formed by disaffected Social Democrats) obtained seats in the Bremen parliament at the 1995 *Land* election.

10 Parties are mentioned specifically only in the constitutions of France, Germany, Greece, Italy, Portugal and Spain.
11 In the Federal Republic of Germany, political parties received financial subsidies from the state before 1967, but the basis of such payments was declared illegal by the Constitutional Court. The Party Law of 1967 introduced the principle of state financial assistance for election campaign costs. The detailed formulae for such payments, and for tax relief on membership subscriptions and donations from individuals or business firms, have been revised at intervals since then.

References

Bille, L. (1992) 'Denmark', in R. Katz and P. Mair (eds) *Party Organizations. A Data Handbook*, London, Sage.

Bull, M.J. and P. Heywood (eds) (1994) *West European Communist Parties and the Revolutions of 1989*, Basingstoke, Macmillan.

Katz, R. (ed.) (1987) *Party Governments: European and American Experiences*, Berlin, de Gruyter.

Katz, R. and P. Mair (eds) (1992) *Party Organizations. A Data Handbook*, London, Sage.

Keman, H. (1995) 'The search for the centre: pivot parties in west European party systems', *West European Politics*, 17(4): 127–8.

Mair, P. (1990) Continuity, change and the vulnerability of party, in P. Mair and G. Smith (eds) *Understanding Party System Change in Western Europe*, London, Frank Cass, pp. 169–87.

Morris, P. (1994) *French Politics Today*, Manchester, Manchester University Press.

Sartori, G. (1976) *Parties and Party Systems*, Cambridge, Cambridge University Press.

Further reading

Broughton, D., D. Farrell, D. Denver and C. Rallings (eds) (1995) *British Elections and Party Yearbook 1994*, London, Frank Cass (and earlier volumes in this series since the 1991 Yearbook).

Bull, M. and P. Heywood (eds) (1994) *West European Communist Parties and the Revolutions of 1989*, Basingstoke, Macmillan.

Frears, J. (1991), *Parties and Voters in France*, London, Hurst.

Gallagher, M. and M. Marsh (eds) (1988) *Candidate Selection in Comparative Perspective*, London, Sage.

Katz, R. and P. Mair (eds) (1992) *Party Organizations. A Data Handbook*, London, Sage.

Mair, P. (ed.) (1990) *The West European Party System*, Oxford, Oxford University Press.

Mair, P. and G. Smith (eds) (1990) *Understanding Party System Change in Western Europe*, London, Frank Cass.

Marcus, J. (1995) *The National Front and French Politics*, Basingstoke, Macmillan.

Padgett, S. (ed.) (1993) *Parties and Party Systems in the New Germany*, Aldershot, Dartmouth.

Richardson, D. and C. Rootes (eds) (1994) *The Green Challenge*, London, Routledge.

Ware, A. (1996) *Political Parties and Party Systems*, Oxford, Oxford University Press.

Wolinetz, S. (ed.) (1988) *Parties and Party Systems in Liberal Democracies*, London and New York, Routledge.

6

Linkage organisations: interest-groups

Politics exists because people have different desires, different needs, different loyalties and different aspirations; politics is a way of accommodating such differences reasonably peacefully. A term which summarily indicates these politically relevant differences is 'interests'. Employed in a political context, 'interests' does not refer to people's hobbies, spare-time activities or choice of television programme. The word refers to the characteristics or affiliations which a person possesses, and which from time to time may stimulate political activity by that person or else by some organisation on her or his behalf.

A man might be a manager of a retail shop, a member of a trade union, a motorist, a house-owner with a mortgage, a father of two children at university and a dog-owner. A woman might be a mother with a part-time teaching job, have an infirm parent to care for at home, be a member of a local protest group seeking to prevent the siting of a nuclear waste processing facility in the neighbourhood, and regularly attend the local parish church. These lists of various characteristics do not, of course, exhaust the 'interests' which each person may have and which may from time to time become politically relevant. They do, though, illustrate how policies may be introduced which affect each of those persons: concerning changes in permitted opening hours of shops or the legal status of trade unions; increases in interest rates affecting mortgage repayments; increased taxes on petrol; financing of students through a loans system; rules affecting dangerous dogs; the legal rights of part-time workers; school testing procedures; tax allowances for care of the elderly at home; planning procedures for hazardous waste sites; the opening of the priesthood to women by the Anglican church and confirmation of that decision by parliament. These 'interests' are taken seriously by politicians, since the interaction of policies with those interests may affect how people vote in elections, how members of the electorate may react to policies, and whether those persons might organise with others who share such 'interests' to exert political influence.

For it is the organisation of persons sharing the same interests which is especially relevant to politics. Interest-groups in a wide variety of forms seek to exercise influence within the political process, to bring about innovations which might otherwise not occur, or to prevent changes which otherwise politicians might introduce. In this way, like political parties, they act as intermediary or 'linkage' organisations between the public and the political authorities. Farmers and railway employees in France, dentists in Germany, fishermen in England, motorists in Switzerland, Welsh-language speakers in Wales, ecologists in Austria: every day, in every European state, at local, regional and national levels and at the level of the EU itself, politicians take into account the demands of such interest-groups and their likely responses to policy initiatives, and interest-groups seek to influence political outcomes, by ensuring that politicians do in fact take their demands into account.

This interaction of, on the one hand, interest-groups and their members or clients or beneficiaries (for some interest-groups act on behalf of those who do not constitute their membership: see below), and of responsible and responsive politicians on the other hand, presupposes the existence of a democratic and pluralist type of political system. This is not to claim that under dictatorships or, earlier, absolute monarchies, interests and even interest-groups could not exist, could not seek to exert influence on political decision-making. But only in a pluralist democracy is such interest-group influence systematically provided with access to political decision-makers, its contribution to the political process welcomed (in principle, if not in every particular case!) and its role in the political system seen as legitimate. Western European political systems all allow for, and even encourage, such interest-group participation as contributing to pluralist politics. Constitutional guarantees of freedom of speech, assembly and organisation are examples of this encouragement (see below).

An interest-group, then, can be defined as any organisation which seeks to exercise influence on political decision-making, in order to promote some change which otherwise might not occur, or to prevent some change which otherwise might occur. As will be discussed further below, interest-groups can vary in all sorts of ways. In particular, some interest-groups have the exercise of political influence as their sole *raison d'être*, while other interest-groups may engage only very rarely and intermittently in politics.

Because interest-groups may seek to exercise influence in politics by bringing some kind of 'pressure' to bear on politicians, the term 'pressure groups' has been used instead in some studies and commentaries (e.g. Alderman 1984; Jordan and Richardson 1987). In some respects, this is a less satisfactory label, because it fails to capture either the whole range of methods which interest-groups may employ, some of which in no way involve 'pressure', or the fact that the status of interest-groups is often founded on the legitimacy and indeed the utility of their activities, so 'pressure' is not a necessary aspect of interest-group activity.

Omitted from the above definition is one very important differentiating factor. Both interest-groups and political parties are organisations which act as intermediaries between the 'people' and the institutions of government (see Chapter 2). However, interest-groups differ from political parties in significant respects. Interest-groups do not normally present candidates for public elective office (though they may occasionally – at least in the UK and in other countries using single-member constituencies – use candidacies as a publicity-seeking measure). However, they certainly may use the elective process as an arena for exercising influence on individual politicians or parties. One reason why they do not present candidates at elections is that interest-groups do not seek to exercise the powers of government themselves (as parties do), but rather hope to influence those who possess political power. Political parties have to be able to compromise and bargain, especially if they aspire to join with other parties in coalition governments. Interest-groups, though, can restrict themselves to the uncompromising representation and advocacy of the interests of a section of the population: members of a profession or trade union, sufferers from some particular physical disability or infirmity, or those concerned with some cause which they wish to promote (such as protection of birds or assistance to prisoners, for example). Whereas in any European state today one can count with a fair degree of precision the number of parties in the legislature and in regional or local elected assemblies, and can assess with some approximation of accuracy the number of parties in existence outside the legislature (e.g. by inspecting the lists of parties which nominated candidates at the most recent election), it is a hopeless endeavour to try to enumerate interest-groups. New ones are constantly springing up in most countries – either as new organisations or as organisations which newly discover a political role – while others go out of existence. Whereas in most countries it would be difficult to identify more than twenty or thirty political parties, there are thousands of interest-groups, active, latent or potentially active.

Interest-groups in western Europe

All European countries, being pluralist democracies, will possess a range of interest-groups which play a role in the political system, and there may be several similarities between these ranges of interest-groups in different countries (for instance, all countries will have one or more trade-union federations, and all will have one or more religious denominations which from time to time engage in political activity). However, at a more detailed level each country will provide a different context within which interest-groups 'live, move and have their being'. This context will affect both the arenas and opportunities for exercising political influence (see below, pp. 147–52) and the numbers, types, structures and other characteristics of the interest-groups which exist in each country.

Transient contextual factors certainly may affect interest-groups, their demands and their activities – such as the party composition of the government of the day; the stage of the economic cycle (recession, recovery or boom); the international situation. More fundamentally, four factors in particular provide the context within which interest-groups exist and operate in each political system.

The first is the set of *laws and other rules* relevant to interest-groups and their political activities. Such laws and rules include, for example:

- Constitutional provisions: e.g. freedom of association, as in the German Basic Law (Art. 9), the Greek constitution (Arts 11, 12) and the constitution of the Netherlands (Arts 8, 9); and freedom of opinion as in the Danish constitution (Art. 77) and the Irish constitution (Art. 40).
- Legal provisions: e.g. the German Party Law of 1967 expressly prohibits corporate membership of political parties, so German trade unions cannot affiliate directly to a political party, in contrast to the many trade unions affiliated to the Labour party in Britain.
- Procedural rules: e.g. the House of Commons requires MPs to register any affiliation from which they may derive financial benefit; the rules of the German Bundestag since 1972 require interest-groups to register with the Bundestag to qualify for the right to be heard before committees and to secure admission of representatives of those groups to the precincts of the Bundestag.

Such laws and rules impose constraints on how interest-groups can behave, but may also provide opportunities for furthering their political activities, for example by offering greater acceptability and status to groups which abide by such rules and procedures.

The second factor is the *structure of the political system* itself. A federal system such as that of Switzerland provides a more decentralised but also a more complex structuring of opportunities for interest-groups to exert political influence than does a more unitary political system such as that of Sweden. The importance of the second chamber in the legislative process, the type of electoral system used, the significance of the party affiliation of high-level civil servants in ministries and agencies – all of these aspects vary from state to state and all may, in that variation, account for the differential status, political significance and success or failure of interest-groups. For example, list-based electoral systems and, to a lesser extent, the Irish STV electoral system (which has some of the features of a list system) allow parties deliberately to provide representatives of certain interests with relatively safe seats. In this way, social democratic parties can ensure the election of trade union officials; Christian democratic parties can give church organisations opportunities to secure the election of favoured candidates; and special interests such as the self-employed, the free professions or representatives of skilled trades might find places on liberal party or conservative party lists. It is important to appreciate that, in such cases, the initiative is that of the party, not the interest-group; it is to the party's advantage that its candidates are seen to appeal to particular sectors of the electorate.

Third, the *political culture* (see Chapter 1) of each country is significant for interest-groups. Political culture is significant with regard to the attitudes of political elites and of the general public towards interest-groups. (Are such groups regarded as contributing positively to the political process? Are some seen as 'unacceptable' or even illegitimate actors in the political process?) It is also significant in terms of the role provided for interest-groups compared to political parties, for instance, or the mass media. The 'direct action' strategies adopted by some French interest-groups, involving mass demonstrations, civil unrest, damage to property and disruption of normal life seem to be regarded sympathetically by the French public. Curiously, this was true even when members of the public themselves are directly inconvenienced by such action, as was illustrated at the end of 1995 by strikes of railway workers in France, perhaps because of traditional French suspicion of 'the state'. Such strategies would be regarded as just a few steps away from revolution by the British or Swiss public. The role of the church in politics is regarded in some (especially Roman Catholic) countries as proper, in other countries – Britain and Germany serve as examples[1] – as a breach of the membrane that should separate church and state. In some countries the degree of individualism in society and a reluctance to join associations may inhibit interest-group activity, at least with regard to certain types of group. Morris (1994:153–6) suggests that France falls into this category.

Though not all interest-groups seek financial benefits, many, and many of the most prominent in political life, do concern themselves with the economic interests of their clientele. The *pattern of the political economy* is therefore a fourth factor which accounts for the different constellations and different modes of operation of interest-groups in western European states. The strength of the agricultural sector in the economy (Spain is an example); the continued existence of extractive or manufacturing industry (traditionally with high-density membership of trade unions, and often locally concentrated in such regions as the Saarland and the Ruhr in Germany, north east and north west England, Clydeside in Scotland, northern Italy, the Basque, Catalan and Asturias areas in Spain, and northern France); the susceptibility of businesses to national policy decisions such as tariff levels (Switzerland, as a non-member of the European Union, is a special case where tariff levels are critical to businesses); the degree of state ownership of industry (France still has a relatively large proportion of its industries, and hence its employment, directly or indirectly in state hands): these are some of the aspects of the political economy of a country which can shape and motivate interest-group activity.

So what do constellations of interest-groups in various countries of western Europe look like? Rather than seek to describe them country by country, it is more useful to identify characteristics which are significant in differentiating groups one from another, and which provide opportunities to refer to interest-groups in a variety of countries.

Characteristics of interest-groups

Type of interest represented
Interest-groups may be of various types with regard to the interests which they seek to represent. While no comprehensive listing or even general classification of such groups can be provided here, a survey of the most common or significant types of interest-group is feasible.

First, in all western European countries interest-groups exist which represent the interests of employees: the trade unions and similar organisations. Such organisations are mainly concerned with the representation of employees in negotiations with employers, and the provision of various services to members. However, many of them (and especially the federations which trade unions may create and join) become involved in politics quite frequently. That involvement takes any of several forms, from sponsoring candidates of labour, social democratic or socialist parties for parliament to negotiating with ministers. Coal miners' unions seek to prevent governments from closing mines, or withdrawing subsidies from commercial operators; car assembly workers' unions battle to secure restrictions on quotas for foreign automobile imports; employees in public utilities use their unions to combat privatisation and the reductions in manning which such transfer to the private sector may bring with it; trade-union federations call political strikes to protest against government policies on a range of issues, such as the strike in Italy in 1994 against the budgetary policies of the Berlusconi government or the strikes and demonstrations in France in 1995 against the Chirac–Juppé government's threats to the welfare benefit levels enjoyed by French employees.

Trade unions and trade-union federations may be closely linked to certain political parties or 'party families'. In some countries there may be a plurality of such federations: in France, for instance, corresponding to communist, socialist and Catholic political tendencies; in Italy, reflecting different political orientations (corresponding to the former communist party, Christian democrats and social democrats); or in the Netherlands, where Protestant, Catholic and socialist trade-union federations exist. In other countries (the UK, Ireland and Germany, for example) a single federation represents member unions.

Parallel to the trade unions, various groups represent employers' interests, providing counterparts to the unions in collective bargaining procedures concerning wage levels or other conditions of employment. In political terms these act sometimes as the opponent of the trade unions (when each side wants a different political outcome on some issue, such as opening hours of shops or extension of employees' legal rights), sometimes as the ally of the unions (when common interests are at stake, such as levels of protective tariffs against cheap imports). As well as such employers' organisations, the owners or managers of business enterprises may have separate agencies of representation. This, for example, is the situation in Germany, where the Federation of German Industry protects business interests, but the Federal Association of German Employers' Organisations (of which *Land* and sectoral employers' associations are members) furthers the interest of employers, which are not always congruent with those of the Federation of German Industry.

Farmers and others engaged in the production of foodstuffs (such as wine-growers and fishermen) have their organisations in every western European state, though in some countries (Norway, Spain, France and Denmark, for example) these agrarian interest-groups will be more widespread and more powerful than in others (such as Britain or Belgium). Despite representing relatively low numbers in relation to those employed in the industrial or service sectors of the economy,[2] agrarian interest-groups often are politically powerful, especially in terms of exercising a veto on changes proposed which might affect their incomes or welfare, such as reductions in levels of price supports by the EU under the Common Agricultural Policy (CAP). Such political power, disproportionate to the numbers of votes which these groups could cast in an election, is based partly on tradition, partly on aggressive political tactics, partly on a system of close links to bureaucrats in relevant governmental ministries, and partly on the fear of governments and voters alike that European countries could suffer if they are not self-sufficient in food supply.

Religion is the basis of another ubiquitous and often still influential class of interest organisations. These organisations may either represent a faith (Christian, Jewish, Muslim, for instance) or a denomination (Catholic and Protestant churches, for instance). Despite the increased secularisation of politics in the second half of the twentieth century, on issues such as divorce law, abortion legislation, even social services and development aid, religious groups are often vocal and sometimes potent actors in the political process.

Beyond these more obvious types of interest-group, many others exist. These include professional organisations for doctors, lawyers, pharmacists, accountants and other such groups; consumer-protection organisations; environmentalist groups; animal-welfare organisations; groups to act as advocates for the homeless or single parents or the physically handicapped; motorists' organisations; and so on. There are also single-issue groups concerned with opposing legalised abortion ('right to life' groups); preventing the construction of nuclear-power facilities or motorways or airport runways which threaten to damage local environments; promoting electoral reform; even with the protection of the production of 'real ale' in Britain! Whatever affects people's welfare or prosperity, whatever touches on their hobbies or charitable concerns, whatever constitutes for them crucial elements of their 'quality of life', can be the basis for organisation with others who share those 'interests', and such organisations can seek to exercise collective political influence.

Temporary and permanent groups
It may seem strange to discuss in the same chapter trade-union federations alongside groups formed to prevent the building of a

new by-pass or to prevent the closure of a local school, to deal both with the Catholic church and an organisation in an applicant country formed to secure a 'yes' vote in a national referendum on the issue of joining the EU. At one level, they are comparable organisations, in that they all seek from time to time to influence political outcomes without acting as political parties. At another level, though, there is a major distinction: some interest-groups have a more or less permanent existence (inasmuch as anything political can be regarded as 'permanent'), while other interest-groups are temporary, concerned with only one issue or set of related issues, which, once settled in an authoritative way, remove the reason for the group's continued existence. The Anti-Corn Law League in Britain, founded in 1839, had no reason to continue to seek to influence politics once the Corn Laws were in fact repealed in 1846. Organisations promoting votes for women found that their cause was successful, eventually, in every western European country, so they had no need for further political activity (though some supporters then took up other feminist issues, but this meant creating organisations for new purposes). Organisations created to promote the case for Berlin or Bonn as the seat of government in the newly reunited Germany were redundant once the Bundestag voted on the issue in favour of Berlin in 1991.

Compare these 'temporary' groups with trade unions, motorists' organisations, pacifist groups or groups to protect the interests and welfare of animals, children, prisoners or racial minorities. These 'permanent' groups may be successful or unsuccessful in relation to any one particular policy proposal or administrative decree, but know that other issues will arise, year in, year out, which will demand from them a political response. Indeed, the largest of these interest-groups sometimes have 'political sections' concerned solely with monitoring legislative proposals and policy implementation, and coordinating responses to these by the group.

Who benefits? 'Self-regarding' and 'other-regarding' groups
Another way of differentiating among types of interest-group is to consider on whose behalf they seek to intervene in the political

process. Many interest-groups act on behalf of their own members: farmers' groups in France; brewers and owners of off-licence shops in Britain affected by heavy taxation and rising imports of duty-free drinks from France; motorists' organisations in Germany defending the absence of speed limits on most German motorways; local groups of residents affected by new road-building projects in various European countries: these are all examples. Other interest-groups, though, hope that their interventions in politics will benefit individuals or groups who are not members of those interest-groups: the Howard League for Penal Reform and Amnesty International on behalf of prisoners, and the Child Poverty Action Group are examples in Britain. Organisations to aid the handicapped and animal-welfare groups exist in many western European countries.

Some groups do not fall neatly into either category, however. Interest-groups to combat racial or gender discrimination, to preserve and protect historical monuments, to promote disarmament or to safeguard the natural environment may all, through their political activities, benefit their own members, but those benefits are equally available to non-members.

Territorial scope

Interest-groups can be categorised according to the different territorial range of their activities. Many interest-groups are localised (especially temporary groups). They are concerned with some local issue or policy area (such as education), and try to influence local political authorities in order to protect the interests with which they are concerned. In some cases the territorial range is regional: Welsh-language groups; the Danish minority in Schleswig-Holstein; the Sorbs in Saxony; groups concerned with protecting Basque and Catalan cultures in Spain; German-speaking groups in South Tyrol; and so on.

The scope of the more significant (and especially of 'permanent') interest-groups tends to be national. This is because the 'interests' which they represent are shared by people scattered throughout the whole country (shop workers, beer drinkers, motorists, parents with handicapped children, owners of small businesses, for example), and because the 'targets' of their political activity tend to be national legislatures and national governments, because it is their decisions which affect the members of those groups.

Interest-groups also exist which have a Europe-wide or even international range. These include, for instance, Greenpeace; the Worldwide Fund for Nature; multinational companies and trade-union confederations. They seek directly (but often collectively) to influence national governments, as well as political authorities such as the EU or the United Nations and its agencies. This is a reflection of the trend towards increasing international regulation of issues such as protection of the environment or regulation of cross-national mass media.

Density of organisation

To what extent are interest-groups in western Europe really representative of the members for whom they speak and act? In some cases, close to 100 per cent of those eligible are registered as members: in certain professions, or some trade unions, for example. In other cases, perhaps only 10 per cent or even 5 per cent of those eligible become members. For certain types of interest-group it is difficult to calculate the eligible population: pacifist groups, for instance, or environmentalist groups. Andeweg and Irwin have collected some figures for the Netherlands. They suggest that 100 per cent of lawyers and doctors, 80 per cent of farmers and 35–40 per cent of retailers and owners of small businesses belong to relevant interest-groups, but that only 24 per cent of eligible employees are members of trade unions – by comparison, density rates for trade unions in Nordic countries are 90 per cent, in Belgium and Austria 60 per cent (Andweg and Irwin 1993:165). Germany, Italy and the UK have trade union membership density rates of about 40 per cent, but France has a rate of under 20 per cent.[3]

Organisational density affects the authority with which interest-groups can exert political influence. Indeed, low density rates can mean either the existence of competing interest-group organisations (the trade-union federations in the Netherlands or Switzerland, or motoring organisations in Britain, for example), or the failure of the interest-group to serve the interests of its 'client group' effectively.

Degree of politicisation

Many organisations are founded for completely non-political purposes: to bring together individuals interested in the same hobby, sport or charitable purpose, for example. Such organisations may operate in those terms perfectly capably, without ever having to come into contact with politics in any shape or form. However, a change in the rules regarding taxation, the imposition of a new tariff, or a proposal to implement some new regulation regarding safety or hygiene or restriction of international contacts may immediately affect the interests of members of an organisation. So it decides to protect its members' interests by engaging in political activity to reverse the proposed change. Such groups (philatelists, racehorse trainers, restaurant owners, banana importers, operators of private homes for the elderly could be examples) have very low degrees of politicisation. They are concerned with politics only rarely and as a consequence of other activities and purposes.

Other organisations, though, may have been created solely for the purpose of promoting, changing or defeating some law or policy. These groups may have few, if any, activities which are not connected with politics, and such other activities would be marginal to, or derived from, these political purposes: educational activities, perhaps, the organisation of occasional social events, or international contacts. Such interest-groups are highly politicised. The Anti-Corn Law League or the Chartists in the 1840s; the 'Bruges Group' of 'Eurosceptics'; the temporary alliances in favour of, and opposed to, deregulation of Sunday opening of shops: these are some British examples. Groups created to promote or oppose referendum proposals concerning entry to the EU (in Norway, Sweden and Austria, for example), changes to divorce law or abortion law (Ireland

and Italy are recent examples), or closer links with the EU (Switzerland) are other instances of such highly politicised groups.

Other groups have levels of politicisation which lie between these two extremes. Trade unions, and more especially trade-union federations, have medium levels of politicisation, being generally more concerned with negotiating conditions of employment than with influencing policy. However, since the standard of living and security of employment of their members depend upon the outcome of economic policies, they are often drawn into campaigns to influence such policy. The Electoral Reform Society is frequently, but by no means solely, concerned with the pursuit of political aims; it also, for example, involves itself in educational matters, and acts as a neutral and expert agency to organise and implement elections for other organisations. Wine-growers in Germany, sheep farmers in France, fishermen in Spain and Portugal need to monitor political events regularly, in order to be able to react to proposed changes in national or EU policy which could affect their livelihoods, changes which occur fairly frequently. It is for this reason that organisations representing industries or employers or commerce almost invariably have 'political sections' in their head offices concerned with monitoring and analysing political developments – domestic and international – likely to impinge upon the interests of their members.

How and where interest-groups operate in politics

Interest-groups may seek to exercise political influence in a variety of ways, in different political 'arenas' and directed at any of several 'targets'. Ultimately, interest-group activity in politics is directed at decision-makers – of which there may be several involved in passing a new item of legislation or in implementing a policy. In addition, indirect pressure as well as direct negotiation may be an appropriate means of securing an outcome favourable to the interest-group.

In a democracy – as all western European states now are – the 'people' are in theory sovereign. So it seems logical that interest-groups should sometimes seek to persuade *the public* of the merits of their case for promoting some change in the law, or preventing some already proposed change. Interest-groups associated with some 'cause' (such as gay rights, disarmament or reform of the law on abortion) often seek to persuade the public in order indirectly to affect the decisions of legislators or governments, as well as to provide public acceptance of their case as supplementary to pressure exerted in other parts of the political system. Demonstrations, acts of civil disobedience, press advertising, posters and petitions are some of the methods used, in the hope of attracting the attention of the mass media, as well as that of the public who come into contact with such activities directly. Campaigns against the poll tax in Britain, against nuclear power installations in Germany, and against changing the minimum-wage laws in France, are all recent examples.

However, three characteristics make 'the public in general' in most cases an inappropriate target for interest-group activity. First, few members of the public have much interest in political issues, so it will be hard to motivate sufficient numbers of people to take action that can be effective (e.g. by contacting MPs or councillors; by voting according to guidelines issued by the interest-group). One exception is when a referendum is called (e.g. in Switzerland, Italy or Ireland), when the members of the public have the power to make a political decision directly. Then interest-group activity may be successful.

Second, even if members of the public are convinced of the merits of a case, in electing members to a local council or a national parliament other factors – especially party loyalties – may override sympathy for the interest-group's stance on some single issue. Rather than vote for a candidate from a different party just because that candidate supports, say, the abolition of some tax which the interest-group opposes, a voter will ignore the interest-group's appeal and vote on wider considerations for the party with which she or he identifies.

Third, MPs tend to ignore the wishes of electors or interest-groups on particular issues, in the interests of party discipline and solidarity, and are intent – when in power – on implementing the government's programme. So even when the public may be in favour of an issue, unless that support is intensely expressed (e.g. by 'direct action', such as often occurs in France), or the issue is seized upon by the mass media and a 'bandwagon effect' develops which the government cannot well ignore, public support for an issue is likely to have little effect on how a parliament or government behaves.

So should an interest-group target instead the *members of a legislature?* After all, if a majority can be found to support a particular line on some issue, that majority can be used to pass or reject relevant legislation. Again, the factor of party discipline applies. Members of legislatures usually vote in support of their party, even if personally (on this particular issue) they would rather vote against the 'party line'.[4] A legislature is principally concerned with the passage of government-sponsored legislation. The issue with which an interest-group is concerned might be broadly supported by the governing party or parties, but the priorities of parliamentary time prevent that issue from reaching the agenda. The British system of private members' bills very occasionally allows such issues to be debated (and interest-groups are very eager to find an MP with a high position in the ballot for the privilege of introducing such private members' bills, so that their 'cause' can be at least debated). Only very rarely, though, do bills introduced under this procedure ever complete their passage into law, and the same is true for other European countries. Only if an issue can be shown to be significant, not damaging to the government in power, and strongly supported is the government likely to 'adopt' the bill and provide parliamentary time for it to become law.

Nevertheless, many interest-groups have their 'representatives' in parliament, either because those representatives are in any case already members of a particular trade union or profession, or have ties to some industry, or because they accept payment to act as watchdogs for a particular interest-group. They can then make known the views of the interest-group on issues brought before parliament, can inform the interest-group of what is happening or likely to happen in parliament, and can seek to persuade colleagues to vote in ways favourable to the group (always, of course, under the obligation to make known to the legislature such an affiliation to the interest-group in order to avoid any suspicion of trying to deceive the legislature regarding the links between the legislator and the group). In particular, where the size of a bloc of representatives from a particular profession is substantial, it might exercise considerable 'veto power', being able to dissuade governments from introducing legislation inimical to that group's interests. Public employees who are members of the German Bundestag are one such group which jealously protects its privileges and status. Doctors in the French National Assembly are another such group.[5] The tendency in some countries (including Britain, Germany and France) for some members of the legislature to have remunerated affilations to 'public relations' firms or other forms of lobbying organisation does suggest that, at times, interest-groups perceive the exercise of influence within the legislature as a worthwhile undertaking.[6] Such associations between legislators and interest-groups may be perceived as beneficial to democracy by their representation and advocacy of the different interests in society at large. One journalist wrote this about the British parliament:

> A deliberative chamber without advocates is a game of charades. To pretend that an MP should sit in Parliament to represent only the interests of a geographic constituency and his party leadership is archaic. It concedes the domination of government business over the vocation of politics. (Jenkins 1995)

In some countries (Germany, the Scandinavian countries and – though not directly concerning pending legislation – the UK are instances) interest-groups obtain access to parliament by being invited to present evidence to *parliamentary committees*. This may not generally be a means of defeating unfavourable legislation, or aiding the passage of favourable legislation, but does offer opportunities to modify legislation in ways favourable to the interest-group, and more generally to 'educate' politicians about the complexities and various issues involved in proposed policy changes.

Since a fundamental feature of parliamentary government in western Europe is the expectation that the governing party or coalition will normally succeed in passing into law those policies to which it gives priority, an interest-group might be well advised to secure the sympathy of the *government* of the day for its case. Whether in the UK, France or Germany, where – in recent years – one party or bloc of parties has enjoyed uninterrupted governing power for well over a decade, or in countries such as Italy, Sweden or the Netherlands, where coalitions are changed or modified with some frequency, an interest-group is most likely to be successful if it can persuade the government of the merits of its case (or at least of the political consequences of resisting the interest-group's arguments).

Interest-groups often manage to persuade governments of the advantages of supporting their case by securing support from within the structure of the governing party or parties. Trade unions and social democratic or labour parties, the Roman Catholic church and Christian democratic parties, farmers and agrarian parties, commercial interests and conservative parties: these are among the more obvious links which western European parties may have with interest-groups. A report in a German news magazine suggested that the Social Democratic Party in Germany obtained 10 per cent of its income from interest-groups, the Christian Democratic Union 20 per cent, while the Christian Social Union in Bavaria and the liberal Free Democrats each received about a third of their income from interest-group sources (*Der Spiegel*, 25 October 1993:56). In Britain, the greater part of the Conservative party central budget comes from donations from companies, and the Labour Party is heavily dependent upon the trade unions for its income, especially at election time. The close, and often illegal, financial links between business groups and Italian political parties have recently resulted in scandal, court cases and the transformation of the Italian party system.

For some interest-groups, close relations may exist with the *civil service*: for farmers with staff of the Ministry for Agriculture, for businesses with officials of the department responsible for industrial policy, for doctors with the Ministry of Health, and so on. Such relationships are useful to interest-groups in several ways. They may receive warning of proposed legislation which may affect their members and, being warned, will be able to take measures to protect members' interests. What is more, once legislation is passed by parliament the civil servants in ministerial departments or government agencies who are responsible for its implementation may be influenced by interest-groups concerning the form or manner of implementation, again potentially to the benefit of the group's members. It is a mutually beneficial relationship: the civil service benefits from information and assistance given by interest-group organisations in various ways. There are big differences, of course, in the efficacy of such links between the 'insider' groups in a country, those that are accepted by governments and bureaucrats as respected and acceptable, even useful, partners, and 'outsider' groups, who have not attained (and who perhaps do not desire to attain) such status, perhaps because of the cause they advocate or the methods of influence which they adopt.

Finally, interest-groups in western Europe are increasingly affected – for better or worse, for richer or poorer – by decisions made within the government machinery of the *EU* (see Chapter 11). Banana importers in Germany, butchers and fishermen in Britain, airline staff in France, businesses in every member state adapting to the internal market all need to direct their lobbying to the Commission, the EP or the Council of Ministers, even if pressure exerted on national governments may be an effective way of conducting such lobbying.

Interest-groups and their effect on democratic politics

More than parties, parliaments or any other institutions within the political system, interest-groups are associated with controversy concerning their contribution to democracy.

On the one hand, their defenders argue that pluralist politics in a democracy depends upon the free, unfettered activities of as many interest-groups as possible. Only in this way can the multitude of varying individual interests be represented in a pluralist democracy. These defenders maintain that the prohibition or restriction of interest-groups is the mark of a dictatorial, not a democratic, political system. They see the existence of a 'balance' of interest-groups on most issues (trade unions and business interests, opponents and proponents of liberalisation of abortion laws, those for and against changes in shop opening hours, car users and public transport undertakings, smokers and non-smokers). They regard such 'balance' as producing a more open and informed type of political debate, with government acting as a kind of scoreboard, registering the relative 'weights' of interest-groups in terms of policy outcomes. In addition, the opportunities for participation which interest-group activity in politics provides to members of the public must benefit democracy.

Those who are more suspicious of interest-groups point to other attributes. They can list cases of corruption, of underhand manipulation of political institutions – the British 'cash for questions' affair is one recent example[7] – of the distortion in the ability of an interest-group-sponsored legislator to represent all her or his constituents properly and fairly. The 'balance' between opposing groups they regard as only partial, since not all issues have only two sides to them, and in the struggle between group interests, the wider 'public interest' may be neglected. 'Insider' groups can appear to distort the neutrality of ministries, for instance. Accusations about the British Ministry of Agriculture, Fisheries and Food being too closely allied to producers to defend the interests of consumers emerged in very explicit form in March 1996 in relation to the 'mad cow disease' scare. In any case, not all groups are equal: in the resources they can command, in their access to the inner circles of government, or in the media attention which their cause can attract.

A more complex issue is the extent to which interest-group politics in some states has moved towards a 'corporatist' mode. A 'corporatist' style of politics exists where significant proportions of policy decisions are normally the result of the interaction of the government with important interest-groups, where those interest-groups have a recognised monopoly of rights of representation of their clientele, and where only a select number of interest-groups are given the degree of access to government (often through the existence of committees, commissions or other structures, but also perhaps more informally) which enables them to influence policy outcomes. The interest-groups involved may also have a role in the implementation of those policies concerning which they have sought to exert influence on government. In particular, trade unions and business groups sometimes have such status, though other groups such as the churches or farmers may be included in corporatist networks. Corporatism, to the extent that it exists, is potentially dangerous for democracy because it has the effect of excluding those interest-groups which are not regarded by the government as acceptable as policy-making partners, because it makes the policy-making process opaque, because decisions are made by organisations non-accountable to the public, and because it may improperly benefit those groups which are involved in the process. It has been suggested that, among western European states, Germany, Austria and Sweden are the closest to the corporatist model.

Whatever the verdict on the contribution which interest-groups make to democracy, interest-group politics is an inescapable feature of democratic politics in a complex, industrialised society. Prohibition of interest-group influence in politics is not just unthinkable because it would be undemocratic; it is unimaginable because it could not conceivably work. At most, regulation can distort interest-group influence in politics.

Participation in some types of interest-group political activity has become increasingly popular, especially among younger citizens. It can appear to be a more satisfying form of political participation than membership of a political party. The consequences of political action can be more obvious and direct (defeating a proposed piece of legislation; preventing some new road or waste dump being built; securing media coverage for a demonstration or rally). Sometimes participation – especially for some 'cause' such as nuclear disarmament or combating right-wing extremism – does not depend on the existence of any particular organisation. Instead, a 'movement' develops, which is only loosely coordinated, and which may include formally organised groups as well as sympathisers who are not members of any of those organised groups. These rather more amorphous groupings, such as the feminist movement, the ecological movement, the pacifist movement and, in some areas, nationalist movements, may nevertheless be significant political actors when certain issues are prominent on the political agenda. Issues associated with postmaterialism, with the 'new politics',[8] have been linked with activity by 'movements' as much as with more orthodox forms of interest-group activity.

So, alongside political parties, interest-groups act as mediators between the public and the political authorities, giving shape to demands from sections of the public, and transmitting those demands (backed by political pressure of various kinds) to those political institutions which have the power to make binding decisions.

Notes

1 In Britain, for example, recent pronouncements by church leaders on social policy, homelessness and the effects of the market economy on family life provoked criticism from politicians and members of the public about such overstepping of the 'proper' role of the churches. In Germany, a recent dispute about the right of Bavaria (a Catholic *Land*) to place crucifixes in school classrooms even against the wishes of parents, and a long history of religious pronouncements on politics during election campaigns, indicate the controversial status of the churches in politics, where echoes of Bismarck's *Kulturkampf* (battle of the cultures) still linger.

2 In Germany, for instance, just 600,000 farmers share subsidies from the state worth DM30 billion (*Der Spiegel*, 25 October 1993:51).

3 A report in the *Sunday Times* (31 October 1993) claimed that only one in eight employees in France belonged to a trade union: the lowest rate of all leading industrialised states. However, 'density' is

not easy to measure accurately, in some cases such as membership of trade unions. For example, some employees in some countries may have no appropriate trade union to join.

4 An exception sometimes is the set of issues which can be termed 'conscience issues': to do with morality, or matters which have no obvious linkage to party ideology (such as the Bonn–Berlin issue in the German Bundestag in 1991). Here a 'free vote' may be permitted, and the governing party or coalition is not affected in its authority or status by the outcome of that vote.

5 An adviser to former French prime minister Balladur is quoted as saying that there are nearly 100 members of the medical profession in the French parliament, and that they also have considerable power in local communities (*Sunday Times*, 19 November 1995).

6 The recommendations of the Nolan Committee, which examined, among other things, the links between members of the House of Commons and commercial interests, may probably have the effect of reducing such paid affiliations in Britain.

7 Some British MPs were accused in 1994 of receiving payments from organisations for asking certain parliamentary questions, for the benefit of those organisations, in the House of Commons.

8 These concepts are discussed in Chapters 3 and 12.

References

Alderman, G. (1984) *Pressure Groups and Government in Great Britain*, London, Longman.

Andeweg, R.B. and G.A. Irwin (1993) *Dutch Government and Politics*, London, Macmillan.

Jenkins, S. (1995) 'A place for advocates', *The Times*, 8 November.

Jordan, A.G. and J.J. Richardson (1987) *Government and Pressure Groups in Britain*, Oxford, Clarendon Press.

Morris, P. (1994) *French Politics Today*, Manchester, Manchester University Press.

Further reading

Berger, S. (ed.) (1981) *Organizing Interests in Western Europe*, Cambridge, Cambridge University Press.

Baggott, R. (1995) *Pressure Groups Today*, Manchester, Manchester University Press.

Jordan, A. and J.J. Richardson (1987) *Government and Pressure Groups in Britain*, Oxford, Clarendon Press.

Rush, M. (ed.) (1990) *Parliament and Pressure Politics*, Oxford, Clarendon Press.

7

Executive government

Parliamentary government in western Europe

Most western European countries share a distinctive pattern of rules and institutions known as parliamentary government. The central feature of parliamentary government is the mutual dependence, or 'fusion', of the legislative and executive branch of government. This mutual dependence is achieved through procedures for the selection and dismissal of members of parliament and the government.

As a democratic form of government, parliamentary government demands that its leaders' authority is tested in periodic selection procedures. MPs in western Europe are chosen directly by the people in elections held at maximum intervals of between four and five years. In a presidential system of government such as the USA, the president, or chief executive, is also directly elected, giving him an independent mandate from the people. In a parliamentary system, however, the choice of prime minister, the head of the government, is not made directly by the people, but is delegated to the people's representatives in parliament. In some countries, a formal selection procedure takes place after an election to determine who will be prime minister. This is the case in Germany, for example, where the Bundestag votes to elect the chancellor. In Britain, there is simply a tacit understanding that the leader of the majority party will form a government.

The process of government formation can be long and complex, particularly in countries where a coalition must usually be forged from several disparate parties, as in Italy or the Netherlands. European prime ministers have the formal authority to nominate the members of their cabinets. With a few exceptions, cabinet members are usually selected through the 'party-cum-parliament' route (Blondel 1985). That is, they are chosen from among the party or coalition supporting the prime minister in parliament, on the basis of their parliamentary work. The fact that they are elected representatives of the people gives them the authority to make rules that are binding on the people. These selection procedures tie parliament and the government closely to one another. The prime minister depends on parliament for selection. In turn, if they hope to gain ministerial office, MPs must be loyal to the prime minister and government.

In most cases, parliaments and governments also have reciprocal powers of dismissal. The prime minister and cabinet are responsible for their conduct of government to parliament. If parliament loses confidence in the ability of the prime minister and cabinet to govern, it has the right to turn them out of office in a vote of no confidence. In turn, the prime minister usually has the authority to have parliament dissolved before it has completed its term of office.

The rules of selection and dismissal which bind the legislature and executive in a parliamentary system were devised to balance the power of these two institutions. This balance has been distorted by the development of party democracy in western Europe. Parties have extended their reach far beyond acting as channels of opinion in elections. They have come to organise the work of parliament and are the basis for recruitment to government. Party loyalty has given the executive the upper hand over parliament, as the government can usually rely on strict party discipline in parliament to translate the main aims of its policy programme into legislation.

Some variants of parliamentary government

In many countries, minor variations can be found on the pattern of reciprocal controls typical of parliamentary systems. For example, Germany, Norway, Sweden and Switzerland have legal or practical limits on the power of the executive to dissolve the legislature.[1] In Norway and Switzerland, there is no constitutional provision at all for the early dissolution of parliament. In the case of Norway, this is one of the peculiarities resulting from an increasingly anachronistic constitution. The Norwegian constitution dates back to 1814 and has never been amended to take account of parliamentary government, which was introduced over one hundred years ago. Following government practices inherited from a pre-parliamentary stage of constitutional development, the Norwegian parliament, the Storting, cannot be dissolved before the end of its four-year term of office. In addition, Norwegian government ministers must resign their seats in parliament when they take office. For Norway, these two constitutional features have produced a weaker link between the legislature and the executive than is usual in western European countries. In other respects though, Norway conforms to a parliamentary system of government.

The same cannot be said of Switzerland. A combination of unusual features makes the Swiss model of government unique in western Europe. In keeping with a parliamentary system, the Swiss government, the Federal Council, is elected by the two houses of parliament which make up the Federal Assembly. However, the Federal Assembly does not have the authority to bring down the Federal Council by a vote of no confidence. The Federal Assembly and Federal Council share the same fixed four-year period of office. The seven members of the Federal Council are generally re-elected until they choose to retire, allowing the Council to 'outlive' the Assembly in practice. The Federal Council consists of a permanent coalition of the four main parties. Appointments to the Council follow an established formula allowing the representation of the different linguistic and religious communities of the Swiss cantons. The members of the Council are equal in rank and power and its decisions are genuinely collective.

This model of government preserves the chronic government stability preferred by the Swiss. It has produced patterns of government markedly different from those elsewhere in western Europe. In particular, these features have stunted the development of partisan competition for the 'prize' of running the government – there is no credible parliamentary opposition in the Swiss Federal Assembly as only minor groups are left out of the government. A fully-fledged parliamentary opposition is in any case seen as unnecessary, since the public has the opportunity to make a direct challenge to laws through the unique system of referenda. While the Federal Council is relatively well insulated from party and parliamentary pressures, it is constrained by the need to represent the demands of organised interest-groups. These have an unusual hold over government because of their power to mobilise the public behind a popular referendum. The Federal Council, then, does not act as a partisan government which develops and implements distinctive policy priorities. Rather, it processes the demands of opposing interest-groups in an 'administrative' style of government.

A few other countries depart significantly from a model of parliamentary government. France and Finland are the best examples of a 'semi-presidential' form of government, in which a strong president with some executive powers works alongside a prime minister. In order to understand how unusual the role of the head of state is in the semi-presidential systems, it is necessary first to examine the conventional place of the head of state in a parliamentary system.

The head of state: a figurehead for the nation

A parliamentary system makes a clear distinction between ceremonial leadership and policy leadership at the highest level. A monarch or president is entrusted with ceremonial duties and a prime minister heads the government. Originally, European monarchs had combined these two aspects of leadership, but over time their power to determine policy was eroded. In some countries, the hereditary monarchy has survived and retained its ceremonial role. In others, the monarchy was abolished and ceremonial leadership was transferred to a president (see Table 7.1). In the twentieth century, attempts to retain or reintroduce joint ceremonial and policy leadership have been associated with the abuse of executive power. In Germany, for example, Hitler, head of the government since 1933, took advantage of President von Hindenburg's death in 1934 to declare himself head of state as well. As head of state he assumed the role of head of the armed forces and launched his programme of military expansion. In post-war Europe, the experience of the Third Reich served as a warning against the concentration of state power under a single leader.

When Greece, Portugal and Spain replaced their authoritarian regimes with democratic government in the 1970s, they too chose to separate the roles of head of state and head of the government. In these countries, the need to legitimise the transition to a democratic system meant that the presidents of Greece and Portugal were initially given a more prominent constitutional role than is the norm in western Europe. However, constitutional revisions of the 1980s reduced their executive powers, leaving them the more conventional ceremonial tasks. King Juan Carlos of Spain also played a leading role in establishing the new democratic state, and has taken decisive action in times of crisis (see below). As the new system has rooted itself, though, he has withdrawn to his ceremonial duties, leaving executive government to the directly elected representatives of the people.

Heads of state, whether monarchs or presidents, perform three main functions: symbolic, diplomatic and procedural (see Gallagher *et al.* 1995:17–23).

The symbolic and diplomatic roles of the head of state
The high symbolic status of the head of state derives from the former power of the European monarchies. The head of state is the personal embodiment of the state, and, as such, contributes to its legitimation. While the prime minister is the highest repre-

Table 7.1 Western European heads of state and their selection, August 1996

	Head of state	*Current incumbent*	*Method of selection*
Austria	President	Thomas Klestil	Universal suffrage
Belgium	Monarch	King Albert II	Heredity
Denmark	Monarch	Queen Margrethe II	Heredity
Finland	President	Martti Ahtisaari	Universal suffrage
France	President	Jacques Chirac	Universal suffrage
Germany	President	Roman Herzog	Electoral college
Greece	President	Konstantinos Stefanopoulos	Electoral college
Iceland	President	Ólafur Ragnar Grímsson	Universal suffrage
Ireland	President	Mary Robinson	Universal suffrage
Italy	President	Oscar Luigi Scalfaro	Electoral college
Liechtenstein	Monarch	Prince Hans-Adam von und zu Liechtenstein II	Heredity
Luxembourg	Monarch	Grand Duke Jean	Heredity
Netherlands	Monarch	Queen Beatrix	Heredity
Norway	Monarch	King Harald V	Heredity
Portugal	President	Jorge Sampaio	Universal suffrage
Spain	Monarch	King Juan Carlos I de Borbón	Heredity
Sweden	Monarch	King Carl XVI Gustaf	Heredity
UK	Monarch	Queen Elizabeth II	Heredity

Sources: Europa (1995); Keesing's (1995); *Financial Times*, 1995–96.

sentative of the government of the day, the president or monarch is the highest representative of the state itself, a position above partisan politics. The head of state is the country's chief diplomat, attending major state occasions at home and abroad to represent the nation and greet other heads of state and leading dignitaries. Much of the day-to-day work of heads of state is routine and low in profile. However, they can make a major and sometimes crucial contribution to public confidence in the state.

West German presidents took on the role of guardian of the country's conscience and morale, working particularly for the people's moral rehabilitation from war guilt. The process of *Vergangenheitsbewältigung* (overcoming the past) turned out to be a lengthy one. Opinion polls show that many Germans continue to feel uncomfortable with their German nationality.[2] In 1985, on the fortieth anniversary of the German capitulation, President Richard von Weizsäcker directly addressed the problem of war guilt, which led to a remarkable country-wide wave of confession and repentance. On the fortieth anniversary of the Federal Republic, he addressed the nation on the importance of avoiding nationalism (hatred of others) while promoting patriotism (love of one's own). With German unification, von Weizsäcker's attempts to promote internal cohesion took on a new focus of reconciling the two German societies.

The task of promoting public confidence in the regime sometimes requires a head of state to take the initiative in a crisis. During an attempted army coup in 1981, King Juan Carlos of Spain acted to preserve the democratic regime established in 1978. While Lieutenant-Colonel Antonio Tejero was holding the MPs hostage, Juan Carlos contacted military leaders not involved in the action to assure them that he did not support it. He then made a television address to the nation, stating that the Crown would not tolerate the coup. He informed the coup leaders that he would not abdicate or leave the country and would rather be shot than accept the army takeover. The coup fizzled out and the MPs were released (Gilmour 1985:241–5). King

Juan Carlos's role in safeguarding Spain's transition to democracy was recognised both in Spain and abroad.

The symbolic and diplomatic functions exercised by the head of state demand a very high standard of personal integrity. The monarch or president must be above reproach. Any lapse in behaviour damages the reputation of the country as well as the individual involved. Modern media coverage of public events has made the head of state ever more vulnerable as a figurehead and results in often bizarre exchanges over standards of behaviour. In a recent television interview, President Ahtisaari of Finland protested that he had not been drunk on a state visit to Stockholm. When asked why he had fallen over and hit his head on a table, he said he had been wearing shoes with slippery leather soles and promised never to do it again (*The Times*, 5 September 1994).

On a more serious note, the disintegration of relationships within the British royal family has degenerated into an unseemly battle played out in public via the press and television. In particular, Prince Charles's television confession of adultery has led to speculation over whether he is a suitable candidate to succeed to the monarchy. His divorce from Princess Diana and the possibility of his remarriage some time in the future are expected to create uncertainty about the constitutional position of all concerned. Moreover, the recent behaviour of the Prince and Princess of Wales and various other members of the royal family appears to have severely dented the standing of the monarchy with the British public.[3] The more the public's respect for the royal family is eroded, the less able the monarchy will be to perform its symbolic, integrative function for the nation.

The past behaviour of heads of state can also be damaging, particularly if attempts have been made to cover up episodes which are judged as unacceptable. François Mitterrand, president of France for fourteen years until May 1995, concealed his collaboration in the wartime Vichy regime and his continuing friendship with a former Vichy police chief almost to the end of his presidency. These revelations could not be shrugged off as easily as his late acknowledgement of his illegitimate daughter, and, on his death in 1996, soured evaluations of his contribution to French politics. Dr Kurt Waldheim, Austrian president from 1986 to 1991, was severely hampered in his role as head of state by allegations surrounding his wartime activities. Even during his presidential campaign, he was accused of having been implicated in atrocities committed by the Nazis in the Balkans in 1942–45. When he took office, he was barred from entering the United States, and Austrian relations with many states, particularly Israel, became strained. In 1988 an international commission of historians concluded that Waldheim must have been aware of the atrocities, but he refused to resign as president. However, he did not seek re-election when his term of office came to an end. His years in office demonstrated how a controversial head of state can be both internally divisive and detrimental to a country's international standing.

The procedural tasks of the head of state
The head of state is called on to legitimise the procedures of government. For example, he or she presides over the orderly transfer of government power from one party or coalition to another, formally appoints key political leaders and promulgates laws. The head of state can usually carry out these procedural functions in a token manner, simply rubber-stamping decisions made by other authorities. However, under certain circumstances, the president or monarch can be involved in far-reaching political decisions. As we will see, the head of state can play a decisive role in selecting the government; arguably the most fundamental political decision in the regular cycle of a parliamentary democracy. Once the government is in place, the responsibility for supervising law-making can involve the head of state in real policy decisions. The head of state's ceremonial position can be consistent with a role in foreign policy. Simply in carrying out their procedural duties, all heads of state have the potential to make politically significant moves. Factors encouraging a politically active head of state include a crisis situation requiring a strong figurehead, a personal mandate conferred by

direct election, and special constitutional powers. A politically active head of state can, of course, erode the model separation of ceremonial and policy leadership which characterises parliamentary government. In most of the western European countries, heads of state have been insulated from regular and substantial involvement in decisions with political implications. In some countries, however, the position of head of state has evolved beyond a merely ceremonial role. These countries are referred to not as parliamentary but as 'semi-presidential' systems.

Semi-presidentialism in western Europe

France represents the most clear-cut example of a semi-presidential system in western Europe. Finland is also termed semi-presidential while Austria, Iceland, Ireland and Portugal have sometimes been referred to in this way on account of special features of their presidencies. In these countries, however, conventions of government are currently more in line with a parliamentary model than a presidential one; the balance of power is tipped in favour of the prime minister rather than the president. In France, the position is reversed, as the president of France has in practice been the key executive leader throughout most of the Fifth Republic.

The first president of the Fifth Republic, General de Gaulle, had the status of a national hero. In exile during the Second World War, he came to symbolise the resistance to the Nazi occupation of France. He was not a member of the political elite associated with the failure of the Fourth Republic and had resolved the Algerian crisis which had brought down the old regime. His popularity allowed him to interpret the Fifth Republic constitution to his liking and created a precedent for active presidential leadership, with the prime minister in a supporting role. In 1962 de Gaulle revised the constitution, by referendum, to arrange for the direct election of the presidency. (The president had previously been chosen by an electoral college.) From this time onwards, the presidency evolved beyond the already generous powers noted in the constitution. Electoral politics came to be dominated by presidential rather than parliamentary elections. As long as the president had a sympathetic majority in parliament, he could in practice appoint and dismiss prime ministers and cabinet ministers, chair cabinet meetings, and dissolve parliament. Only in the two periods of 'cohabitation', where the president has found himself facing a hostile majority in parliament, has the prime minister (representing that hostile majority) been able to salvage his control at least of domestic policy. At other times, de Gaulle and his successors have been able to dominate all areas of policy.

The president of Finland also has wide-ranging constitutional powers, including the power to dissolve parliament, to appoint ministers and leading civil servants, to reject or revise proposed government legislation, to veto bills already approved by parliament (in practice, a president's suspensory veto has rarely been overridden by parliament), and to preside over foreign policy. Finnish presidents have played a leading role in foreign policy, but otherwise have tended to underuse their constitutional authority. As in France (especially in the early years of the Fifth Republic), the Finnish president has stood out as a figure of national unity against the potential threat posed by Finland's shared border with the former Soviet Union and by the uncertainties of a complex multi-party system. The direct elections introduced in 1994 have given a boost to presidential legitimacy. This might see an expansion of the president's role, unless proposed reforms are carried out as a countermeasure to reduce some of his constitutional powers.

Selecting the head of state

The ability of the president or monarch to provide cohesion and legitimacy for the state and to exercise any political discretion wisely depends very much on the qualities of the individual incumbent. How should the country's ceremonial leader be chosen? The selection process is a foregone conclusion in the constitutional monarchies of Belgium, Denmark, the Netherlands, Norway, Spain, Sweden and the UK, the Grand Duchy of Luxembourg and the Principality of Liechtenstein. One argument against selection by heredity is that it is a hit-and-miss affair. Chance and the rigorous training provided within the royal family might produce a suitable leader, but there is no certainty of this.

Also, it is often argued that the involvement in policy matters of a person owing his or her position to heredity is inappropriate for a modern democracy. Some monarchies retain quite considerable formal constitutional powers. In Britain, Queen Elizabeth appoints ministers, dissolves Parliament, and gives her assent to all bills passed by Parliament. As in all but the most archaic countries of western Europe, it would now be unthinkable for the British monarch to make any independent judgement when carrying out these procedural tasks.[4] Attempts to intervene directly in politics can prove to be disastrous for the monarchy. The abolition of the monarchy by referendum in Greece (1974) and Italy (1946) was in each case fuelled by public resentment over the king's mishandling of political matters. In 1940, King Leopold III of Belgium acted against the advice of his generals and surrendered to the Germans. After the war, the monarchy narrowly survived a referendum, but the issue of the return of the disgraced king provoked severe social unrest between royalists and anti-royalists. Leopold abdicated in favour of his son Baudouin, who during his reign of forty-two years effectively restored the standing of the Belgian monarchy.

The hereditary monarchs do enjoy some advantages over their presidential counterparts. The former powers of the monarchy mean that they remain the object of reverence for at least some of their subjects. Presidential incumbents have to earn the respect of the people. The archaic mode of 'selecting' monarchs by heredity makes them part of their country's historical tradition: monarchs embody the continuity of the state. It also underlines their independence from party political forces. Monarchs are neither associated with any political party, nor do they owe their selection to party politicians. These factors allow the monarch to transcend everyday politics, an important advantage in carrying out the symbolic functions of the head of state.

Where a president is responsible for ceremonial leadership, a decision must be made as to how the incumbent should be chosen: by direct popular election or by an electoral college. Each method has its own advantages. The president is chosen by universal suffrage in Austria, Finland, France, Iceland, Ireland and Portugal. As long as it produces a conclusive result, direct election confers legitimacy on the president, giving the incumbent a sound basis for carrying out the tasks of the office. The two-ballot election of the president of France is designed to ensure that the president is supported by the majority of the electorate. In the first ballot, any candidate who wins more than 50 per cent of the vote is elected. If no candidate secures an absolute majority, a second ballot is held to choose between the two leading candidates of the first poll. A similar method was introduced in Finland in 1994 (Anckar 1994:272). The disadvantage of direct election is that this can be interpreted as a personal mandate, encouraging the president to encroach into government affairs. This has been the case in the 'semi-presidential' system of France, and, to a lesser extent, in Finland.

Outside the semi-presidential systems, the president has been confined to a ceremonial role by, for example, a clearly defined (and thereby restricted) constitutional role, or by the public expectation that presidential authority will be exercised in a nonpartisan way. Some countries have also opted to select their president by means of an electoral college, denying them a direct mandate from the people. This applies to Germany, Greece, Italy and Switzerland. The presidential electoral colleges include the MPs. Reflecting the need for a president who can unify the people, the regions are usually represented too. They may be involved through their regular channel of parliamentary representation, as in the case of the Swiss Council of States, or they may attend as delegates from the regional parliaments, as in Germany and Italy. One disadvantage of selection by electoral college is that the choice of president can be too strongly influenced by partisan considerations, undermining the president's ability to represent the nation as a whole. In West Germany, the selection of the president was sometimes linked to the subject of wider coalition dealings between the parliamentary parties. One example was the presidential contest of 1969, when the liberal FDP voted for the social democratic candidate Gustav Heinemann in order to open up the opportunity of forging a new coalition with the SPD.

Presidents have a fixed term of office of between four and seven years.[5] The presidential term of office is usually longer than the standard parliamentary electoral cycle. This gives the president the necessary independence to carry out procedural tasks associated with the dissolution and appointment of governments. Some countries impose a limit on the number of times an individual may hold presidential office. For example, the German president may be elected for only two successive terms of office (Basic Law, Article 54). Elsewhere, regular elections are seen as an adequate check on presidential powers. In 1992, President Vigdís Finnbogadóttir of Iceland was re-elected unopposed for her fourth four-year term of office.

Executive government in western Europe: the principles of cabinet government

In western Europe, the executive branch of government is made up of a cabinet, or committee, of senior party politicians. Most cabinet members head a government ministry, although in some countries it is possible to hold a cabinet seat 'without portfolio', that is, without having the responsibility for a ministry. The cabinet is chaired by the prime minister, except in France, where the president 'presides' over the Council of Ministers. Cabinet government follows two main principles: collective cabinet responsibility and individual ministerial responsibility.

Collective cabinet responsibility concerns the relationship between the executive and the legislature. It means that the prime minister and cabinet are *together* ultimately responsible to the elected representatives of the people for executive decisions and actions during their term of office. Once the cabinet has made a decision, each cabinet member should be prepared to defend it in public, or resign. If the prime minister should step down, the whole cabinet goes too.

Individual ministerial responsibility concerns the relationship between the executive and the administration. Each minister is held to be responsible for the decisions and actions of his or her own ministry. Ministers must police their department, or pay for a serious mistake or corrupt activities with their resignation. Individual ministerial responsibility is a means of holding the non-elected civil service accountable to the public.

The prime minister and the cabinet

As head of the cabinet, the prime minister is sometimes referred to as the 'chief executive'. This term is misleading, as it implies that the prime minister is personally responsible for policy and can take decisions independently. Parliamentary procedures can personalise 'the government' in giving the prime minister the role of government spokesperson. The media backs up this personalisation by focusing attention on the prime minister. In principle and in practice, though, prime ministers must work closely with other individuals and institutions of government and must often struggle to maintain their authority as head of the government. All prime ministers are not equally powerful. Some are able to initiate policy and manage their cabinet colleagues largely on their own terms, while others can at best coordinate the work of the government. The strength of a prime minister rests partly on rules and traditions governing the prime minister's relationship with the cabinet and with parliament, and on the personality and leadership style of the incumbent. Much also depends on the circumstances under which a prime minister must operate, particularly the government's parliamentary majority (or absence of it) and the cohesion of the party or coalition of government.

Cabinet conventions

Not every country understands the concept of collective cabinet responsibility in the same way. The prime minister has a better chance of exercising active leadership of the cabinet where this is supported by constitutional rules or conventions. In some countries, including Britain, Ireland and Germany, there is a tradition of strong executive leadership from the prime minister. In contrast, in Italy, neither the political elite nor the public has expected the prime minister to be the dominant force in government. In the Benelux and Scandinavian countries, tradition dictates that the cabinet as a whole should exercise executive power, with the prime minister in the role of a chairman. Scandinavian prime ministers are 'link men', who integrate and coordinate the policy activities of government, rather than policy leaders (Arter 1984:115). In countries where the prime minister has a coordinating role, cabinet government was sometimes established long before the office of prime minister was introduced. In the Netherlands, the office of prime minister was created only after the First World War. In Belgium, the term 'prime minister' was not used officially until 1918 (King 1994: 160–1).

The prime minister's role within the cabinet is also linked with traditional perceptions of how governments ought to act. In Britain, France and Ireland, for example, government is expected to set partisan policy guidelines: there is an overtly political style of government. In other countries, including Austria, Sweden, Switzerland and the Netherlands, the cabinet is expected to filter policy preferences expressed by different social and economic groups, and to try to resolve conflicts between them. There is a more consensual approach to policy-making, and the style of government can be described as administrative rather than political. Even in these countries, the increasing tendency for political parties to organise the work of government has helped to politicise government. Nevertheless, it is still possible to distinguish between countries according to their perceptions of the proper role of the cabinet in policy formulation.

The working practices within the cabinet can also help to determine the prime minister's capacity for leadership. For example, it can be difficult for a prime minister to monitor the work of cabinet where it is common practice for pairs or small groups of ministers to meet informally to exchange information. Most countries now use cabinet committees to assist in the preparation of cabinet decisions, and sometimes, as with the Italian 'interministerial committees', to make decisions in their own right. In West Germany, a 'coalition committee' was formed in 1961 to coordinate relations between the parties in the government coalition. The coalition committee has become increasingly institutionalised and is growing so politically important that there are now fears of it threatening to undermine the cabinet. Developments such as these are contributing to a fragmentation of cabinet work in western European countries. In a few countries, there has been a determined effort to resist any erosion of collective cabinet responsibility. Sweden has no cabinet committees but holds regular 'informal' meetings of the whole cabinet. Here, working practices confine the prime minister to a coordinating role, but simultaneously limit the individual ministers, who are not permitted to take decisions independently of the full cabinet (Arter 1984:100–2). To help in the increasingly complex task of co-ordinating the cabinet, many European prime ministers now make use of a group of personal advisers loyal to themselves rather than to the cabinet as a whole.

The prime minister's power of appointment

Much of a prime minister's power rests on the authority to make political appointments – the power of patronage. Prime ministers typically have the formal right to nominate their own cabinet ministers. (Exceptions are Switzerland, where all seven members of the Federal Council are chosen directly by parliament, the Federal Assembly; and the Netherlands.) However, their freedom of choice can be restricted in a number of ways. A prime minister might be obliged to represent competing party factions in the cabinet. In some countries where coalition cabinets are the norm, the parties will present their own nominees for appointment to their share of cabinet posts. In the 'corporatist' democracies such as the Scandinavian countries, economic interest-groups are closely involved in government decision-making. Here, cabinet appointments must enjoy the tacit approval of the major organised interests. Together, these factors can leave the prime minister with very little real choice over cabinet members. As a Norwegian prime minister once remarked, 'If you cannot get the ministers you love, you have to love the ones you get' (Arter 1984:120). The more complex the process of government formation, the more likely it is that the head of state, who appoints the prime minister and cabinet ministers, will influence the composition of the government. In France, the choice of cabinet ministers can in certain circumstances be 'hijacked' by the president.

The prime minister's power to make political appointments varies widely from country to country. The British prime minister controls an exceptionally wide range of posts, comprising cabinet ministers and the less senior positions of minister of state and parliamentary under-secretary – a total of some 100 posts (King 1994:155). The power to reshuffle the cabinet can add to the prime minister's ability to keep his or her cabinet colleagues in check. The British prime minister makes relatively frequent use of cabinet reshuffles. In the Netherlands, however, the prime minister does not have the right to remove a cabinet colleague or to reshuffle the cabinet, once appointed, before the end of the government's period in office. Some prime ministers have the power to organise and reorganise government ministries as they choose. The flexibility this entails can promote efficient government, but it also has implications for patronage. The prime minister may create a portfolio to reward a loyal supporter, or to 'buy' the support of an opposing faction within the party, or that of a coalition partner.

The prime minister and government

Each country, then, has evolved specific rules and traditions which together define the office of prime minister within the wider institutional framework of government. This is the context within which each individual prime minister must operate. Some countries give the office of prime minister greater powers or more freedom of action than others. This means that it is easier to be a strong prime minister in some countries than in others. The British prime minister has considerable powers of appointment and patronage, can reshuffle the cabinet at will and can alter the organisation of the cabinet and government departments. At the other end of the scale, the Norwegian prime minister has little say in the choice of cabinet and cannot alter the government ministries, or even dissolve the Storting. King (1994) has attempted to rank prime ministers according to their degree of influence within their own system of government (see Table 7.2).

Personality and leadership

The personality and leadership style of individual prime ministers affect the way they interpret their office and are perceived by the public. Margaret Thatcher's combative leadership style at home and abroad earned her the nickname of the 'iron lady';

Table 7.2 Prime ministers ranked according to their degree of influence within government[a]

High	Medium	Low
Germany	Austria	Italy
UK	Belgium	Netherlands
Greece	Denmark	Norway
Ireland	Sweden	
Portugal		
Spain		

Source: King (1994:153, Table 9.1).
[a] The French, Finnish and Swiss prime ministers are not included because these countries do not fully conform to a model of parliamentary government.

political columnists seized with glee on the term 'handbagging' to describe her *modus operandi*. Following such a strong character, her successor, John Major, struggled to shake off the image of the 'grey man'. Chancellor Kohl of Germany has often styled himself 'Adenauer's grandson'. At least in terms of the two chancellors' leadership styles, certain similarities can be seen. Both could be high-handed with their cabinets and were adept at disposing of potential rivals within the party. Both preferred pragmatic or *ad hoc* decisions to the grand designs espoused by Erhard or Brandt. Recent French prime ministers could hardly have demonstrated a wider range of personality, including the *soignée* but rash and tactless Edith Cresson, the down-to-earth, dependable Pierre Bérégovoy and the patrician Édouard Balladur.

The circumstances of office

Some prime ministers find themselves in office under more favourable circumstances than others. British prime ministers have usually enjoyed a triple advantage: as the leader of the party of government, in having a majority in parliament, and in heading a single-party government. It cannot be taken for granted that a European prime minister will simultaneously head his or her party. While this is the custom in Britain and Ireland, it is not necessarily the case in Germany, for example. It is rare for British prime ministers to have to contend with minority rule, yet this has been relatively common in the Scandinavian countries and in Italy. Also, most western European countries are governed by coalition rather than a single party of government. The prime ministers of West Germany have shown that it is possible to exercise firm leadership of a government coalition. However, where many parties are involved, or where the coalition is unstable, the prime minister is more likely to take on the character of a coordinator rather than the leader of government policy.

In the countries of western Europe, increasing party discipline has strengthened the hand of the executive as a whole. It is more difficult to judge whether, overall, the role of prime minister is becoming more important within the political systems of western Europe. Prime ministers are certainly becoming more visible, as the media cover their activities at home and at international meetings. The profile of the office can be raised by strong-minded individuals such as Adenauer in West Germany, Andreotti in Italy, or Thatcher in Britain. On the other hand, the ability of prime ministers to lead the executive is severely restricted by the expansion and diffusion of government decision-making. Also, most European countries remain attached to the idea of consensual rather than leader-dominated government.

Choosing the government

When cabinet government first developed in western Europe, the members of the government were chosen by the monarch. Until the 1983 constitutional revision, the Dutch constitution stated that 'the king appoints and dismisses ministers at his pleasure'. While it has long been accepted that a monarch should not have the power to determine the government of a democratic society, most heads of state still retain the formal power to appoint the government. (In Sweden, the power of appointment was transferred to the Speaker of the parliament in 1975.) In Britain, elections have usually given a clear majority to a single party, which then forms the government. In most western European countries however, this is not the case. It is rare for an electoral system based on proportional representation to return an absolute majority. Frequently, there is a real choice to be made between alternative coalitions of parties for the country's leadership.

Each country has developed a set of conventions to guide the process of government formation. One common concern has been to shield the head of state from having to make a political choice between alternative governments. A head of state must often appoint a *formateur*. A formateur, usually a senior MP, is designated as a potential prime minister and his or her task is to try to put together a viable government. Where heads of state must exercise their own judgement in appointing a formateur, they are clearly making a decision with potentially profound political implications. The head of state can sometimes fall back on a set of established guidelines. In Greece, for example, if the election does not result in an absolute majority, the president must invite each of the leaders of the four largest parties to form a government, working from the largest party to the smallest in terms of parliamentary strength. If none of these leaders is successful in forming a government, the president must try to assemble an all-party government. If he fails, he must appoint a caretaker cabinet, led by a senior judge, to hold office until fresh elections can be held.

In multi-party systems where the process of government formation can be lengthy and arduous, simple formula choices are not always possible. Where government formation might involve protracted bargaining, in Belgium and the Netherlands for example, the head of state might first appoint an intermediary, or *informateur*. The informateur is ideally a trusted elder-statesman figure, who no longer has any personal stake in the outcome of the bargaining process. The informateur's task is to negotiate with the parties represented in parliament and then to report back to the head of state with the name of a likely government formateur. The informateur acts on behalf of the head of state, leaving him or her to preside, at a safe distance, over the government negotiations.

However, even the appointment of an informateur cannot always prevent the head of state from becoming involved in the choice of government. Andeweg and Irwin (1993:109–11) describe how the monarch of the Netherlands influences government formation. The party background of the formateur or informateur is significant. If, for example, someone with a centre-left party background is chosen, this is taken to indicate the monarch's preference for a centre-left coalition. The monarch then issues directions which guide the subsequent negotiations. She might, for example, require that the government formed has the confidence of a majority in parliament – this means that minority governments are to be excluded. The instruction to form 'a cabinet that enjoys the broadest possible support' in parliament is interpreted as one to include the Christian Democratic Appeal (CDA) and the Labour Party (PvdA) in the cabinet, as these are usually the two largest parties.

Conventions of coalition bargaining differ from country to country. In Belgium the parties are represented by the party chairmen, in the Netherlands by the leaders of the parliamentary party groups. In all countries, any parties entering a coalition agreement will expect a share in the rewards of government. Cabinet portfolios can be considered as currency in coalition dealing: they represent value to the holder in offering the status of cabinet membership and the opportunity to influence policy in a particular area of government. Coalition negotiations can be expected to cover the distribution of cabinet portfolios and will sometimes also involve specific prior agreement on aspects of the future government's policies. In the Netherlands the agreed government programme is very comprehensive and is considered binding. It leaves the incoming prime minister and individual ministers little room for manoeuvre over issues which might split the coalition.

How should cabinet portfolios be divided among the parties forming a coalition government? A common solution is for parties to control a share of cabinet posts in proportion to the number of seats each contributes to the government's majority in parliament. Sometimes a party is in a position to claim more than its fair share of posts. In Germany, both the CDU and SPD have had to rely on the small FDP to ensure a government majority and each has been prepared to 'overcompensate' the FDP to this end. The question of which parties should control which particular ministries is less easily resolved. First, some ministries are considered inherently more important than others. Key posts include those associated with taxation, budgetary control and internal security. Typically, the party leading the negotiations in forming the government will try to consolidate its leadership position within the coalition by controlling the most important portfolios. Also, parties have their own preferences, determined by their ideological aims. Socialist and social democratic parties have, for example, a fundamental interest in influencing welfare policies. An important party representative might have personal ambitions to lead a particular ministry. The more parties involved in coalition negotiations, the more these interests are likely to come into conflict. Another question is whether parties should be entitled to determine their own candidates for 'their' share of ministries. This is the case in Sweden, for example. In the Netherlands, parties nominate their own candidates, but these must be acceptable to all the coalition partners.

Staying in power

Once a government has been formed, its chances of survival for its full electoral term are greater in some countries than in others. Everywhere except Switzerland, constitutional principles require that the government retain the confidence of parliament in order to stay in power. However, 'confidence' is an elastic concept and has different implications in different countries.

Some countries' constitutions demand a formal vote of investiture. This is a parliamentary vote of confidence on the government's proposed policy and cabinet team which it must pass in order to take office. In other words, the government must demonstrate majority backing in order to come to power. This is the case in Belgium, Greece, Ireland, Italy, Portugal, Spain and Switzerland. In Sweden, the prime minister alone must face a formal vote of confidence. Prior to the vote, he should give notice of his proposed programme and indicate which parties, if any, would join his own in forming a government coalition. Once approved by parliament, the prime minister appoints his cabinet team, which takes office without having to submit to a vote of investiture. In countries which do not observe a vote of investiture, even a minority government can survive as long as it is not successfully challenged by a parliamentary vote of no confidence. Parliament might be more reluctant to challenge a minority government if there is no acceptable alternative to the current cabinet. In most countries, it is considered important for a government to be able to pass its main legislative proposals. Even where this is the tradition, though, a government might sometimes try to stay in power after losing an important vote. The British Callaghan government of the 1970s did not offer to resign in spite of some defeats on major items of proposed legislation.

In Britain, there is a widespread belief that coalition government is inherently unstable. This is not necessarily true. Since 1945, Austria, Ireland and Luxembourg (all with experience of coalition government) have, with Britain, had stable cabinets with an average life-span of around three years. In other countries, though, particularly in Italy and Belgium, coalition government has been far more fragile, with cabinets lasting on average around one year (Gallagher *et al.* 1995:327–33). What makes coalitions in these countries more prone to collapse? Countries with short-lived governments tend to have large, complex party systems in which the parties represent radically different ideological and policy positions. Often, several parties are required to form a viable government. These factors make the task of maintaining the coalition in government much more difficult than one made up of only two or three parties with a moderate stance and flexible policy positions.

Patterns of executives: majority and minority government, single-party and coalition cabinets

Within each country, factors such as social cleavages, electoral and constitutional rules and conventions of government formation often combine to produce a distinctive pattern of government. For some, majority government is the norm, while in others a minority government is tolerated. Some countries are often led by a single-party government, others by a coalition cabinet. Single-party majority government has been fairly common in Ireland and Norway, but Britain is the archetypal 'majoritarian' system.[6] In Britain, a country dominated by the class cleavage, much of the vote falls to the two major parties, Conservative and Labour. The first-past-the-post electoral system tends to create a clear majority for either Labour or the Conservatives in parliament, so that the 'choice' of government is determined by the election. The style of government is partisan rather than administrative and adversarial rather than consensual. The prime minister is the leader of the majority party and is in a powerful position in comparison to most of his western European counterparts. On the occasions when the government has fallen short of a majority in parliament, it has preferred (in peacetime) not to draw another party into the cabinet in a formal executive coalition. Instead, it has relied on the support of another party or parties to vote legislative proposals through parliament. For example, during the Lib–Lab pact of 1977–78, Labour and the Liberals agreed to cooperate in parliament, but the Liberals did not receive any cabinet posts. In this way, Britain has kept at least the appearance of single-party government.

Coalition government is much more common than single-party government in most western European countries, where the class cleavage in society is often cross-cut with other significant cleavages such as religion or region. Electoral systems based on proportional representation reproduce the voters' choice more faithfully than a first-past-the-post system. As a result, numerous parties, representing a wide range of ideologies, may gain seats in parliament. Majority coalition government depends on the continued support of its constituent parties. If one or more of these parties should withdraw its support, the coalition cabinet could lose its majority in parliament. Depending on the circumstances and country conventions, it might then be necessary to call a general election to replace the government. Alternatively, it might be possible for the remaining parties of the coalition to continue as a minority cabinet. Or, if appropriate, the party groups in parliament might agree on a replacement coalition. A mid-term change of government without an election is not unusual in, for example, Italy or Germany. In some countries, this practice is considered unacceptable on the grounds that it distances the electorate from the choice of government. Between 1963 and 1967, three coalitions of quite different partisan composition governed the Netherlands, with only the first formed after an election. After this experience, it was accepted as a convention that a new government should be formed only after an election.

Minority cabinets can be formed by a single party or a coalition of parties. Minority government is the norm in Denmark. Eighteen of the twenty governments formed between 1945 and 1987 were of this type. During this period, minority governments were also very common in Italy and in Finland, Norway and Sweden (Laver and Schofield 1990:100, Table 5.4). The idea of minority government would seem to go against the grain in a parliamentary system. How can a government claim to have the confidence of parliament when it has the support of less than a majority of MPs? The point is that although the majority of members supports parties outside the government, this majority is not a united force. It might not actively support the government, but cannot agree on a preferable alternative. The government represents the least worst option and can therefore claim the confidence of parliament by default. Minority governments often make use of shifting legislative majorities in order to stay in power. Lacking the support in parliament for their policy programme as a whole, they will negotiate separate agreements with different parliamentary party groups on each policy issue. In this way, the majority supporting the government shifts with each piece of legislation.

The constraints and opportunities of parliamentary government

In sum, while parliamentary government imposes a recognisable pattern of behaviour on government institutions and actors, it also leaves room for the development of distinctive country conventions and specific styles of leadership. Most western European heads of state are not actively involved in executive decision-making, but some have nevertheless played an important role in the political life of their respective countries. The prime minister's leadership of the government can amount to little more than a coordinating role, or it can be directional or even domineering. As noted above, the key characteristic of parliamentary government is the mutual dependence of the legislative and executive branches of government. The balance of parties in parliament helps to determine whether a government is made up of a single party or a coalition of parties, and whether or not it enjoys the support of a stable majority in parliament. Irrespective of its strength at the outset, every cabinet operating within the framework of parliamentary government must maintain a working relationship with parliament in order to stay in power. The following chapter examines this dependent relationship from the other side: that of the western European parliaments.

Notes

1 In Germany, the government has no formal right to dissolve the Bundestag and the president may only do so under clearly specified circumstances. However, an early dissolution has twice been contrived by the government, in 1972 and in 1982, through special provisions concerning parliamentary confidence in the government (for details see Paterson and Southern 1991:85–9). While the Swedish government may dissolve parliament by calling an early election, in practice this has been strongly discouraged by the fact that, in this event, the constitution requires an additional election to be held between ordinary elections (Swedish Instrument of Government of 1989, Art 4; Elder *et al.* 1982:122–3). Since the Swedish constitution provided for a regular electoral cycle of three years, an early dissolution would have resulted in a very short maximum period in office for the successor government. (In 1994, the regular electoral cycle was changed from three years to four years.) In the semi-presidential systems of France and Finland, it is the president who holds the power to dissolve parliament. Article 12 of the constitution of the Fifth French Republic states that this power can only be exercised once in a year.

2 For example, in 1983, a Eurobarometer survey showed that 56 per cent of West Germans were either 'very' or 'quite' proud to be German. This level of positive identification was well below that of the other countries in the survey – the average for the EC was 77 per cent; Britain registered 92 per cent. Many West Germans were reluctant to answer the question (11 per cent responded 'don't know' or

gave no reply). Also, the 1983 study found that national pride was especially low among those respondents who were born just after the First World War and who therefore experienced the Third Reich as young adults. A follow-up poll conducted in 1994, after German unification, confirms these findings for Germany as a whole. Whereas seven out of ten EU citizens were found to be proud of their nationality, only 45 per cent of Germans were 'very' or 'fairly' proud to be German. As many as 19 per cent of Germans questioned would not answer or responded 'don't know'. Differences in the responses between eastern and western Germans were not substantial (Eurobarometer 1983; 1995).

3 A MORI poll of November 1995 confirms this. Classing the royal family as a 'profession', MORI asked people to indicate which professions they had most and least respect for. In August 1989, the royal family scored +24 points on the 'respect index', showing that they were the third most respected group after doctors and the police. In the 1995 poll, the index for the royal family stood at -6 points, sixth in ranking. Comparing the two polls, the royal family had declined in public respect more than any other group during this period (*The Times*, 24 November 1995).

4 In tiny Liechtenstein, the monarch still plays an active constitutional role long forgotten elsewhere in western Europe. As recently as 1993, Prince Hans-Adam imposed his will on the twenty-five-member parliament. Annoyed because the parliament had dismissed the prime minister in a vote of no confidence, Prince Hans-Adam dissolved the parliament and called fresh elections for the second time that year (*The Times*, 16 September 1993).

5 The exception is Switzerland, where the presidency rotates annually among the members of the cabinet, the Federal Council. Within Switzerland's unique system of government, the president carries out necessary procedural tasks but does not have any of the special political powers or privileges usually associated with a prime minister. Selection by rotation and the president's very short period in office keep to a minimum any personal status from holding the office. These features help to preserve the collegial character of the Swiss government.

6 Lijphart (1984) distinguishes between two models of parliamentary government which he terms 'majoritarian' and 'consensus'. The majoritarian model consists of nine related elements: the concentration of executive power in one-party and bare-majority cabinets; the

fusion of power and cabinet dominance; asymmetric bicameralism; a two-party system; a one-dimensional party system; a plurality system of elections; unitary and centralised government; an unwritten constitution and parliamentary sovereignty; and exclusively representative democracy. The consensus model has eight elements which are in sharp contrast to those of the majoritarian model: executive power-sharing and grand coalition; the formal and informal separation of powers; balanced bicameralism and minority representation; a multi-party system; a multi-dimensional party system; proportional representation; territorial and non-territorial federalism and decentralisation; and a written constitution and minority veto.

References

Anckar, D. (1994) 'The Finnish presidential election of 1994', *Electoral Studies*, 13:3, 272–6.

Andeweg, R. and G.A. Irwin (1993) *Dutch Government and Politics*, Basingstoke, Macmillan.

Arter, D. (1984) *The Nordic Parliaments: a Comparative Analysis*, London, Hurst.

Blondel, J. (1985) *Government Ministers in the Contemporary World*, London, Sage.

Eurobarometer (1983) *Public Opinion in the EC*, No. 19, Brussels, European Commission.

Eurobarometer (1995) *Public Opinion in the EU*, No. 42, Brussels, European Commission.

Europa (1995) *Europa World Yearbook*, London, Europa Publications, 36th edn.

Elder, N., A. Thomas and D. Arter (1982) *The Consensual Democracies? The Government and Politics of the Scandinavian States*, Oxford, Martin Robertson.

Gallagher, M., M. Laver and P. Mair (1995) *Representative Government in Modern Europe*, New York, McGraw-Hill.

Gilmour, D. (1985) *The Transformation of Spain. From Franco to the Constitutional Monarchy*, London, Quartet.

Keesing's (1995) *Keesing's Record of World Events*, Vol. 41, Harlow, Longman.

King, A. (1994) '"Chief executives" in Western Europe', in I. Budge and D. McKay (eds) *Developing Democracy*, London, Sage.

Laver, M. and N. Schofield (1990) *Multiparty Government. The Politics of Coalition in Europe*, Oxford, Oxford University Press.

Lijphart, A. (1984) *Democracies. Patterns of Majoritarian and Consensus Government in Twenty-One Countries* New Haven, CT, Yale University Press.

Paterson, W. and D. Southern (1991) *Governing Germany*, Oxford, Blackwell.

Further reading

Blondel, J. and F. Müller-Rommel (eds) (1988) *Cabinets in Western Europe*, Basingstoke, Macmillan.

Jones, G. (ed.) (1991) *West European Prime Ministers*, London, Frank Cass (originally published as a special issue of *West European Politics*, 14:2).

Laver, M. and K. Shepsle (eds) (1994) *Cabinet Ministers and Parliamentary Government. The Political Economy of Institutions and Decisions*, Cambridge, Cambridge University Press.

8

Accountable government: parliaments

European parliaments can trace their roots back to medieval times. They began as assemblies of aristocrats convened by the king whenever their support was needed to levy taxes or to go to war. These early, *ad hoc* assemblies became institutionalised. They came to meet regularly, to serve as a forum for communication between the king and powerful local leaders and to act as a check on the king's executive power. As the power of monarchs declined and modern institutions of government developed, parliaments survived and adapted to new circumstances. In the nineteenth century, parliament became the main symbol of national independence in new nation-states such as Belgium, Germany, Switzerland and Italy. Throughout Europe, acceptance of the principles of liberal democracy strengthened the position of parliament as an institution of government (see Chapter 2). The directly elected parliament represented the sovereignty of the people. When the vote was extended to mass publics, parliament's symbolic status rose still further.

It has often been asserted that parliaments have been in decline since the 'golden age' of the nineteenth century. Following the extension of the franchise, influential critics felt that the development of organised parties and interest-groups was undermining the independence and dignity of parliament. Various leaders and institutions of government have since been charged with encroaching on parliamentary authority, including popularly elected presidents, policy experts in the bureaucracy, military leaders and constitutional courts. Also, until recently, it was common for parliaments to be evaluated solely on their influence on policy-making. In the twentieth century, the ability of governments to initiate and determine policy has increased through the development of parliamentary party groups loyal to the government. Judging parliaments by this single criterion, this development seems to confirm the theory of parliamentary decline. If parliaments are judged on the full range of their activities, though, it is clear that they continue to perform tasks which are essential to democratic government. In some countries, parliament has become more significant in recent years (see Mezey, 1995). This chapter examines the organisation of western European parliaments, the tasks they perform, and the way in which they interact with their cabinets.

Parliamentary organisation

Bicameralism and unicameralism

In terms of organisation, western European parliaments share many similarities. Most are bicameral. That is, they are composed of two chambers, or, in British terminology, two houses (see Table 8.1). The bicameral structure is a product of the long evolution of parliament. Originally, upper (or second) chambers represented the aristocracy and lower chambers the commoners. The lower chambers were strengthened by the acceptance of ideas of popular democracy and by progressive extensions of the franchise. In all of the bicameral systems, the lower chamber is now directly elected by universal suffrage and is the more active and more politically significant of the two. Upper chambers had in effect become superfluous by the time of mass enfranchisement. Since then, their purpose and even their existence have frequently been challenged. All surviving upper chambers play a part in the legislative process and some have a special role in representing regional interests.

Various methods are used to select the members of upper chambers. A few are directly elected, as in Italy, Spain and Switzerland. Usually, though, they are selected by political elites. For example, the French Sénat is selected by an electoral college of politicians from national and subnational parliaments or councils. Members of both the Austrian and German Bundesrat are selected at the level of the *Länder* (see Table 8.1). Some upper chambers are selected by mixed methods, with a set proportion of seats allocated by a specified method (direct election, indirect election, appointment or co-optation). The membership of the House of Lords reflects the former structures of power in British society. The aristocracy is represented by the 'lords temporal': the hereditary peers of England, Scotland, Great Britain and the UK. The hereditary peers account for around two-thirds of the members of the House of Lords. In practice, the hereditary members are self-selecting; many rarely attend the House. The 'lords spiritual' comprise the Archbishops of Canterbury and York and twenty-four senior bishops of the Church of England. The lords spiritual are members of the House of Lords only during their period in ecclesiastical office. All others are members for life. The 'law lords' are judges appointed by the Crown to participate in the House of Lords in its role as the final court of appeal. The Life Peerages Act of 1958 introduced a new category of non-hereditary peer, a title bestowed on an individual for his or her lifetime, but which cannot be passed on to the next generation. There is no limit to the number of members of the House of Lords. In the parliamentary session of 1988–89, it had 1,183 members; in 1994–95, 1,194 members. In general, selection by political elites or by indirect means is more likely to represent entrenched interests and therefore to result in a more conservative upper chamber than the directly elected lower chamber or unicameral parliament.

Unicameral parliaments are directly elected and carry out the function of a lower chamber in a bicameral system. Unicameral parliaments are found in Denmark, Finland, Greece, Iceland, Luxembourg, Norway, Portugal and Sweden. Although technically unicameral, Norway's Storting emulates a bicameral parliament in the way it organises internally. After an election, it forms two divisions for the scrutiny of legislation: the Lagting (made up of around one quarter of MPs) and the Odelsting (the

Table 8.1 The structure of western European parliaments, 1996

	Lower chamber	*Upper chamber*
Austria	Nationalrat seats: 183 term: 4 years	Bundesrat seats: 64 term: 5 or 6 years[a]
Belgium	Chambre des Représentants seats: 150 term: 4 years	Sénat seats: 71 term: 4 years
Britain	House of Commons seats: 651 term: 5 years	House of Lords seats: 1,194[b] term: Life or duration of Church office
Denmark	Folketing – unicameral seats: 179 term: 4 years	
Finland	Eduskunta – unicameral seats: 200 term: 4 years	
France	Assemblée Nationale seats: 577 term: 5 years	Sénat seats: 321 term: 9 years[c]
Germany	Bundestag seats: 656[d] term: 4 years	Bundesrat seats: 69 term: varies[e]
Greece	Vouli ton Ellinon – unicameral seats: 300 term: 4 years	
Iceland	Althingi – unicameral seats: 63 term: 4 years	
Ireland	Dáil Éireann seats: 166 term: 5 years	Seanad Éireann seats: 60 term: 5 years
Italy	Camera dei Deputati seats: 630 term: 5 years	Senato seats: 323[f] term: 5 years
Luxembourg	Chambre des Députés – unicameral seats: 60 term: 5 years	

Table 8.1 *Continued*

	Lower chamber	*Upper chamber*
Netherlands	Tweede Kamer seats: 150 term: 4 years	Eerste Kamer seats: 75 term: 6 years
Norway	Storting – unicameral seats: 165 term: 4 years	
Portugal	Assembléia da República – unicameral seats: 230 term: 4 years	
Spain	Congreso de los Diputados seats: 350 term: 4 years	Senado seats: 256 term: 4 years
Sweden	Riksdag – unicameral seats: 349 term: 4 years	
Switzerland	Nationalrat seats: 200 term: 4 years	Ständerat seats: 46 term: 4 years

Sources: country constitutions; Elder *et al.* (1982:119–22);
Fitzmaurice (1991:163–4); Inter-parliamentary Union (1986); Lane
et al. (1991); Smith (1992: Tables 4.3, 6.1), Vacher's (1995).

[a] The term of 5 or 6 years depends on the term of the *Land* (provincial)
legislatures. Each *Land* legislature elects its share of the members of
the Bundesrat by proportional representation after the *Land* election.
Bundesrat members need not necessarily be members of the Landtag
which selects them.

[b] The number of members of the House of Lords varies with each
parliamentary session. In 1995, there were 1,194 members.

[c] One-third of the membership retires every three years.

[d] While the standard membership of the Bundestag is 656 members,
the electoral system can sometimes produce a small number of
additional mandates. The election of 1994 produced a Bundestag
comprising 672 members.

[e] Members of the Bundesrat must be members of *Land* governments.
Each *Land* selects its share of Bundesrat members after the formation
of a new *Land* government following the *Land* elections.

[f] Of these, 315 senators are directly elected.

remaining three quarters). Given the enduring controversy over the role of upper chambers, it is possible that some of the remaining bicameral systems might choose in future to abolish their upper chamber in favour of a unicameral system.

Rules of procedure and the presiding authority

MPs are required to resolve conflict over contentious issues. In order to do this efficiently, fairly and without coming to blows, they agree on a set of rules of procedure (in Britain, standing orders) to regulate the conduct of parliamentary business. In most western European countries, the parliaments are free to determine their own rules of procedure.[1] This autonomy is important, as the rules of procedure do not only concern internal parliamentary matters, but also affect the way in which parliament interacts with the executive. All of the parliaments have a presiding authority to ensure that the rules of procedure are kept, to maintain order during parliamentary sessions and to take responsibility for the administration of parliament. These important tasks are headed by a single individual: the president of the parliament (in Britain, the Speaker). In most cases, he or she is supported by a small group of parliamentarians known as the bureau or presidium. Ideally, the president of the parliament should be a non-controversial choice, acceptable to all parliamentary parties. In 1994, the Italian prime minister, Silvio Berlusconi, broke with tradition when he selected candidates from his own party coalition, the Freedom Alliance, for the posts of president of the Camera dei Deputati (Chamber of Deputies) and president of the Senato (Senate).

Parliamentary committees

Parliamentary committees have become a standard feature of western European parliaments. Created by their 'parent' chambers to help them with their work, the committees are composed of MPs. The organisation and use of committees have become more systematic as parliamentary business has increased. All of the lower chambers and some of the upper chambers have a number of permanent committees in key policy areas, usually corresponding to government ministries; these are convened for the duration of the session of parliament. Specialised committees have been introduced relatively recently in some countries. Britain, for example, has had a specialised committee system only since 1979, and Ireland since 1983 (Norton 1990a:145). They may be supplemented by *ad hoc* committees, appointed as required to deal with a particular policy area or to investigate a matter of public concern, and then disbanded.

The use of committees offers several advantages. They can bring together known specialists in a particular policy area to give expert attention to a proposed bill. A greater volume of work can be completed by a number of small groups than could be achieved in the cumbersome plenary (full) sittings of parliament. A committee can get to grips with the details of a proposal, leaving questions of broader importance to the plenary sittings. While committees were originally intended to support the work of parliaments, they have become increasingly important in their own right, so that, in many countries, decisions made in committee are now simply confirmed in parliament. Depending on the circumstances, a strong committee system can strengthen parliament in its dealings with the executive. It can enhance the quality of parliamentary representation by giving backbenchers or opposition members an opportunity to contribute. In some countries, MPs can use committee work to further their parliamentary career.

Party groups
Within the formal structures of parliament's plenary sittings and committee meetings, political parties exert an informal but very significant influence on the organisation of parliamentary activity. After an election, the MPs band together to form parliamentary party groups, headed by a party group leader and governed by internal rules. Although these organisations are neither required nor foreseen by most constitutions, they have achieved a

de facto legitimacy within parliaments and may be awarded rights and access to facilities under parliamentary rules of procedure. Recognised rights may include, for example: membership of important parliamentary bodies, representation on committees, speaking time in debates, special privileges for party group leaders, parliamentary office space and secretarial assistance. In Spain, parliamentary groups (and not individual deputies) introduce legislation. The importance of party group status was illustrated in France following the 1988 parliamentary election. At this election the representation of the Communist Party had fallen to twenty-seven seats, three short of the thirty required to constitute an official party group with its accompanying privileges. The Communists struck a deal with the Socialist Party to reduce the number of seats needed to form a party group in return for the Communists' support of the Socialist candidate for president of the Assemblée Nationale (National Assembly) (Machin 1994:40).

Given the strength of party discipline, the party groups effectively structure parliamentary debate. Since many of the 'real' decisions of parliament are now taken in committee, a party line is often decided in advance of committee meetings, to be represented by party group members on the relevant committee. Particularly in countries prone to coalition government, control of the parliamentary committees has become a vital issue for the parties. Party groups compete to gain control of important committees by securing the committee chair (and thus the ability to set the agenda and possibly a deciding vote in cases of deadlock) and by ensuring if possible that their party or alliance has a voting majority. In many cases, parliamentary guidelines have been devised to determine how these important posts are filled.

The work of parliaments

In general terms, parliaments act as a means of communication between the people and the government. They (or at least their lower chambers) are composed of elected representatives of the people. Together, these elected representatives have the authority to hold the government accountable to the people. As such they symbolise the consent given to government by the people to make binding decisions for society. Western European parliaments enjoy a relatively high level of acceptance by their citizens. In this they help to legitimise the regime, as well as the government of the day. Of course, some parliaments are more respected than others. Recent evaluations have shown that the parliaments of Sweden and (West) Germany enjoy the highest levels of public confidence in western Europe, while the Italian parliament is the least trusted (Norton 1990a:146). In Italy, the low level of public confidence in government in general has contributed to the current constitutional review which is hoped to give the system more credibility.

Parliaments are not the only means of communication between government and the people. The mass media provide a channel of communication through news coverage and lately also through the televising of parliamentary sittings. Interest-groups act on behalf of their own members to provide links to government officials. Political parties act as channels of political opinion and have come to structure the work of parliaments. Nevertheless, none of these alternative channels of communication enjoys a direct mandate from the whole electorate which is periodically renewed in free elections. It is this mandate which distinguishes parliaments as channels of communication in democratic systems and which gives them the authority to hold governments to account.

Within their general function of linking government and the governed, parliaments in western Europe are expected to engage in representation, legislation, the selection and control of governments, and to provide a forum for debate.

Representation

An MP might be called on to represent various interests, including those of the nation, territorial constituency, individual constituent, parliamentary party group or faction. An MP might also be guided by his or her own conscience. These interests can easily conflict with one another. In deciding how to argue or how to vote in parliament, how do individual members resolve conflicting demands?

Increasingly, the parliamentary party group has come to dominate such choices. As parties have come to organise the work of government, individual MPs are expected to vote in line with the wishes of their party group. Members are customarily granted a free vote over matters of conscience, such as the death penalty. Party groups may also make allowances for a 'deviant' vote on a matter which directly affects a member's constituency. Otherwise, party group pressure can be strong, but may be offset by the method of voting used. It is much more difficult for the party groups to police a vote taken by a secret ballot than an open ballot in which individual votes are identifiable.

In some countries, MPs are also expected actively to represent the interests of their local constituency. This tends to be given higher priority where the electoral system allows the residents of a constituency to identify a single individual as their parliamentary representative. In Britain, for example, an MP will be expected not only to lobby for national funds to be spent on local projects, but also to intervene directly on behalf of individual constituents over complaints of bureaucratic inefficiency or corruption. MPs in France are also concerned with their constituents' needs, but here public expectations have a different emphasis. The French are less likely to seek help over the redress of grievances. Instead, they tend to approach their 'deputy' in the hope that he or she can arrange a favour of some kind; perhaps a social security benefit, a civil service posting or promotion, or a special licence. In contrast, voters in the Netherlands are unlikely to approach MPs with their problems. The Netherlands has an electoral system of proportional representation in which there are no local constituencies.

The parliamentary structure can help to determine how particular interests are represented. In some bicameral systems, territorial interests are assured of permanent representation: the lower chamber represents the needs of the electorate as a whole while the second chamber represents the regions, or, in a federation, the provinces or 'states'. Territorial interests are particularly well represented in the German Bundesrat. Although the Austrian Bundesrat was devised along the same lines as its German namesake, it is more tied by constitutional and party political constraints and has in practice been less effective in representing the interests of the *Länder*. Upper chambers without a territorial base are less easy to justify in terms of representation. (Except, of course, the directly elected upper chambers, which can claim to represent the people.) In some of the Scandinavian countries, the upper chamber has been abolished fairly recently. Denmark's parliament has been unicameral since 1953, Sweden's since 1969 and Iceland's since 1991. In these relatively small countries with homogeneous societies, there was no need for a second chamber to represent and resolve territorial differences. Of all the upper chambers, Britain's House of Lords is least concerned with representation: 'peers are deemed formally to represent no one but themselves' (Norton 1990b:13).

Although parliamentary committees are not primarily concerned with representation, the committee structure can affect the range of views expressed in parliament. During plenary sittings of parliament there is only a limited time available for members to speak. Internal arrangements allocate speaking time to important individuals such as cabinet members and party group leaders, but an ordinary backbencher will rarely get the opportunity to speak. A parliament with an extensive committee system will offer more opportunities for input from all members (Lees and Shaw 1979:370, 426).

Legislation

Parliaments are usually associated with their function of legislation or law-making. In practice, they share this task with many other groups including the executive, the electorate (through referenda), regional parliaments and local councils, parliamentary committees and party groups, bureaucracies, economic interests, the courts, and the institutions of the EU. Parliaments may be excluded altogether from some measures which are binding on society. In France, for example, parliament may only deal with measures classified in the constitution as a law. Other measures are dealt with by government regulation and the Constitutional Council ensures that parliament does not legislate outside its competence. In federal or strongly regionalised countries, the constitution may reserve certain matters for the subnational parliaments. In most countries, routine regulatory matters may be dealt with by the civil service. Once a law is passed, parliament generally has little further influence over it. Committees may be charged with overseeing the work of a parallel government department, but legislation may still be implemented with considerable discretion. It may also be subject to review by the courts or by a referendum (see Chapter 9).

Usually, laws are initiated by the executive. Parliaments do have the opportunity to initiate a law through individual members or groups of parliamentarians, such as Britain's 'private member's bill'.[2] Such bills rarely gain the government backing which would guarantee them a safe passage. However, while parliamentary initiatives of this sort usually fail to become law, they can place controversial issues and minority interests on the political agenda and can help to counter the major parties' dominance of parliamentary debate. In spite of the high risk of failure, many MPs and party groups take this provision very seriously.

While most parliaments are all but excluded from the initiation and first elaboration of a law, they and their committees take responsibility for the next stages in the legislative process: detailed redrafting, debating and amendment. According to the established procedure in each country, a bill passes between the one or two chambers of parliament and relevant committees. While each country has its own requirements as to how many readings a bill must have or the way in which committees are involved, the principle is the same everywhere: a bill should receive more than one stage of careful scrutiny by elected representatives in parliament.

Even where an upper chamber plays an active role in the legislative process, the lower chamber enjoys a higher status because it is directly elected. This is evident in special circumstances or when particularly important legislation must be passed. In France, for example, each of the two chambers must pass a bill before it becomes law. In the case of deadlock between the chambers, the government may intervene and ask the National Assembly to take a final decision. Also, bills involving finance must be introduced in the National Assembly. In Austria, the Nationalrat has exclusive powers concerning the budget. Overall, the main legislative role of upper chambers in bicameral parliaments is to give a final reading to legislation before it is passed. This final reading acts as a check on majority government in the lower chamber. While these tasks are seen as important, it is by no means agreed that upper chambers in their traditional form are needed to undertake them. Upper chambers are frequently criticised over their role in legislation, either for being too weak or too powerful. Some upper chambers can only delay rather than prevent the passage of legislation. This applies, for example, to the British House of Lords, which may delay legislation passed by the House of Commons for a year. Those which are more powerful, such as the Italian Senate, are often criticised for being obstructive when they use the measures at their disposal. Also, the need to coordinate the work of two chambers inevitably slows and complicates the legislative process. Unicameral Denmark and Sweden have compensated – apparently quite successfully – for the loss of their upper chambers by introducing alternative institutional and procedural checks on the passage of legislation. Moreover, in many countries, the courts are gradually usurping the traditional revising role of upper chambers by exercising judicial review of legislation.

The legislative powers delegated to parliamentary committees vary considerably from country to country. Some have the power to initiate legislation. In Sweden all committees may introduce legislation; in Finland this right is restricted to the finance and bank committees. In Austria, a permanent committee can make drastic changes to the content of a bill referred to it by the government or an MP, effectively initiating legislation of its own. In Italy, Spain and Sweden, parliament may even delegate full legislative competences to its committees. Italy makes such frequent use of this procedure that most legislation is passed in the committees. This has helped to speed up the passage of uncontentious legislation in a particularly cumbersome parliamentary system, leaving the plenary sittings to deal with more controversial and important topics. It can be argued, though, that this increased efficiency has been at the cost of accountability, as many laws are passed without the public debate they would receive in a full sitting of parliament.

The Swedish Riksdag and Danish Folketing have a wider legislative role than their counterparts in other countries. In fact, the Riksdag is involved at every stage of the legislative process: formulation, deliberation and implementation (see Arter 1990). In Sweden, commissions are set up on a systematic basic to formulate public policy, and around a third of the places on these bodies are taken by Riksdag members. In keeping with the consensual style of decision-making in Sweden, members of the opposition are not excluded from serving on the commissions, although pro-government members almost always dominate. Elsewhere, the regular involvement of parliamentarians in prelegislative work is rare. The British House of Commons, for example, has an essentially reactive role in the legislative process. Pre-legislative select committees are only occasionally used to evaluate a subject and recommend legislation. The government might test out parliament's opinion by issuing discussion papers (green papers) and papers outlining its proposals (white papers). Debates on white papers are held occasionally, allowing MPs to express their views before legislation is introduced. Such debates have included problematic topics such as industrial relations (1969) and Britain's membership of the European Communities (1975). However, these measures allow little initiative for Parliament and certainly no regular input (Norton 1981:85).

In Sweden, the Riksdag continues to be influential at the deliberative stage of legislation. The rationalisation of the committee system in 1971 has helped parliament to scrutinise bills more effectively. Also, since 1971, it has become more common for Riksdag members to be appointed to the boards and agencies which supervise the implementation of legislation, an important site of control located outside parliament. One of the advantages of the Swedish practice is that it provides regular channels of contact between parliament, government, administration and corporate interests. This promotes parliament's role as an intermediary between government and the governed.

The role of parliaments in legislation depends partly on the rules and forms of organisation outlined above. Another important factor is the strength of the government in office. A government with secure parliamentary backing (a majority of seats and a disciplined party group or coalition) can use this advantage to dominate legislation. It might be able to channel the detailed elaboration of legislation through executive departments or through government committees, excluding MPs from opposition groups (Lees and Shaw 1979:367). It might arrange the parliamentary timetable in order to influence the degree of scrutiny a particular bill will receive. On the other hand, a less secure government will have to tread more carefully when it introduces legislation and might have more difficulty in influencing the deliberative stage. If the government anticipates strong opposition to a bill in parliament, it might reluctantly decide to postpone the bill's introduction until a more favourable reception is likely. It might have to make prior concessions to members or party groups outside the government to 'buy' parliamentary support for a measure. When minority governments became more common in Denmark, Norway and Sweden, their parliaments made more active use of their powers and became less subordinate to the government of the day (see Mezey 1995: 197, 209). While parliaments cannot control the legislative process, then, they can be very influential within it.

The selection of executives

In a parliamentary system of government, the institution of parliament selects the executive, maintains it in power and, under certain circumstances, brings it down before the end of its maximum term of office. Parliaments therefore play an important part in bringing about the orderly succession of governments.

The choice of executive depends on the relative strengths of the individual party groups and party group alliances in parliament. Even in the anomolous case of France, the confidence of the parliamentary majority is crucial to the composition of the government. While the French president is directly elected, the prime minister, as head of the government, must be acceptable to the majority in parliament. This was demonstrated by the two 'cohabitation' governments in France following the general elections of 1986 and 1993. On each occasion, the elections returned a centre-right majority. In order to respect the electorate's choice, the Socialist president, François Mitterrand, was obliged to select a prime minister from the centre right (Jacques Chirac in 1986 and Edouard Balladur in 1993).

While the government must have the confidence of the parliament to survive, certain circumstances can reduce the parliament's control over the choice of government (see Chapter 7). In complex party systems, a formateur or informateur may be appointed to direct coalition negotiations between the party groups. Some countries do not require governments to submit to a formal vote of investiture, so that the confidence of parliament is assumed unless the government is actively challenged. In Switzerland, the role of parliament in choosing the executive is nominal. The composition of the Swiss federal executive is largely determined by convention and its term of office is fixed in the constitution.

In addition to selecting and maintaining the executive, parliaments are the chief source of recruitment to executive office. In Britain, cabinet members must be drawn from either of the two Houses of Parliament. However, the Life Peerage Act of 1958 has enabled prime ministers to award cabinet posts to individual non-parliamentarians by first giving them a place in the House of Lords. In France, the constitution of the Fifth Republic (1958) tried to enforce a separation of powers along American lines between the executive and legislative branches of government.

While government ministers are responsible to parliament as in Britain, members of the executive are banned from simultaneously holding a seat in parliament. As a result, many career bureaucrats have been recruited to government posts. In practice, however, the traditional link between government and parliament has reasserted itself. Goverment ministers have found that winning a parliamentary seat gives them legitimacy in the eyes of the electorate. Would-be ministers frequently contest a seat, handing it to their elected substitute if they are appointed to office. (The substitute obligingly resigns the seat if the minister should lose the post.) During their period in office, ministers cultivate close links with 'their' constituents in preparation for the next election.

In selecting the government and providing a large share of its members, parliaments act as an agent of socialisation for the country's government. Those who are recruited from parliament to executive leadership tend to support the current regime (anti-system parties are rarely involved in government). The shared experience of parliamentary activity produces political leaders who, partisan differences aside, respect the same set of values and operate by the same rules and conventions. While this arguably helps to provide stability in government, it can also lead to public resentment over a 'political class' that is distanced from the needs of the general population.

The control of executives

One of the traditional roles of parliaments is to hold executives accountable to the electorate for their decisions and actions. Parliaments may call their executives to account by various means. These include motions of no confidence, interpellations (questions followed by debate on the response), written or oral parliamentary questions, parliamentary investigative committees, and audit committees for the oversight of financial matters.

Smith (1989:191–2) has noted that parliamentary controls of governments are 'double-edged' in nature. This is a product of the mutual dependence of the legislative and executive branches of government under a parliamentary system. The motion of no confidence appears to be a powerful weapon in holding governments to account, but, if it results in a national election, it also dissolves the parliament. Party elites in the government rely on the support of their party colleagues in parliament to stay in power, but in turn have the power of patronage over those who want to join the government in the future.

Also, controls do not always work as anticipated. For example, the Swedish Riksdag did not receive the 'classic' right to initiate a motion of no confidence against the government until the constitutional revision of 1971. Paradoxically, since its introduction, minority governments have found it easier to stay in power as the defeat of a bill need not bring down a government unless it is specifically designated a question of confidence (Arter 1990:132). A parliament can have a full complement of formal controls but still be unable or unwilling to challenge the government effectively. The parliamentary control of governments depends very much on the context and circumstances in which it is exercised. (This is illustrated below in the country studies of France and Germany.) Even where the institutional balance of power favours the executive, though, the executive can never take its advantage for granted. The Spanish parliament has been judged the most docile in Europe: constitutionally weak in relation to the executive, taking its lead from government and unable to make use of its control functions (see Heywood 1995: 99–102). In October 1995, the usually passive parliament inflicted two major defeats on the socialist government. The government lost its first vote in the Senado (Senate) when it failed to prevent an inquiry into the 'Gal' case (an alleged state campaign of murder and kidnap directed against Basque terrorists). The following week, parliament rejected the government's annual budget for the first time since the restoration of democracy in the late 1970s (*Financial Times*, 26 October 1995).

Parliament as a forum for debate
Parliaments have traditionally provided a forum for debate on issues which directly affect their nation. In this respect, Britain's

House of Commons is generally held in high esteem. In comparison with the parliaments of, for example, France, Germany, Denmark and Sweden, the House of Commons generates a healthy and topical public debate. Many countries have tried to introduce a version of the British 'Prime Minister's Questions' in the hope that this will stimulate a more meaningful parliamentary debate. (Ironically, many British MPs would welcome a reform of 'Question Time', described by a recent Commons report as a 'partisan joust' between noisier MPs.[3]) In fact, parliaments are debating matters of public interest, but this is increasingly taking place behind the closed doors of committee and party group meetings rather than in the plenary sittings of parliament. In some countries, France and Britain for example, the upper chamber is noted for the high quality of debate. However, the activity of upper chambers receives far less public attention than that of lower chambers.

While western European parliaments may be failing in their task of providing public debate, they are providing more public information. Parliamentary information services distribute documents, sometimes with commentaries; they publish communiques and organise press conferences. During the twentieth century, advances in media technology have meant that the public can have first-hand access to some of the work of parliament rather than depending on a journalist's interpretation. Politicians were initially quite wary of broadcasting coverage of their work. There were fears that some of the more obscure rituals of parliament might make the sessions appear trivial or out of touch with reality. Also, MPs might be tempted to play to the camera. However, the broadcasting of parliamentary activity is now widely accepted. By the mid-1980s, all western European countries except Finland, Ireland, Luxembourg and Liechtenstein had made provision for the televising of parliamentary debates. It should be noted, however, that a relatively small proportion of the public takes advantage of this access to parliamentary business. For example, in Austria, only 2–8 per cent of the public watch the televised proceedings of parliament (Fitzmaurice 1991:85).

Parliaments in context

While parliaments in western European countries perform similar tasks, they do not perform them equally well. Some parliaments display strengths in some areas and weaknesses in others. Some are altogether more efficient and powerful institutions than others. These variations can be accounted for by differences in the historical evolution of a country's institutions of government and different ideas as to what role parliament should play within this institutional framework. The parliaments of France and Germany can serve to illustrate some of these differences. In each case, the drafters of the current constitutional framework had a clear role in mind for parliament. While both parliaments have been shaped by this constitutional design, each has developed in slightly unforeseen ways in the process of adapting to new circumstances.

France

The French Third and Fourth Republics (1870–1940, 1946–58) had been based on a constitutional framework in which parliament was the dominant institution of government. Unfortunately, while parliament dominated government activity, it was also grossly inefficient. At this time, parliamentary activity was not structured by disciplined political parties. There was no concept of a government party which was responsible to the country in return for the power to govern. Parliament was fragmented by deep class, ideological and local differences. MPs formed loose associations, often acting on behalf of powerful interest-groups. These groups effectively blocked each others' initiatives. The result was *immobilisme* – the parliament was strong enough to block the executive, but was incapable of performing decisively or consistently.

The drafters of the constitution of the Fifth Republic were determined to redress the balance of the institutions of government to enable the executive branch to engage in firm leadership. The French president was given constitutional powers designed to avoid or break a deadlock in parliament. The important task of appointing the prime minister was taken away from parliament and given to the president. The president was given the authority to oversee the calling of a referendum. He could dissolve the National Assembly once in a period of twelve months. The constitution also limits the length of parliamentary sessions.

Parliament's legislative powers were drastically reduced and control of the legislative process was transferred to the executive. The constitution spells out in detail the limits of parliamentary competence. It lists those subject areas which are regulated by 'laws' and which therefore fall under the competence of parliament, while other measures are dealt with by the executive. Under Article 38, the government may encroach on the legislative powers of parliament. It may ask parliament to delegate its power of law-making to the government (on a specific subject and for a limited period). In addition, there are a number of procedures the government may use to promote its legislative initiatives. The new Constitutional Council was charged with policing parliamentary legislation. It was to rule on which new issues came under the classification of 'laws' and on the constitutionality of laws passed by parliament. The constitution limits the number of permanent committees to six for each chamber of parliament – considerably fewer than in other western European countries. They are large and unwieldy and are easily controlled by the government because they are chaired by members of the government party or coalition.

In spite of the constraints imposed on them by the constitution, parliamentarians of the Fifth Republic have taken their legislative role seriously and have exercised it to the full. MPs make use of their right to introduce private members' legislation, even though few of these measures are passed. The legislative committees (with their government majorities) propose numerous amendments to bills, over 75 per cent of which are accepted (Frears 1990:42). Amendments are proposed by individual members of all parties in parliament, even though those originating with pro-government members are much more likely to succeed.

The French parliament has also been severely restricted in its ability to control the executive. In particular, there was until recently almost no role for opposition forces in parliament. The constitution does provide for the parliamentary questioning of executive decisions and actions, but the means available are not very effective. The effectiveness of oral parliamentary questions is limited by lengthy delays before they appear on the agenda, or by scheduling them on Fridays when most deputies are absent from the National Assembly. A form of Britain's 'Question Time' was introduced to the National Assembly in the 1970s and to the Senate in 1982, but has had little impact. In practice, written parliamentary questions are tabled largely for the benefit of a member of parliament's home constituency, to demonstrate that local interests are being represented.

Two types of committee may be set up on an *ad hoc* basis: committees of inquiry and committees of control. However, a majority is needed to convene them, and so the government can usually block any which are likely to delve too deeply. Requests for committees of inquiry, which have become more frequent since the early 1970s, are usually rejected. Those which get through tend to have all-party support, to be concerned with non-partisan topics such as the state of the French language, or to investigate the conduct of a previous government. These committees have only six months in which to produce their reports, which receive little media attention. Also, ministers may refuse to cooperate with them and may instruct their officials not to attend the hearings (Frears 1990:35–6).

As a last resort, the National Assembly (but not the Senate) may issue a motion of censure against the government, which, if successful, forces the government to resign. The special procedure required ensures that only a determined effort and an absolute majority of the National Assembly can bring a government down. In attempting to redress the balance of power between the institutions of government, the constitution of the Fifth Republic has trimmed the control function of the parliament to the very minimum acceptable in terms of democratic accountability.

In sum, the constitution of 1958 has left the French parliament in a very weak position in comparison with that of the Fourth Republic and most other western European countries. It gives the executive firm control of the legislative process, restricts the terms of debate largely to those set by the government, and gives parliament very little opportunity for scrutinising the executive and holding it accountable for its decisions and actions.

In spite of all its weaknesses, Frears (1990) concludes that the French parliament has managed to prove its worth in the Fifth Republic. While politicians as a breed are mistrusted by the public, both the institution of parliament and the local MP are highly valued. This high esteem rests partly on the republican values deeply embedded in French political culture. MPs have worked hard with the little influence they have over legislation and with the inadequate means at their disposal to oversee the government. Particularly since changes in the rules of access to the Constitutional Council in 1974 and the transfer of power to the socialists in 1981, the parliamentary opposition has become more self-aware and more active. More important in the eyes of the public, MPs have retained their traditional commitment to their local constituency. One development which could not have been foreseen in 1958 was the emergence of disciplined party groups in parliament. (This was prompted by the presidentialisation of French politics set in motion by de Gaulle.) The new-found party discipline in parliament has made majority government possible, which in turn has helped to stabilise the Fifth Republic.

Germany

The reunification of Germany in 1990 brought the former East and West Germany together under the constitutional framework which had been in force in West Germany since 1949. Whereas France's Fifth Republic constitution had set out to weaken parliament in relation to the executive, the West German *Grundgesetz* (Basic Law) had a different aim. It was to create a balanced and stable system of government in which the executive could not act arbitrarily as it had during the Third Reich. One element in this was the clear demarcation of responsibility. The chancellor (prime minister) was to be the undisputed head of the executive, leaving the president the ceremonial tasks of a head of state.

The drafters of the constitution were at pains to create a responsible parliament as well as a responsible government. The chancellor and his government are responsible to the Bundestag. The Bundestag formally elects the chancellor. It can remove the chancellor and his government, but only by means of a majority vote in favour of a new chancellor. This 'constructive vote of no confidence' does not detract from parliament's traditional right to dismiss a government, but avoids the possibility of a power vacuum. While the constitution set the guidelines for a responsible parliament, the Bundestag had to earn the high esteem it now enjoys. In 1949, Germans had seen five changes of regime in under eighty years. Initially, the West German Bundestag could not count on public support. However, by the 1980s, opinion polls suggested that the West Germans had more confidence in their parliament than was the case in comparable countries such as Britain and France.

The parliamentary party groups play a key role in the German Bundestag. Changes in government have usually been brought about neither by electoral upheavals nor by a challenge from the Bundestag as a whole. Instead, they have resulted from the withdrawal of one of the parties from the coalition government. Chancellors have had to cultivate their relationships with their coalition partners in order to stay in power, carefully balancing the demands of their own party with those of their partners. This has led to the development of strong channels of communication within and between parties. It has also given an unusually high profile to party group interests as opposed to those of the individual MP. The procedures of the Bundestag are based on the unit of the party group. For example, Bundestag committee places and committee chairs are allocated not to individual MPs, but to the party groups in proportion to their representation in the chamber. These then distribute the posts to their members. While the Bundestag is in session, time is set aside to allow the party groups to meet and prepare their positions. The party groups are formal organisations, each with its own set of rules of procedure, chairman and executive. They are allocated office space, administrative support and public funding. They form working groups (which in turn form subcommittees) to parallel the committees of the Bundestag and whose task it is to develop party policy. The party groups have effectively become 'mini-parliaments' (Paterson and Southern 1991:116), acting as a forum for debating legislation and deciding party policy. Before tabling a parliamentary question, or making a point in a Bundestag committee, a member of parliament must first receive clearance from the party group. The party group decides which of its members may speak, and for how long, in a plenary sitting of the Bundestag.

The government, the Bundesrat and the Bundestag may initiate legislation. The Bundesrat can veto legislation of the Bundestag. This veto cannot be overridden by the Bundestag if the bill affects the administrative organisation and powers of the *Länder*, or if it affects the division of taxes between the federation and the *Länder*.

The legislative work undertaken by committees dominates the life of the Bundestag, at the expense of parliamentary scrutiny and plenary debate. Most of the permanent committees of the Bundestag correspond to a single government department. Departmental committees do not have the power to initiate legislation, nor do they have autonomous decision-making powers. Their task is to scrutinise executive activities and bills that have passed their first reading in the Bundestag. The committees are a focus for bargaining between the government, parliament and interest-groups. Interest-groups present their views to committees, either directly, or else indirectly, through sympathetic or affiliated MPs. In spite of the party groups' attempts to coordinate the activities of their members, committee decisions have proved difficult to control. This is because the groups appoint long-serving subject specialists to the committees. In the resulting non-partisan atmosphere, government representatives are often prepared to make minor concessions and some 60 per cent of bills are amended at this stage in the legislative process.

As in all western European countries, the Bundestag's ability to scrutinise executive decisions is limited by the fact that many important decisions, particularly those involving economic planning, simply by-pass parliament. In Germany, the problem is exacerbated by the federal system, which creates a diffuse bargaining and decision-making network between the federal and *Land* governments. The main problem, however, has been that the means available for parliamentary control of the government have not been used as extensively as they might. Investigative committees may be set up to examine claims of government maladministration or wrongdoing. However, only twenty-six such committees were convened between 1949 and 1987 (Saalfeld 1990:81). Until recently, the various forms of parliamentary questioning appeared to have little effect. The *Aktuelle Stunden*, introduced in 1965, made it possible for a minority group to initiate short, adversarial debates on topical issues. This failed to invigorate parliamentary scrutiny until 1983, when the Green party's entry into the federal parliament ensured a more spirited opposition. In the parliamentary session of 1983–87, the Greens initiated forty-two debates under Aktuelle Stunden and the SPD, not to be outdone, initiated forty-eight. Other questioning procedures were also used more aggressively at this time: the Greens and the SPD making more active use of the *Grosse Anfrage* (interpellation), a form of parliamentary question which allows a meaningful debate between the party group tabling the question and the government (Saalfeld 1990: 78–81).

A long-standing criticism of the West German parliament has been its failure to develop as a forum for political debate. With about sixty plenary sittings in a year, the Bundestag meets less often than most other western European parliaments. A consensus between the leading parties is hammered out in the powerful party groups and legislative committees, leaving the plenary sittings to formalise the agreements reached beforehand. These highly structured decision-making processes have been beneficial in some ways. They have helped to 'domesticate' conflict and have thereby contributed to stabilising and legitimising the Bonn regime (see Mezey 1979:10). They have both helped and hindered the development of a parliamentary opposition. On the one hand, the opposition has enjoyed a consistent and constructive role in formulating legislation. On the other, in cooperating so readily, parties in opposition have tended to be half-hearted in their criticism of the government (although the Greens have prompted a more outspoken opposition) and have failed to offer much of an alternative at elections. Moreover, removing parliamentary decision-making from the public sittings of parliament to the closed sittings of parliamentary committees and party groups has compromised the accountability of the system. As we will see in the following chapter, this lack of accountability has been partly compensated by the development of the *Bundesverfassungsgericht* (Constitutional Court) as a major institution of government.

Parliaments today

Parliaments are amorphous institutions, performing such a wide range of activities that their function in contemporary European politics is difficult to pin down. In some ways they appear outmoded. Their task of representing the people is now channelled largely through the political parties. They continue to produce legislation, but share this function with many other bodies and institutions. Their ability to control the executive is limited, particularly given the expansion and diffusion of executive decision-making in the twentieth century. Their provision of public debate is overshadowed by the modern media. Their strength lies in their longevity and adaptability. Modern institutions of government have developed around the pre-existing parliaments, the institutional and symbolic hub of liberal democracies. Parliaments retain their special role in linking the government and the people, sanctioned by elections. The symbolic status of parliaments remains important in western Europe, and has been restated in post-communist eastern Europe. In the west, parliaments have continued to adapt, for example through party group activity, committee specialisation and the televising of plenary debates, to the changing circumstances of the late twentieth century.

Notes

1 The exceptions are Finland, the Netherlands and Sweden. In Finland and the Netherlands, the basic rules of procedure are set out in the country's constitution, and the parliaments may operate as they choose within these limits. In Sweden, the Riksdag is limited by the constitution and the Riksdag Act. In France, the parliamentary rules of procedure must be submitted to the Constitutional Council for verification before they can take effect. In Austria and Germany, they may be checked by the Constitutional Court, but only if their constitutionality is in doubt (Inter-parliamentary Union 1986 (Vol. I): 236, Table 7).

2 MPs have a traditional right to put forward proposals for legislation, but some countries place restrictions on this right of initiative. For example, in Austria, a private member's bill must be supported by at least eight MPs, in Spain by twenty-five members or a parliamentary party group. This requirement for group support of a proposal effectively filters out truly idiosyncratic personal crusades. In France, deputies may not introduce bills which diminish public revenue or increase expenditure. This is a much more far-reaching restriction, designed as one of many to restrict the activity of the parliament as an institution of government (Inter-parliamentary Union (Vol. II): 1986 863, Table 29).

3 A survey of 167 MPs conducted by Harris Political Research Unit showed that two-thirds were in favour of reform (*The Times*, 17 July 1995). An inquiry conducted by the House of Commons Select Committee on Procedure recommended that questions on one of the twice-weekly sessions should be on specific issues notified in advance. This would restrict the number of 'open' questions, which allow MPs to raise any point they wish (see House of Commons Select Committee on Procedure 1995).

References

Arter, D. (1990) 'The Swedish Riksdag: the case of a strong policy-influencing assembly', *West European Politics*, 13:3, 120–42.

Elder, N., A. Thomas and D. Arter (1982) *The Consensual Democracies? The Government and Politics of the Scandinavian States*, Oxford, Martin Robertson.

Fitzmaurice, J. (1991) *Austrian Politics and Society Today. In Defence of Austria*, Basingstoke, Macmillan.

Frears, J. (1990) 'The French parliament: loyal workhorse, poor watchdog', *West European Politics*, 13:3, 32–51.

Heywood, P. (1995) *The Government and Politics of Spain*, Basingstoke, Macmillan.

House of Commons Select Committee on Procedure (1995) *7th Report. Prime Minister's Questions: Together with the Proceedings of the Committee Relating to the Report, Minutes of Evidence and Appendices*, Sir Peter Emery (Chairman), HC 555, Session 1994–95, London, HMSO.

Inter-parliamentary Union (1986) *Parliaments of the World*, Vols I and II, Aldershot, Gower, 2nd edn.

Lane, J.-E., D. McKay and K. Newton (1991) *Political Data Handbook: OECD Countries*, Oxford, Oxford University Press.

Lees, J. and M. Shaw (eds) (1979) *Committees in Legislatures: a Comparative Analysis*, Durham, NC, Duke University Press.

Machin, H. (1994) 'Changing patterns of party competition', in P. Hall, J. Hayward and H. Machin (eds) *Developments in French Politics*, Basingstoke, Macmillan, 2nd edn.

Mezey, M. (1979) *Comparative Legislatures*, Durham, NC, Duke University Press.

Mezey, M. (1995) 'Parliament in the new Europe', in J. Hayward and E. Page (eds) *Governing the New Europe*, Cambridge, Polity Press.

Norton, P. (1981) *The Commons in Perspective*, Oxford, Martin Robertson.

Norton, P. (1990a) 'Legislatures in perspective', *West European Politics*, 13:3, 143–52.

Norton, P. (1990b) 'Parliament in the UK: balancing effectiveness and consent?', *West European Politics*, 13:3, 10–31.

Paterson, W. and D. Southern (1991) *Governing Germany*, Oxford, Blackwell.

Saalfeld, T. (1990) 'The West German Bundestag after 40 years: the role of parliament in a "party democracy" ', *West European Politics*, 13:3, 68–89.

Smith, G. (1989) *Politics in Western Europe*, Aldershot, Gower, 5th edn.

Smith, G. (1992) 'The nature of the unified state', in G. Smith, W. Paterson, P. Merkl and S. Padgett (eds) *Developments in German Politics*, Basingstoke, Macmillan, pp. 37–51.

Vacher's (1995) *Vacher's Parliamentary Companion* No. 1079, Berkhamstead, Vachers Publications.

Further reading

Mezey, M. (1995) 'Parliament in the new Europe', in J. Hayward and E. Page (eds) *Governing the New Europe*, Cambridge, Polity Press.

Norton, P. (ed.) (1990) *Parliaments in Western Europe*, Frank Cass, London (first published as a special issue of *West European Politics*, 13:3).

9

Accountable government: judicial review and civil rights

During the early part of the twentieth century, the collapse of parliamentary democracy in Germany and Italy highlighted the weaknesses of the democratic form of government. It showed that neither constitutions nor elected parliaments could necessarily prevent governments from abusing the powers entrusted to them. In Germany, the democratic constitution of the Weimar Republic had included some of the most progressive ideas of its day and yet it had allowed the anti-democratic National Socialist Party to come to power under Hitler. Once at the head of the government, Hitler had used his position to suspend democratic government and to introduce state persecution of political rivals such as communists and socialists, and minorities including the Jewish community and homosexuals.

After the Second World War, many European countries amended their constitution or even fundamentally recast their constitutional order in an attempt to guard against the possibility (or the recurrence) of such abuses. While some countries made substantial changes to their institutions of government, others were content to preserve the existing pattern of institutional competences, but to build up procedural safeguards against abuse. Two related areas of constitutional innovation were considered particularly important. First, safeguards were needed to ensure that legislatures and executives observed the limits of their constitutional authority. A way had to be found to assess alleged breaches of constitutionality which was independent of legislatures and executives themselves. Second, there was a need for clearer regulation of relationships between the state and the individual.

The most common institutional solution to the problem of alleged breaches of the constitution was to upgrade the role of the judiciary: often a special constitutional court was empowered to decide such disputes. Otherwise, each country devised its own checks on the abuse of executive power. These included the office of ombudsman, or parliamentary commissioner, appointed to act as a special representative of the citizen in disputes with public authorities. Some countries introduced the national referendum so that the electorate had the right to decide certain issues. Some of the innovations were by no means painless. They threatened firmly established ideas about the proper role of institutions in a representative democracy and promised to constrain the power of political and judicial elites. Their effectiveness as safeguards on executive decisions and actions has varied considerably from country to country.

After the Second World War, statements of basic rights began to be codified on a supranational level. The Charter of the United Nations of 1945 and the 1948 Universal Declaration of Human Rights was followed in 1953 by the European Convention for the Protection of Human Rights and Fundamental Freedoms. These statements represented internationally accepted standards concerning state–citizen relations and were reflected – if not reproduced – in post-war constitutions. In western Europe, adherence to these principles has been promoted by the work of the European Commission of Human Rights and the binding judgments of the European Court of Human Rights (both institutions of the Council of Europe).

Other influences have contributed to the acceptance and standardisation of rights provision throughout western Europe. As the modern states of the post-war period became involved in areas of life previously outside government regulation, it became necessary to adopt guidelines for the increasingly complex relations between the state; the individual, both as a citizen and as a member of numerous groups (religious, ethnic, gender, trade union, and so on); and society as a whole. While the details of these relations are regulated by statutory law, a statement of the principles behind them can now often be found in a country's constitution. Also, as society has changed, so too have citizens' expectations of government. Following the civil rights movement which began in the United States in the 1960s, state–citizen relations became a matter of controversy. The western European students' protests of 1968 focused on an active defence of the rights of the individual against the state. This theme was later taken up by the new social movements of the 1970s and the green parties of the 1980s.

The new constitutional courts: accountable government and the judiciary

Traditionally, the judiciary had been a relatively insignificant branch of government in western Europe. Law-making was seen as the exclusive preserve of the elected representatives of the people: the role of judges was merely to interpret and enforce the law. In practice, there was never a complete separation of political and judicial functions. After the Second World War, though, the need to uphold constitutional law assumed a higher priority, which inevitably brought the work of politicians and the judiciary into closer contact. Going against the traditional conceptions of the separation of powers, some countries opted to establish a special constitutional court to guarantee the constitution. The success of the constitutional courts has depended on a number of factors, such as the powers allocated to them; whether they have opted for judicial restraint or judicial activism (that is, the extent to which they have chosen to exercise their powers); and the relative strength or weakness of other institutions of government.

Constitutional courts have been introduced in Austria (revived in 1945), (West) Germany (1951), Italy (1956), Portugal (1982) and Spain (1981).[1] In France, the Constitutional Council (1959) is a unique body which exercises some of the functions usually associated with a constitutional court. Belgium's Court of Arbitration (1984) is still developing its role within the new Belgian federation and is taking on more of the functions of a constitutional court. The new constitutional courts have been placed in an ambiguous and often difficult position. Meny (1993: 342–3) describes them as hybrid institutions, semi-judicial and semi-political. The courts declare the law at the highest level, that of the constitution. In this, they act as judicial bodies. They must also ensure that the other institutions of government do not exceed their authority and abuse their powers. In this they act as mediators in a highly political role. Moreover, as new institutions carrying out functions of judicial review foreign to the legal and democratic traditions of western Europe, they have had to establish credibility in the context of the traditional institutions of legislature, executive and the existing courts. Initially, the new constitutional courts often met with resistance from judges and politicians alike, who realised that the powers of judicial review would in practice allow these new bodies to influence legislation and policy. In Italy, for example, the constitutional court provided for in the constitution of 1948 did not become active until 1956 because of resistance from the political establishment. Even then, it initially used its powers very cautiously in the face of hostility from senior judges of the ordinary courts.

Membership
The need to establish the credibility of the constitutional courts with the political and judicial establishment is reflected in the set procedures for choosing their members. As Table 9.1 shows, the political establishment dominates the process of selecting constitutional court judges. Particularly in France, the party political affiliation of judges has been a significant qualification for appointment. Generally, most of the members of the French Constitutional Council are former government ministers and MPs. In addition, all of the members of the Council are appointed rather than elected. This contrasts with Germany, for example, where all members are elected, or Spain and Italy, where some are appointed and some elected. In these countries, elected members

Table 9.1 The selection of members of the constitutional courts

	Number of members	Selection by political bodies	Selection by legal bodies
Austria	14	Cabinet[a] (8) Nationalrat (3) Bundesrat (3)	–
Germany	16	Bundestag (8) Bundesrat (8)	–
France	9	President (3) Pres. of National Assembly (3) Pres. of Senate (3)	–
Italy[b]	15	President (5) Parliament (5)	Court of Cassation (3) Council of State (1) Court of Accounts (1)
Portugal	13	Parliament (10)	Constitutional Court (3)
Spain	12	Congress (4) Senate (4) Cabinet (2)	General Council of the Judiciary (2)

Sources: Constitution of the Portuguese Republic (second revision of 1989), Article 224; Balsemao (1986:202); Stone (1992a: Table 9.1, p. 232); de Franciscis and Zannini (1992:70); Hine (1993).
[a] The Austrian cabinet's nominations include the president and the vice-president.
[b] The members selected by the Italian judiciary must come from the highest ordinary and administrative courts (the Court of Cassation, the Council of State and the Court of Accounts).

of the constitutional courts must have the support of a specified qualified majority, so that a purely partisan choice of candidate is less likely. In Spain, for example, a three-fifths majority is needed for election.

It is difficult to tell the extent to which politicised selection procedures have affected the decisions of a constitutional court. The decision-making processes of the courts are shrouded in secrecy. In France and Italy, decisions of the court must be unanimous. In Germany and Spain, dissenting opinions may be given, but in practice this is very rare. In the early years of the courts' operation, it might have appeared that politicised selection procedures were responsible for the courts' rather passive approach. However, in most countries the constitutional courts are growing increasingly confident (see below) and apparently independent of their political selectors. In Austria, for example, the *Verfassungsgerichtshof* (Constitutional Court) initially deferred to government decisions, but a new generation of judges has shown itself to be more independent of party interests (Müller 1992:115–18).

In an attempt to make the constitutional courts acceptable also to the legal establishment, all countries except France require members of the constitutional court to be top legal specialists, either as practitioners or as academics. In addition, some countries require a number of constitutional court judges to be drawn from the highest levels of the ordinary courts. This applies, for example, to six of the sixteen members in Germany. Again with the exception of France, most countries have awarded their constitutional courts the power of concrete judicial review, allowing their ordinary courts the right of appeal to the new constitutional court to rule on questions of constitutionality that arise during a regular court case. This measure has helped to link the work of the ordinary and constitutional courts.

Powers

The powers awarded to the constitutional courts vary from country to country. All of the courts exercise some form of legislative judicial review: the power to declare a law or other measure to be invalid, on the grounds that it is incompatible with the constitution. There are two main categories of legislative judicial review: concrete and abstract. Concrete judicial review is undertaken when an existing law is challenged in the course of, or following, a specific court case; the constitutional court then passes judgment on the constitutionality of that law. Concrete review is essentially retrospective (it is exercised *a posteriori*). Under abstract judicial review, the constitutionality of a law may be challenged on principle alone, allowing it to be examined without reference to a specific court case. Abstract review may be exercised *a posteriori*. In this case, a law is referred to the court after its promulgation. In some countries, it may be exercised *a priori*, in which case a law is referred after the final adoption by parliament, but before promulgation.

Table 9.2 shows the combination of legislative review powers allocated to the main constitutional courts of western Europe. In each case, the character of these 'hybrid' institutions, with their uneasy combination of judicial and political tasks, is influenced by the particular powers at their disposal. In exercising concrete judicial review, the courts function recognisably as judicial bodies. This form of retrospective, case-specific review is most compatible with the civil law traditions of western European countries. The introduction of powers of abstract review has been a controversial development in western Europe, as it erodes the traditional boundary between politics and the law, giving the courts a political role. Abstract review is initiated by politicians

Table 9.2 Legislative review powers of the constitutional courts

	Concrete review	*Abstract review* a priori	*Abstract review* a posteriori
Austria	Yes	No	Yes
Germany	Yes	No	Yes
France	No	Yes	No
Italy	Yes	No	Yes
Portugal	Yes	Yes	Yes
Spain	Yes	No[a]	Yes

Sources: Constitution of the Portuguese Republic (second revision of 1989), Articles 278–281; Stone (1992a): Table 9.1, 231–2; 1995: Table 10.1, 290–2.
[a] Spain's powers of *a priori* abstract review were abolished in 1985 on the grounds that they were incompatible with parliamentary democracy.

and requires the courts to undertake a final 'reading' of a disputed bill or law, in effect extending what would otherwise be a concluded legislative process (Stone 1992a:231). This effect is particularly marked in France, as *a priori* abstract review is the only form of legislative review undertaken by the Constitutional Council. Given the absence of provision for concrete review, the fact that referrals for abstract review may be made only by political authorities, and that neither the ordinary courts nor members of the public have access to the Council, Stone (1992a:234) concludes that the Council is 'something other than a court, . . . fulfilling more a legislative than a judicial function' (see also Cappelletti 1971:4–6).

With the exception of France, the proportion of the courts' caseload concerning abstract review remains small. However, its political impact has been significant. In spite of the reservations of politicians and the legal profession alike, minority interests are learning to use abstract review as a means of challenging dominant political views. In Germany, abstract review cases have usually been petitioned by a minority parliamentary party or by a national or regional government challenging an action of another level of government controlled by an opposing party or coalition. There have been objections to this alleged manipulation of the judicial process for political ends.

The constitutional courts may also be charged with adjudicating disputes between institutions of government with the aim of preserving the institutional balance established in the constitution. In states whose territorial structure is specified in the constitution, the constitutional courts decide on conflicts between the levels of government. This applies to the federal states of Germany, Austria and Belgium, and also to the regions of Spain and Italy (see Chapter 10). An increasingly important aspect of the courts' work, discussed below, is to adjudicate conflicts between the state and the citizen over basic rights. They may also be given further 'watchdog' tasks specific to the needs of their country. For example, the Austrian, German and Italian courts may be involved in impeachment trials. Since 1953, the Italian court has had the power to determine the validity of referendum proposals. While the courts may rarely be called on to exercise their watchdog role, the fact that they are entrusted with such powers adds to their political significance.

The German Federal Constitutional Court (FCC), the most powerful of the constitutional courts, serves to illustrate the political status and the potential of these new institutions of government. The president of the FCC occupies the fifth highest office of the Federal Republic, after the federal president, the federal chancellor, and the presidents of the two houses of parliament. Following an amendment to the Basic Law in 1968, there may be no interference in the work of the FCC and its judges even during a state of emergency. The FCC enjoys unusually wide powers which in turn give it a high political profile (see Kommers 1989). These include the authority to declare unconstitutional political parties that 'seek to impair or abolish the free democratic basic order or to endanger the existence of the Federal Republic of Germany' (German Basic Law, Art. 21(2)). Two political parties were banned in the 1950s: the neo-Nazi SRP in 1952 and the communist KPD in 1956.

Since 1993, the Italian Constitutional Court and magistrates have assumed a central role in the country's 'democratic revolution', which aims to root out the corruption endemic in Italy's political class and to restore the credibility of parliamentary government (see the appendix). The crisis of legitimacy in Italy has justified a far greater intrusion of the judiciary into politics than would normally be considered appropriate. The Constitutional Court has sometimes had to take action to keep essential reforms on course. In January 1993, when a parliamentary constitutional reform commission failed to arrive at consensus, the Constitutional Court ruled that referenda on electoral and other reforms should take place later in the year. Initially, the magistrates' contribution to the investigations was welcomed by the public. Now, however, the scope of the inquiries threatens to endanger the delicate process of relegitimation. Unless an amnesty is introduced, Italy could continue to be disrupted by increasingly complex legal inquiries. By the autumn of 1995, more than three-quarters of those accused of crimes related to corruption had yet to be tried; and the procedures of trial and appeal could take ten years to conclude. The magistrates themselves have recently been accused of abusing human rights by making undue use of arrest and preventive detention and by leaking extracts of testimony to the press (*Financial Times*, 18 August 1995).

From judicial restraint to activism

With the exception of the West German FCC, the new post-war constitutional courts were at first rather restrained in the use of their powers of judicial review. One reason for this was the active resistance of the political and legal establishment noted above. This was compounded by the judges' adherence to restrictive legal traditions, according to which the role of the judiciary was to enforce the law as it was written. Judges limited themselves to a formal interpretation of the text of a law rather than a substantive interpretation of the principles behind it. However, after an initial period of caution, the courts began to use their powers more creatively.

From the 1970s onwards, the Italian Constitutional Court was active in the reform of church–state relations, establishing religious freedom as a reality and acting as a progressive force in the reform of social policy. In Austria, the Court has adopted a more active approach since the mid-1980s. In France, the watershed came in 1971 when the Constitutional Council annulled a government-backed law on the grounds that it would have restricted freedom of association, a right recognised in the preamble of the 1958 constitution and dating back to 1789. This ruling was particularly significant within the French context, as, since its inception in 1958, the Council had previously functioned as de Gaulle had intended, by consistently protecting the decisions of the government (as led by the president) against the parliament. In 1974, a revision to Article 61 of the constitution allowed sixty members of the National Assembly or of the Senate to submit legislation to the Constitutional Council for scrutiny. This gave the parliamentary opposition their first access to the Council and began the development of its role as a constitutional control. Between 1981 and 1990, about one-third of legislation adopted was first referred to the Council; 54 per cent of the referrals resulted in censure (Stone 1995:296). These figures indicate that the Council is reviewing major legislation on a systematic basis and playing an active part in the legislative process.

The level of activism of the courts is also partly determined by the strength or weakness of the other institutions of government. For example, it has been argued that the Spanish Constitutional Court is likely to retain a political role because of the very limited rights of the Senate, the upper house of parliament, to delay or amend proposed government legislation. Rather than rely on the Senate, the opposition in the lower chamber has sometimes referred laws to the Constitutional Court in an attempt to check the government (Donaghy and Newton 1987: 20–1, 57–8).

The courts as legislators
Typically, the constitutional courts may not act on their own initiative, but only on the request of another agency, such as a national or regional government, or a parliamentary party. The courts deal only with the issues that are referred to them by others. In view of this, it is unlikely that the courts, through their rulings, could contrive to control policy-making with any consistency. However, with the increasing willingness of the judges to interpret the substance of a law and to make fuller use of their powers, the constitutional courts have begun to exert a significant influence over legislation and policy-making. They have the final word in the disputes which are referred to them. Each ruling they make sets a precedent for future decisions, not only of the courts, but also of the legislative and executive branches of government. This is particularly important where the court has not simply annulled a piece of legislation, but has issued detailed guidelines regarding its implementation on the grounds that

only one interpretation is compatible with the constitution. These guidelines then bind any decisions of the current or future parliaments. The percentage of decisions containing guidelines has risen steadily in France and Germany, and in Italy has increased sharply since the late 1980s (Landfried 1992:52; Stone 1995:299).

Particularly in France and Germany, some parliamentary debates are now strongly coloured by the anticipation of the Council or FCC's likely reaction to a piece of legislation. These forms of judicial influence on policy-making are all the more significant because the rulings of the courts often concern matters which are politically controversial. While this policy-making role is sometimes criticised as being inappropriate for non-elected bodies, it is perhaps unavoidable, resulting from the courts' exercise of their competences. However, it has been argued that the German FCC has exceeded its competences on some occasions by making decisions which should be made only by parliament. In practice, the parliament has encouraged this encroachment on its competences by deferring to the FCC over controversial political and social issues (Landfried 1992).

In Germany, the FCC's rulings in the area of abortion have proved particularly controversial. The FCC has twice overturned parliamentary legislation on abortion on the basis of pro-life arguments. In 1975 it struck down legislation passed by the centre-left government to legalise abortion during the first three months of pregnancy. The FCC prescribed alternative legislation for more restrictive measures, defining abortion as an 'act of killing' and therefore a criminal act. The Bundestag adopted the FCC's guidelines. When German unification took place, the Bundestag passed new legislation in an attempt to end the discrepancy between the existing liberal abortion laws which applied in east Germany and the more restrictive ones which applied in the west. In a complex ruling of 1993, the FCC again overturned the proposed legislation and issued an interim regulation to serve until the Bundestag could produce legislation which complied with the FCC's decision.

Accountability without a constitutional court

Many western European countries have no separate constitutional court. In these countries, the judiciary is used in a variety of ways to enhance the accountability of government. A regular court of appeal may have the power to check the actions and decisions of the legislature and executive. In some countries, all the courts are permitted to carry out the judicial review of legislation. These 'diffuse' systems include Greece, Ireland and most of the Scandinavian countries (Brewer-Carias 1989:91). The Greek constitution of 1975 states that 'The courts shall be bound not to apply laws, the contents of which are contrary to the Constitution' (Art. 93(4)). The Greek system can lead to conflicting judgments concerning the constitutionality of laws and it falls to the Special Highest Court to resolve these. In the Scandinavian countries, procedures of judicial review are complex and tightly restricted.[2] In Sweden, in spite of constitutional provision for judicial review, judges have been reluctant to exercise their powers to the full. Here, judicial review has been confined largely to low-level administrative regulations or local ordinances, judged by the Supreme Administrative Court. The Swedish Supreme Court has yet to declare any law to be unconstitutional (Board 1991:179–80). In Portugal there is an unusually wide provision of judicial review. In common with 'diffuse' systems, the ordinary courts may declare laws invalid within the context of a concrete case. In addition, the Portuguese Constitutional Court can review both proposed and enacted legislation. Switzerland too has a 'mixed' system where the ordinary courts share review powers with the Federal Tribunal. However, only cantonal laws (and not federal laws) may be subject to judicial review.

Other countries have remained so committed to the ideal of parliamentary sovereignty that they do not allow their courts to review laws passed by parliament (primary legislation). These include the UK, Luxembourg and the Netherlands. (Until recently, Belgium belonged to this tradition, but with its evolution into a federal state has had to introduce some elements of judicial review.) Where judicial review is not permitted or is little used in practice, other institutions and procedural measures have been adopted to ensure that governments and parliaments legislate responsibly and can be held to account for their decisions. Some countries have chosen to 'preview' legislation for potential flaws, rather than have the courts review it when a problem arises. In Sweden, for example, the courts may be consulted prior to the drafting of new legislation. In Finland, the Supreme Court may advise on the constitutionality of proposed legislation. Traditionally, Finland's president has refused to approve laws found wanting by the Supreme Court, giving this body an effective power of veto. In the Benelux countries, a body called the Council of State has acted as a check on legislation. It advises on the constitutionality of bills before they are presented to parliament and plays a role in reviewing cases of alleged maladministration. Belgium's evolution into a federal state has meant that executive and legislative decision-making is no longer confined to the national level. In 1984 a Court of Arbitration was established to check that the state, community and regional legislatures act within their competence. Since 1988, the Court may also determine whether legislation complies with three fundamental rights: equality, non-discrimination and freedom of education. The case law of the Court of Arbitration has in practice addressed other fundamental rights enshrined in international treaties. It appears, then, that the Court of Arbitration is developing the functions of a constitutional court (Alen and Ergec 1994:20–2).

In the UK, the objection to a constitutional court centres on the doctrine of parliamentary sovereignty, by which the judiciary is constitutionally subordinate to parliament. The courts do not have the power to annul legislation or executive actions. Not even the House of Lords, the final court of appeal, may declare an Act of Parliament unconstitutional. In the UK, judicial review is exclusively an instrument of administrative law. It is limited to challenging acts and decisions by ministers, government officials and public bodies on the grounds that they have acted unlawfully or improperly. In contrast to the practice elsewhere in western Europe, UK legislation is drafted in great detail so as to anticipate all likely contingencies (Drewry 1992: 13). The judiciary has shied away from becoming involved in political controversies. Taken together, these factors would appear to limit the courts' role to terms set by parliament itself and to rule out any scope for the courts to influence policy or legislation.

However, even in the UK there is room for judicial creativity. This has been in evidence since the 1960s, and particularly over the last decade or so. In part this can be put down to a gradual change in attitude as to 'appropriate' judicial activity. Also, since the late 1970s, procedural reforms have helped to facilitate the process of judicial review. The courts now rule on areas of government that would have been regarded as beyond judicial competence even twenty or thirty years ago, including education policy, television licensing, airline regulation, local government finance and social welfare. In 1984, a significant case established that the British government is no longer immune from a legal challenge on the grounds of the ancient prerogatives of the Crown.[3] So, while the potential for control of government decisions and actions and the scope for creative rulings remains very limited in the UK in comparison to many of its western European neighbours, even here the separation of the legislature and the judiciary is becoming less clear.

Similar developments can be seen in the Netherlands. Here, the introduction of the judicial review of primary legislation was explicitly rejected as recently as the constitutional reform of 1983, and yet the Supreme Court is increasingly substituting for the legislature in certain areas. The Court has produced case law on controversial issues where parliament has been unable to pass legislation, such as the right to strike, euthanasia and abortion. This development has been encouraged by the precarious nature of Dutch government coalitions, which has often stifled legislation even when there might be a parliamentary majority to support it. The risk of offending a coalition partner has also tended to result in legislation couched in vague terms, requiring substantial interpretation by the Court before it can be implemented (ten Kate and van Koppen 1994:144–6). Another factor which is increasing the potential for legal challenge in countries without primary legislative review is the growing body of EU legislation. A UK or Dutch act of parliament can be declared invalid if it is found to be inconsistent with treaties of the EU.

Individual liberties and civil rights

The first attempts to regulate the relationship between the state and the citizen were conceived as principles preventing arbitrary actions of government against individual citizens. The French Declaration of the Rights of Man and the Citizen (1789) and the American Bill of Rights (1791) helped to define these civil liberties and to establish principles which continue to influence western European constitutions. These included the right to a fair criminal trial and freedom of speech, expression and association. In constitutions introduced from the inter-war period onwards, these liberties of the person began to be combined with social and economic rights. The short-lived German Weimar constitution of 1919 included fifty-six articles devoted to 'the individual', 'social life', 'education' and 'economic life', which included social security.

   The totalitarian regimes of the inter-war period showed a blatant disregard for these principles. The early post-war period saw a move towards, a commonly accepted standard of human rights and, with this, a greater standardisation of provision in western European constitutions. A milestone in this development was the European Convention on Human Rights, which came into force in 1953. Provisions of the Convention cover the rights of the individual *per se* (personal rights) and the individual as part of a wider community (social rights). Basic guarantees include the right to life; the right to liberty and security of the person; freedom of thought, conscience and religion; freedom of expression; freedom of association, including right to form and join trade unions; the prohibition of torture, inhuman and degrading treatment, and forced labour; and the right to a fair trial in civil and criminal proceedings. The Convention stresses that these rights and freedoms are held by virtue of the citizen's humanity alone, irrespective of gender, race, religion or political opinion.

These values were given high priority in those western European constitutions introduced or updated after the Second World War. Some countries – Austria, Denmark (1953), the Irish Republic, Italy, West Germany and Switzerland – included a formal bill of rights in the constitution conforming to these accepted standards. In the West German Basic Law, the bill of rights was given pride of place. It is the first part of the constitution (Articles 1–19), coming before even the definition of the state. In general, legislatures and executives were no longer trusted to uphold the principles set out in the bill of rights in the post-war constitutions. Typically, the bill of rights could be changed only by a set constitutional procedure more complex than was needed for the amendment of ordinary legislation and with a more substantial level of parliamentary support. West Germany's Basic Law went further still, allowing for no dilution of the essential content of the bill of rights short of replacing the constitution itself.

While the French constitution of 1958 did not contain a bill of rights *per se*, the Constitutional Council decision of 1971 (see above) in practice established the preamble as a functional equivalent. The preamble incorporates the Declaration of the Rights of Man and the Citizen of 1789; the Fundamental Principles Recognised by the Laws of the Republic; and a number of progressive principles established in the constitution of 1946. The principles of 1946 include the equality of the sexes; the right to work, to join a union, to strike and to social security; the state guarantee of a secular education system; and the state guarantee of the nationalisation of all industries that have taken on the character of a monopoly or public service.

This ill-assorted collection of rights illustrates a problem common to constitutions of the post-war period. In many constitutions, a list of economic, social and cultural rights has simply been added to the long-recognised classical civil liberties, irrespective of the fact that the pre- and post-war principles represent very different ideas of individual and collective rights and of the proper relationship between state and society. These principles can come into conflict with one another, as was illustrated by a ruling of the French Constitutional Council of 1982. With this decision, the Council vetoed part of the Socialist government's nationalisation programme subject to a detailed compensation package. In doing so, it established a constitutional hierarchy whereby the principles of 1789 take precedence over those added in 1946 (Stone 1992b:36–7).

The inclusion of economic and social rights as basic constitutional principles causes a further problem when it comes to the fulfilment of constitutional guarantees. Unlike the 'defensive' classical civil liberties, they require positive action on the part of the state. A state's ability to realise these rights depends on determined government action and ultimately on the health of the country's economy. For this reason, these new rights cannot be enforced by the courts. Some constitutions recognise that their provisions in the field of public welfare represent an intention only and cannot be guaranteed. For example, Article 45 of the Irish constitution is entitled 'Directive Principles of Social Policy', but states that the principles it contains are intended for the general guidance of parliament and 'shall not be cognisable by any court'.

The recent unification process in Germany was accompanied by a lengthy debate on reforming the Basic Law. Although no fundamental amendments resulted from this debate, one of the issues examined was the introduction of *Staatsziele* (state objectives) into the Basic Law.[4] The debate showed that there was a fairly broad-based consensus in favour of state action to shape economic, social and cultural life beyond the reach of basic rights. The main objections were that such measures might restrict the legislative scope of parliament or result in an excessive 'judicialisation' of politics. There has been less concern over the ability of the state to realise any constitutional objectives. Indeed, most of the new *Länder* of the former GDR – those least able to command the necessary resources – have adopted constitutions listing numerous 'state' objectives (Cullen and Goetz 1994: 162–9). In practice, experience has shown that the state might be in no position to effect such guarantees. The Italian state has patently failed to realise its constitutional commitments to the right to work and the right to free medical treatment for the poor.

In addition to a bill of rights, some countries have opted to hold their new constitutional courts responsible for adjudicating disputes between the state and the citizen over basic rights. Where the courts have this responsibility, the bulk of their workload is taken up with this type of dispute. This is certainly the case for the German FCC. The FCC may rule on cases originating in the ordinary courts. Moreover, any person who claims that a basic right has been violated by a public authority may make a direct 'constitutional complaint' to the Court. This form of direct appeal had historical precedents in Switzerland, Austria and the former kingdom of Bavaria. Originally authorised by law, the constitutional complaint came to be seen as a fundamental right and in 1969 it was incorporated into the West German Basic Law (Art. 93(1) (4a)). The procedure, relatively straightforward and inexpensive, left the FCC a victim of its own success. In spite of a low success rate (2.7 per cent), 97,007 constitutional complaints were filed by February 1995 (*Frankfurter Allgemeine Zeitung*, 20 February 1995). In 1975, a constitutional amendment allowed all individuals the right of appeal to the Austrian Constitutional Court. This too resulted in a tremendous increase in workload, from under 200 appeals in 1973 to almost 2,000 in 1987 (Müller 1992:116). In both cases, the resulting overload of the court could only be eased by a progressive restriction of direct access. While the right to appeal to the German FCC remains unrestricted, screening committees now weed out frivolous complaints and fines are imposed against those who are judged to have abused the Court's provisions. Since 1981, the Austrian Court may reject individual appeals against administrative decisions where these are not likely to be successful. Since 1984, it may also reject those which are not likely to contribute to the clarification of constitutional issues.

In western European countries with no constitutional court, other bodies may be charged with protecting the rights of citizens. In Belgium, for example, the administrative sector of the Council of State (introduced in 1946), whose members are appointed by parliament, has been responsible for ensuring that the rights of citizens are protected in their dealings with the government. Of course, these countries are also subject to the rulings of the European Court of Human Rights.

The office of ombudsman

The principle of safeguarding the citizen against the public authorities' misuse of their powers had long been accepted in western European countries. When, in the post-war period, these countries sought to improve the provision and quality of such safeguards, they did not rely exclusively on the courts. Some chose to appoint an ombudsman or parliamentary commissioner. This office originated in Sweden (see al-Wahab 1979). The post of *Justitieombudsman* (JO) was established in the Swedish constitution of 1809 in the context of a range of reforms informed by long experience of absolutist, authoritarian monarchy, under which anyone in a position of power had been likely to abuse it. Independent of the executive, the Swedish ombudsmen supervise the work of judges and civil servants and have the right to prosecute those who act illegally, misuse their powers or neglect their duties. While the prosecution of officials was common until the start of the twentieth century, this measure is now limited to serious cases. In Sweden, the office of ombudsman became a respected and trusted means of recourse against the misuse of executive power. The ombudsmen are elected by each new parliament and may only be removed by parliament. They have usually been drawn from the higher ranks of the administration or judiciary.

This century, many other countries have attempted to borrow the institution and graft it on to their own systems of government. These attempts have met with mixed success. They have perhaps worked best in the other Scandinavian countries, where the office has been only slightly adapted and where the traditions and institutions of government are closer to the Swedish original than elsewhere. Other western European countries have introduced the office with more far-reaching modifications, which have considerably reduced its potential. Some have limited the role to a particular function. The Federal Republic of Germany introduced a military ombudsman in 1957. Italy has a number of regional ombudsmen, the first introduced in Tuscany in 1974.

The British parliamentary commissioner for administration (PCA) was introduced in 1967 and has since been supplemented by further offices, including health service commissioners and commissioners for local administration (Greenwood and Wilson 1989:310–24). In terms of the Scandinavian model, British PCAs' independence of the executive has been questionable, as they are appointed by the government and they and their staff have been drawn largely from the civil service. However, PCAs can be removed from office only by both Houses of Parliament and their activities are closely tied to the work of the Commons. The House of Commons Select Committee on the Parliamentary Commissioner for Administration receives the PCAs' reports and oversees their work. Grievances may not be registered directly with the PCA, but only through an MP. This is an unusual restriction for an ombudsman post: only the British PCA and French *médiateur* cannot receive complaints direct from the public. The PCA's jurisdiction is considerably narrower than that of other ombudsmen, excluding important areas such as civil and criminal proceedings and government commercial activities. Moreover, the PCA is limited to investigating complaints of injustice caused by alleged maladministration, rather than injustice caused by an unfair decision following appropriate procedures. While PCAs have wide investigative powers and may propose remedial action, they have no powers of enforcement.

Referendums

Another means of ensuring government accountability is the popular referendum. Originally used as an instrument of direct democracy in small communities, the referendum has been adapted to the needs of parliamentary democracy. In a referendum, the electorate votes on a specific issue. Usually, the referendum presents two mutually exclusive alternatives – this virtually ensures an absolute majority for one of the options. Occasionally, however, three choices have been presented to the electorate, as for the referendum on the Prohibition Act in Finland (1931) or the Swedish nuclear energy vote (1980). Provision for national referendums can be found in the constitutions of Austria, Denmark, France, Greece, Iceland, Ireland, Italy, Liechtenstein, Luxembourg, Spain, Sweden and Switzerland (see Suksi, 1993). They have also been used in Britain. Taken at face value, the referendum might appear to give the people a means of checking government decisions. Although a referendum can work in this way, it can also be used by the government, parliamentary opposition forces or interest-groups to by-pass regular decision-making channels by manufacturing a popular mandate on an issue. The function of referendums in any given country depends to a large extent on the regulations determining their use. Much depends on which individuals or institutions are entitled to initiate the referendum and to formulate the question; whether the referendum is used on an *ad hoc* basis or is regularly used as a standard procedure; and on whether the referendum is decisive or consultative.

Since the emergence of the modern nation-state, Switzerland has made by far the greatest use of national referendums: a total of 403 between 1848 and mid-1993. Here, regular use of the referendum has inhibited the development of 'normal' parliamentary government. Switzerland is the only country in which referendums play a fundamental role in the legislative process.[5] While the Swiss electorate has unusually wide powers in initiating referendums, the government is unusually tied. On the basis of a given number of signatures, a petition may be submitted by citizens to challenge federal legislation, or to propose a constitutional amendment. This is called the 'initiative'. For its part, the Federal Council is obliged to submit any proposed change in the constitution to a referendum. If the vote is passed by the required majorities, a referendum is binding. Historically, the initiative has been the main recourse of non-establishment movements and pressure groups in their attempts to influence federal decision-making. During the post-war period, pressure groups have also begun to make tactical use of referendums: putting forward an initiative only to withdraw it in return for policy concessions.

The value of the referendum has been accepted in some western European countries as a means of legitimising important or controversial decisions, or even as a check on legislation. In others, though, it is viewed with suspicion and seen to interfere with the proper working of representative democracy. Curiously, Germany and Italy, the two countries with the most direct experience of totalitarian rule, have adopted opposing views on the referendum. The abuse of the referendum in Weimar Germany arguably helped Hitler's rise to power and only marginal provision for referendums was incorporated into the Basic Law of 1949. Most of the West German *Länder* introduced the referendum for internal use without ill effect. The new east German *Länder* also provide for referendums in their constitutions. However, as the recent debate on constitutional reform has shown, many still consider its use inappropriate at the federal level.

Italy, on the other hand, has gone so far as to include provision for the abrogative referendum (one which, if successful, repeals current legislation) in its 1948 constitution. The Italian rules include provision for the electorate to initiate an abrogative referendum. With the exception of financial laws, pardons and treaty ratification, ordinary legislation can be subject to a referendum on the request of 500,000 voters or five regional councils. The Constitutional Court must confirm the validity of a referendum proposal for it to proceed. This measure has aroused controversy, as the Court has on occasions ruled a referendum inadmissible on rather spurious grounds. To obtain the repeal of all or part of a law, a majority of the electorate must vote, and there must be a majority in favour of abrogation of those who vote. By 1991 there had been eighteen referendums on legislation (Hine 1993:154–6).

Outside Switzerland, Italy and Liechtenstein, the role of the electorate in referendums is less active, but can still be significant. The constitutions of Ireland and Denmark make provision, under specified circumstances, for referendums on legislation and the constitution. In Denmark, these referendums are seen to have a general legitimising function and to protect minority interests in parliament and in society. More specifically, though, they are used as an alternative to the checks formerly carried out by the upper chamber of parliament, which was abolished in 1953.

Elsewhere, referendums have been used less regularly and primarily to decide conflicts which the political parties would rather not resolve through the normal parliamentary channels. Depending on the circumstances, a referendum might be called in the hope of avoiding government responsibility for a controversial decision, to avoid splitting the party or coalition, or to rally the support of the electorate in advance of an election campaign.

Constitutionalism and the judicialisation of politics in western Europe

Since the Second World War, western European countries have agreed on the need for independent constraints on government power and the active protection of individual and civil rights. There has been a growing acceptance of the ideology of 'constitutionalism': the belief that, in a constitutional democracy, all government acts must conform to constitutional law to be considered legitimate (Stone 1995:307). This has encouraged the 'judicialisation' of politics, a development in which political debate and decision-making are becoming more strongly influenced by legal norms and court rulings. Under such favourable conditions, the new constitutional courts have flourished. In a short space of time, they have established themselves as active and respected institutions of government. As the courts become powerful political actors in their own right, concerns continue to be voiced about their role in parliamentary democracy. As Bogdanor (1988:12) notes, a constitution 'is not something that can be defended only, or even mainly, by the courts' but must depend primarily on the practice of free and fair elections and the potential for the alternation of parties in government. While such doubts persist, in practice, many European governments, parliaments and administrators are now governing in conjunction with constitutional court judges. Even in countries without a constitutional court, the decisions of politicians are subject to specific forms of judicial review and to the requirements imposed by international law and treaty agreements. The new constitutionalism in western Europe has also been expressed through the standardisation and active pursuit of individual liberties and civil rights, whether through the courts or through alternative channels.

Notes

1 The dates given refer to the year in which the courts came into operation.
2 For the Scandinavian countries, some general patterns of judicial review can be identified. All judges have the power of judicial review; there are no special courts in charge of the control of constitutionality; the question of the constitutionality of a law must be raised in cases in ordinary civil, criminal or administrative litigation; the constitutional issue must only be decided upon if it is unavoidable for the resolution of the concrete case; and the effect of the judicial decision only applies to the concrete case in question – the judges do not annul the law itself (Brewer-Carias 1989:173).
3 The government had debarred staff of the Government Communications Headquarters (GCHQ) from trade-union membership. GCHQ staff then challenged the ban on the grounds that it had been made without consultation. One of the government's arguments was that prerogative powers could not be reviewed by the courts. While the

GCHQ challenge was finally lost on the grounds of the interests of national security, it was established that a decision taken under prerogative powers may be the subject of judicial review (Hogwood 1987:196–7; Sunkin 1994:128).

4 In the event, the only two state objectives to be introduced into the Basic Law were the protection of the environment and the equal treatment of women and men. Other issues under consideration included animal welfare protection; the protection of ethnic minorities; the right to work, to adequate housing, and to education; the maintenance of a system of social security; and human fellowship (*Mitmenschlichkeit*) and public spiritedness (*Gemeinsinn*). In contrast with the definition of a state objective found in Article 45 of the Constitution of the Irish Republic, the German Joint Constitutional Commission saw state objectives as 'Typically . . . addressed to the legislature, though this does not exclude the possibility that the norm is also an interpretative guideline for the executive and the judiciary' (Cullen and Goetz 1994:168–9).

5 Four different types of federal referendum are currently used in Switzerland. First, the constitutional or 'obligatory' referendum is required to approve any constitutional amendment or revision proposed by the government. A 'double majority', comprising over 50 per cent of the national vote and a majority in more than half of the cantons, is required for passage. Second, the constitutional initiative requires 100,000 signatures to qualify for a ballot and a double majority for passage. The government may put forward a counterproposal in response. Third, for the legislative (facultative) referendum 50,000 signatures are required, legislation is subjected to the referendum and only a simple majority is required for passage. Finally, any treaty may be subject to a referendum, provided that 50,000 signatures have been collected (Kobach 1993:363, n. 1).

References

Alen, A. and R. Ergec (1994) *Federal Belgium after the Fourth State Reform of 1993*, Brussels, Ministry of Foreign Affairs.

Balsemao, F. (1986) 'The constitution and politics: options for the future', in K. Maxwell (ed.) *Portugal in the 1980s. Dilemmas of Democratic Consolidation*, New York, Greenwood Press.

Board, J. (1991) 'Judicial activism in Sweden', in K. Holland (ed.) *Judicial*

Activism in Comparative Perspective, Basingstoke, Macmillan, pp. 175–87.

Bogdanor, V. (ed.) (1988) *Constitutions in Democratic Politics*, Aldershot, Gower.

Brewer-Carias, A. (1989) *Judicial Review in Comparative Law*, Cambridge, Cambridge University Press.

Cappelletti, M. (1971) *Judicial Review in the Contemporary World*, Indianapolis, Bobbs-Merrill.

Cullen, P. and K. Goetz (1994) 'Concluding theses on constitutional policy in unified Germany', *German Politics* 3:3, 162–78.

de Franciscis, M. and R. Zannini (1992) 'Judicial policy-making in Italy: the Constitutional Court'. *West European Politics*, 15:3, 68–79.

Donaghy, P. and M. Newton (1987) *Spain: a Guide to Political and Economic Institutions*, Cambridge, Cambridge University Press.

Drewry, G. (1992) 'Judicial politics in Britain: patrolling the boundaries', *West European Politics* 15:3, 9–28.

Greenwood, J. and D. Wilson (1989) *Public Administration in Britain Today*, London, Unwin Hyman, 2nd edn.

Hine, D. (1993) *Governing Italy. The Politics of Bargained Pluralism*, Oxford, Clarendon Press.

Hogwood, B. (1987) *From Crisis to Complacency? Shaping Public Policy in Britain*, Oxford, Oxford University Press.

Kobach, K. (1993) 'Recent developments in Swiss direct democracy', *Electoral Studies*, 12:4, 342–65.

Kommers, D. (1989) *The Constitutional Jurisprudence of the Federal Republic of Germany*, Durham, NC, Duke University Press.

Landfried, C. (1992) 'Judicial policy-making in Germany: the Federal Constitutional Court', *West European Politics* 15:3, 50–67.

Meny, Y. with A. Knapp (1993) *Government and Politics in Western Europe*, Oxford, Oxford University Press, 2nd edn.

Müller, W. (1992) 'Austrian governmental institutions: do they matter?', *West European Politics*, 15:1, 99–131.

Stone, A. (1992a) *The Birth of Judicial Politics in France. The Constitutional Council in Comparative Perspective*, Oxford, Oxford University Press.

Stone, A. (1992b) 'Where judicial politics are legislative politics: the French Constitutional Council', *West European Politics*, 15:3, 29–49.

Stone, A. (1995) 'Governing with judges: the new constitutionalism', in J. Hayward and E. Page (eds) *Governing the New Europe*, Cambridge, Polity Press, pp. 286–314.

Suksi, M. (1993) *Bringing in the People. A Comparison of Constitutional Forms and Practices of the Referendum*, Dordrecht, Martinus Nijhoff.

Sunkin, M. (1994) 'Judicialization of politics in the United Kingdom', *International Political Science Review*, 15:2, 125–33.

ten Kate, J. and P. van Koppen (1994) 'Judicialization of politics in the Netherlands: towards a form of judicial review', *International Political Science Review*, 15:2, 143–51.

al-Wahab, I. (1979) *The Swedish Institution of Ombudsman. An Instrument of Human Rights*, Stockholm, LiberFörlag.

Further reading

Shapiro, M. and A. Stone (1994) *Comparative Political Studies*, 26:4 (special issue on the new constitutional politics of Europe).

Volcansek, M. (ed.) (1992) *Judicial Politics and Policy-Making in Western Europe*, London, Frank Cass (originally published as a special issue of *West European Politics*, 15:3).

10

Federalism, devolution and local government

The structure of the state

Western European politics is not simply the politics of central government. There is a complex and important process of multi-level bargaining and negotiation, of resource distribution and policy coordination, between central government and lower levels of government.

The significance of territorial factors for politics has already been illustrated in Chapters 1 and 3. Territorial conflicts have been persistent throughout history. They have arisen, for example, when a state has attempted to extend its authority to new territories, or, alternatively, when peripheral areas already integrated into the state have demanded a share of autonomy which the central government has been reluctant to concede.

The actual form which the structure of any state in western Europe possesses is the result of decisions about the advantages and disadvantages of the concentration of power at the centre. The territorial organisation of western European states varies considerably. Three basic categories of state structure can be distinguished: *unitary*, *federal* and *confederal*.

The difference between the formal structure of government in a unitary state and that in a federal state is straightforward. A unitary state has a single source of ultimate sovereignty, the central government. A federal state has a dual location of sovereignty, with authority divided between central government and a set of regional governments. These regions may be variously called cantons (as in Switzerland), *Länder* (in Germany and Austria), or communities and regions (Belgium); in countries outside Europe they can be called states (the USA, India), or provinces (Canada), for instance. To avoid confusion, the term *provinces* will be used in this chapter to refer in general to such sovereign regional territories within a state, and the term *region* will be reserved for territories which are part of a unitary state and which do not possess their own form of sovereignty. Of course, when particular countries are under discussion and use of these terms would be confusing (Belgian regions, for instance) the appropriate local term will be used.

In addition to the distinction between unitary and federal states, there is as well a distinction between federal states and *confederations*. Whereas federal states have a defined arrangement of divided sovereignty, but otherwise possess the normal attributes of a state (such as defined territorial boundaries, claim to monopoly of the use of legitimate coercive force, and expectation of long-term continuing existence), a confederation is a looser arrangement of sovereign states, which have voluntarily surrendered control over one or more specific functions (e.g. defence; monetary issue and banking; trade controls) to some joint authority which acts on behalf of the member states. The United States of America – as its name suggests – was initially a confederation of colonies formed to oppose the British and to attain independence. Only when the limitations of that confederal arrangement became apparent was a federation created in its stead. Switzerland also began as a confederation. The EU (formerly the EC) could be also regarded as a kind of confederation.

In the period of the development of state identities and of liberal democracy, there was a tendency to see the unitary form of state structure, with power concentrated at the centre, as an ideal to strive towards. Federal states, or states with some significant measure of decentralisation, were seen as diverging from this ideal, though perhaps for good reasons. Indeed, as will be illustrated below, in certain cases the very creation of the state originally might have been conditional upon the development of a federal form of state structure, which would accommodate regional loyalties and interests by ensuring the retention of constitutionally guaranteed regional autonomy in certain sectors of political life. The persistence of peripheral nationalisms (in Scotland, Wales, Northern Ireland, Corsica, parts of Spain, for instance) and regional loyalties (in parts of Italy, in Belgium, in Bavaria), as well as new ideas about the democratic importance of local or regional self-government and the vexed question of the relationships between 'Brussels', the governments of member states and the regions within the EU, have all led to questioning of this old idea about the primacy of the territorial concentration of power in the state.

The distinction between unitary and federal state structures is a formal one: some commentators might argue that the pattern of regional devolution in Italy or Spain is in actuality a more effective form of diffusion of power than the federal arrangements of Austria, for instance. But formal arrangements can be very important, as demonstrated by the recent Belgian decision to formalise what had already become in essence an informal federal pattern of state organisation.

In a federal state, the division of sovereignty is enshrined in a written constitution. This requirement has several corollaries. First, it means that a federal state must possess a constitutional regime, and thus must operate under the rule of law. Any federally structured state where a written constitution does not exist, or where a written constitution can be ignored (as it was in the USSR because of the overriding authority of the Communist party), cannot be regarded as a proper federation because there is no guaranteed protection of the sovereign rights of the provinces *vis-à-vis* the central government. Second, it means that there must be some source of adjudication, such as a constitutional court, to make authoritative and binding judgments where the allocation of sovereignty (and therefore the right to make legitimate decisions) is in doubt: for example, in cases where the written constitution is ambiguous, or has not anticipated some set of functions or responsibilities which now exist, such as television broadcasting regulation, the extension of powers of the EU, or data protection legislation. (These first two requirements of a federal state are also, of course, found in most unitary liberal democratic states as well.) Third, there must be mechanisms for coordinating policy-making at central and at provincial levels (to ensure, for instance, that economic policy strategies are harmonised for both levels of government). In unitary states, where only one source of sovereign authority exists, powers – sometimes quite extensive powers – may be devolved to regional authorities, but these may be amended or withdrawn by the central government at will, so neither a means of adjudication regarding allocation of sovereignty nor methods of policy coordination between two sovereign levels of government are so necessary.

Why should some states be federations, while others remain as unitary states? Certainly, the unitary form of state structure is more usual, and better corresponds to ideas about states possessing a single, undisputed and unrestricted source of ultimate authority: the 'sovereign power'. Federal states exist either because of special historical circumstances which were the context within which the state was created, or because of some development in a previously unitary state which produced a change to a federal structure. In either case, a federal structure is introduced because some looser, more flexible arrangement of governmental power than exists in unitary states was thought to be desirable or necessary. Federation can be a method of integrating otherwise disparate regional, ethnic, religious or linguistic groups within a common state organisation (Belgium, Switzerland, Germany in 1871, are all examples). It can also be perceived as a more democratic form of government, bringing areas of decision-making to a more localised level, and, as the post-war Federal Republic of Germany illustrates, providing a constitutional bulwark against possible dictatorial tendencies.

Federalism can give rise to disputes that would not exist, or that would be easier to resolve, in a unitary state. It can appear cumbersome, and may provoke seemingly unnecessary and inefficient regional variations (e.g. the different school curricula which exist in the *Länder* of Germany, causing problems when a family with schoolchildren moves from one *Land* to another). Especially where the provinces have responsibilities for implementing federal policies (as in Germany), there can be a lack of control by central government over the speed, modes and effectiveness of such implementation.

But federalism also offers undoubted advantages. It is an attractive solution to the problem of how best to delegate power from the centre, so that regional or local problems can be dealt with swiftly, so that the needs and aspirations of regionally distinct groups can be satisfied, so that responsiveness of government can match the democratic expectations of the citizen. It also offers the chance to try out new policies or modes of governing at a fairly local level, before extending them to the whole country.

In all modern states several reasons exist for instituting procedures by which decision-making and administration of policy are delegated to local levels: because of the need to take account of local conditions, for instance. In unitary states, a variety of devices have been tried which delegate power from the centre to more local structures of government, but which stop short of the creation of two distinct levels of sovereign authority. Some of these devices approximate quite closely to those utilised in federal states. Others – and the UK is one example – involve delegation of powers to particular regions, without producing a systematic form of devolution over the whole country. Because the constitutional constraints of a federal state do not apply, it is in principle (but not always in practice) simple in a unitary state to amend and expand such arrangements of delegation to meet changing circumstances.

All states have a system of local government, delegating governmental responsibilities and obligations to district authorities. These arrangements for local government will be considered at the conclusion of this chapter, together with some of the more frequent problems which systems of local government produce. The basic distinction between local government in unitary and in federal states is that in federal states local authorities have powers and responsibilities delegated to them by the provincial legislatures; in unitary states the central government and parliament delegate such powers and responsibilities. Indeed, federal states (such as Germany) can have patterns of local government which vary from province to province.[1]

Federal states in western Europe

To understand how federal states are structured and operate in western Europe, the examples of Germany, Austria, Switzerland and Belgium will be described.

Germany

After the Second World War, the West German state designed by the Parliamentary Council was given a federal structure for three reasons. First, since its formation in 1871, the modern German state had always been organised as a federation until the Third Reich substituted a centralised, dictatorial one-party state in its place. This tradition of federalism was therefore easy to carry on into the post-war period.

Second, the allied occupying powers (and especially the USA, itself a federal state) favoured a federal form of state organisation for West Germany as a more democratic, less authoritarian model, and one likely to act as a bulwark against any new Nazi takeover of the state. After all, the Nazi regime of the Third Reich had – through the process known as *Gleichschaltung* (meaning, in effect, the 'Nazification' of every institution) – created an extremely centralised state system.

Third, the Parliamentary Council was itself composed of representatives drawn from the legislatures of the already existing *Länder*. They were predisposed to retain the existence and the autonomy of their *Länder* (despite the fact that several of these *Länder* were new, artificial creations of the occupation regime, and thus lacking in tradition). Indeed, any attempt to abolish the *Länder* might have jeopardised the venture of creating a West German state altogether.

When the two states of West and East Germany were unified on 3 October 1990, the method chosen was that provided by Article 23 of the version of the Basic Law (the constitution) which then existed.[2] This meant that the Basic Law became applicable in the territory of the former GDR. Since that constitution applied a federal structure to the state, new *Länder* had to be formed in that territory. This was done, and the five new *Länder* joined the eleven west German *Länder* at the moment of reunification.

The Basic Law enshrines the principle of federalism as an unamendable part of the constitution. It spells out the powers which shall be exercised by the federal government: matters such as national defence, foreign affairs, the national budget, social security, international trade and some transportation responsibilities (such as the motorway network). It lists powers specifically reserved to the *Länder*, including local government, policing, education (including universities), broadcasting, local transport and industrial development policy. In certain areas of policy (such as aspects of environmental protection, control of nuclear energy, employment law and commercial regulation) both the federal and the *Land* governments may exercise authority, though the need to ensure uniformity of standards and, indeed, the need for compliance with an increasing number of regulations from the EU have now left the *Länder* little room for independent action in most of these fields of policy. Areas of responsibility not specifically mentioned in the Basic Law remain under the authority of the *Länder*. Arrangements are specified by which the *Länder* are given shares in national revenues, as well as having autonomous sources of finance, and there are mechanisms for transferring some revenues from the wealthier to the less prosperous *Länder*. Disputes between the federal government and the *Länder*, between the *Länder* themselves, or between a citizen and the government of either the federation or the *Länder*, are to be settled by the Federal Constitutional Court.

A federation needs more than just a constitutional basis in order to function successfully. Coordinating arrangements must be developed. One of the most important institutions which serves this purpose is the Bundesrat, the second chamber of the national legislature. This is composed of representatives of the *Land* governments, and has powers to discuss legislation, and to veto any such legislation which cannot command a majority in the Bundesrat. For legislation directly affecting the responsibilities or status of the *Länder*, such a veto is absolute. For other legislation, the Bundesrat veto can be overruled by a majority in the Bundestag. However, disagreements between the two chambers are frequently resolved by a 'mediation committee' of equal numbers of representatives from each chamber, drawn proportionally according to the strength of the parties in each chamber.

In the case of policies which are the responsibility of the federal government, their administration is often delegated to *Land* governments, and in this way too coordination is fostered. For matters where both the federal and *Land* governments have responsibility (such as university planning, or some matters of financial planning and cooperation), joint committees exist, under the provision of treaties signed by all the governments involved. On other matters less formal cooperation is produced through joint committees composed of the responsible federal minister and counterpart ministers from the *Land* governments: environment, education, criminal matters (such as combating extremism) and transport are examples. Each *Land* also has its own 'embassy' in Bonn.[3] These institutions serve as coordinating and 'representative' agencies, under the direction of the *Land* minister responsible for dealing with the federal government.

All the *Länder* have their own constitution (each very much resembling the Basic Law in terms of content, differing only in detail). Each *Land* also has its own government, judiciary and legislature. In a majority of the *Länder*, the legislature is normally elected every four years, though several *Länder* (such as North Rhine-Westphalia and Saarland) have five-year legislative periods. Electoral systems are variations of that used to elect the Bundestag, though some *Länder* have single-vote proportional representation systems, while others have separate votes for candidates and for party lists. The party systems of the *Länder* are very similar to those of the Federal Republic as a whole, though of course the relative strengths of parties may differ markedly between different *Länder*.

Differences in the size of territory and of population (see Table 10.1), and in financial resources, cause problems for German federalism. The small city-states of Bremen and Hamburg have to fulfil the same range of functions as *Länder* such as North Rhine-Westphalia, Baden-Württemberg and Bavaria, which are wealthier, larger and more populous (and which all contain cities comparable in size to Hamburg, but which are not independent *Länder*). The addition of the 'new' *Länder* in eastern Germany, which are all far from prosperous, exacerbates this situation. Suggestions are made from time to time that there should be a reorganisation of the *Länder*, perhaps merging Bremen,

Table 10.1   The *Länder* of the Federal Republic of Germany

Land	Population (millions)	Area (sq.km)	Votes in the Bundesrat
Baden-Württemberg	10.234	35,751	6
Bavaria	11.863	70,554	6
Berlin	3.475	883	4
Brandenburg	2.538	29,060	4
Bremen	0.683	404	3
Hamburg	1.703	755	3
Hesse	5.967	21,114	5[a]
Lower Saxony	7.648	47,439	6
Mecklenburg-Vorpommern	1.843	23,835	3
North Rhine-Westphalia	17.759	34,068	6
Rhineland-Pfalz	3.926	19,848	4
Saarland	1.085	2,568	3
Saxony	4.608	18,300	4
Saxony-Anhalt	2.778	20,445	4
Schleswig-Holstein	2.695	15,680	4
Thuringia	2.533	16,251	4

Source: *Statistisches Jahrbuch für die Bundesrepublik Deutschland*, 1995. Data refer to 31.12.1993.
[a] Hesse qualified for a fifth vote in 1996, on account of its increased population. Previously it had had four votes.

Hamburg, Lower Saxony and Schleswig-Holstein in the north, and some of the southern *Länder* (Saarland, Hesse and Rhineland-Pfalz are the most obvious candidates) to create a smaller number of more equal-sized and financially more viable *Länder*. It is probable that Berlin and Brandenburg will eventually merge: this was anticipated at the time of reunification and discussions about merger have commenced. However, the opportunity offered by reunification to redesign the federal structure was not seized, partly because of pressure of time in 1990, and partly because of opposition to loss of identity by some of the *Länder* which would have been affected by such redesign.

Austria

Austria is also, formally, a federal state, as it had been before it was forcibly joined to Germany by Hitler in 1938. In terms of state structures, the Austrian federal model is similar to that of Germany: the constituent units are the nine *Länder*, and the upper chamber (the Bundesrat) represents the constituent *Länder*. However, Austria in practice resembles unitary states with strong regional devolution, rather than the German or Swiss models of federalism. In particular, though constitutionally residual powers remain within the *Länder*, in practice most powers have been assumed by the federal government, with the *Länder* as units for the administration and implementation of policy. The powers of the Bundesrat to veto or delay legislation passed by the lower chamber of the legislature are also much weaker than in Germany.

Switzerland

The origins of the Swiss state go back to a defence pact among three cantons in the thirteenth century, but the modern federation dates from the peace settlement following the Napoleonic wars and the revolutions in Europe in 1848. Like Germany's federal structure, federalism in Switzerland is a mode of accommodating historical differences among formerly independent regions wishing to form a single state. Unlike Germany, regional differences in Switzerland are reinforced by the existence of various languages and religious denominations: some cantons have a majority of French speakers, some of German speakers, one of Italian speakers; some are strongly Catholic, others have more Protestants. There is now a total of twenty-six cantons, counting six 'half-cantons' separately.[4]

The traditional neutrality of Switzerland and its relative unimportance in international relations have meant that domestic policies, rather than foreign affairs, have been all-important. Since domestic policies and issues often involve local interests, this reinforces the political significance of the cantons compared to the national level of government. Identification of citizens with their canton is still very strong (much more so than of German citizens with their *Land*). Use of the referendum to settle issues locally, as well as nationally, helps to preserve the significance of cantonal and local political structures and organisations. Rejection on 6 December 1992 by referendum of a proposal to take Switzerland into the European Economic Area was indicative of the importance both of the referendum device and of cantonal veto over federal government policies.

The Swiss constitution reserves only a very restricted range of functions to the federal government. Among these are foreign relations; defence policy; banking and coinage; the railway system; and immigration (Switzerland has one of the highest ratios of foreign residents to native-born inhabitants in Europe, and is a highly desirable destination for would-be immigrants). All other functions remain the responsibility of the cantons: policing; local government; local transport; education; tourism; cultural affairs; environmental protection and planning among them. Each canton has its own constitution, elected legislature, government and courts, and cantons have protected sources of finance which are independent of federal government decisions. As is the case with the *Länder* in Germany, cantons take responsibility for the administration of many of the federal government's policies.

The influence of the federal principle is seen in the structures of the federal government. While the National Council (Nationalrat) reflects the distribution of population and is elected by the people directly, the second chamber, the Council of the

States (Ständerat), is composed of nominees of the cantons, who choose their two representatives (one for half-cantons) by whatever mode of election and for whatever term of office each canton thinks appropriate. The federal council (Bundesrat), the equivalent of the cabinet, has seven members, and they must be drawn from seven different cantons when they are elected by a joint session of the two legislative chambers.

Though suggestions are made from time to time concerning revision of cantonal boundaries, the only example of the creation of a new canton in recent years was in 1979, when Jura became a canton following a referendum. In general, neither the relatively large number of cantons in such a small country, nor the vast differences which exist in their territorial or population sizes, are serious matters for political concern. Yet differences are at least equivalent to those found among the *Länder* in Germany: Graubünden has 7,109 square kilometres, and Bern 6,887, but Basel City covers only 37 square kilometres and Zug 239.

Federalism seems to suit the Swiss, and is itself not an issue for political debate. There has inevitably been a strengthening of the centre in recent years, but the deep differences in the social, cultural and economic composition of the cantons mean that local autonomy is still regarded as the most appropriate, most democratic and most efficient method of conducting politics within a national framework.

Belgium[5]

Belgium has become a federal state gradually and in stages. The existence of two main language areas in the Belgian state became increasingly a matter for conflict in the 1950s. The decline of traditional industries in the Walloon (French-speaking) part of the country and the swifter economic development of the Flemish-speaking area exacerbated the divisions related to the language issue. It seemed then that only the symbolic figure of the monarch could prevent the state from distintegrating.

However, the introduction of legislation to give greater autonomy to the component language areas improved the situation. Laws of 1962 and 1963 established the boundaries of linguistic areas in Belgium, recognising the fact that the country was divided into French-speaking and Flemish-speaking areas, with a very small German-speaking area as well. Then a first constitutional reform in 1970 established 'cultural communities' as area authorities with powers to issue decrees on linguistic, educational, artistic and broadcasting matters, for example. A second constitutional reform in 1980 added executive governments to the legislative bodies of the cultural communities, and the competences of the communities were extended to cover matters such as health and family policy. At the same time, the regions of Flanders and Wallonia (though not the bilingual region of Brussels) were also given restricted legislative and executive powers, covering matters such as economic development, land-use planning, agriculture, some energy and transport responsibilities, and the environment. A Court of Arbitration was created to give judgment in cases where the competences of the Belgian state, the regions or the cultural communities were contested, conducting, in effect, the functions of a constitutional court (Belgian Constitution of 1994, Art. 142). Further reforms in 1988–89 extended the powers of the communities and regions, and gave Brussels its own regional executive and legislative organs.

In 1993, Belgium formally became a federal state; the first article of the 1994 constitution (which consolidated the constitutional reforms which had occurred up to 1993) now reads: 'Belgium is a federal state, composed of communities and regions'. Further reforms were instituted to provide for the direct election of regional legislatures (previously they had been composed of the members of the Belgian parliament from the region). Coordination mechanisms have been further developed: federal–region, federal–community and region–community coordination are all necessary from time to time. Some joint committees exist, and there are inter-ministerial conferences involving representatives of the governments of the federation, the communities and the regions, which go some way towards coordinating policy and its implementation (Hooghe 1995:143; Alen and Ergec 1994:38–9).

So Belgium is a complicated form of federal state, with dual and overlapping sets of constituent units: the communities and the regions. The upper house (Senate) consists now of forty directly elected senators representing the linguistic areas and twenty-one senators chosen by the community councils; in addition, these sixty-one Senators co-opt ten other senators. Both regions and communities have powers to negotiate and conclude international treaties. Unusually for a federal state, residual powers (powers not allocated specifically to the federal government or to the regions or communities) remain with the federation (Art. 35 of the Belgian constitution).

The great significance for Belgians of their language differences has led almost inevitably to the creation of a federal state to accommodate those differences without allowing them to break the state apart. However, the fact that the political parties are almost all divided on linguistic lines (so that there are French-speaking and Flemish-speaking Christian democratic parties, French-speaking and Flemish-speaking socialist parties, and so on) means that the parties cannot act as cross-regional integrative institutions. The requirement that Belgian cabinets be balanced linguistically and the effective veto which each language group has over legislation means that changes and adaptations by the government only find agreement with difficulty.

Regional decentralisation

While federalism is one method of accommodating local and regional differences within a state, a more widespread mode is some form of regional decentralisation within a unitary state. In this way, regions obtain considerable autonomy over their own affairs, but their rights and powers may be amended – or, indeed, abolished – by the central government; they are not 'constitutionally protected' rights and powers. A growing sensitivity to the need for more localised democracy, and recently the recognition of the status and importance of regions by the EU through the creation of a Committee of the Regions, have encouraged the extension of powers to the regions in several countries.

Spain is perhaps the European country with the most powerful set of regional units (outside the federal states described above). Because of the pressures for autonomy, especially in the Basque and Catalan regions, which re-emerged after the death of Franco, a system of autonomous regions was introduced from 1980, to cover those two regions and Andalucia and Galicia. Though some consideration was given to the idea of making Spain a federal state, the situation following the death of Franco, the power of the military and the fragility of constitutional and democratic ideas in Spain all made federation an unviable alternative.

This establishment of autonomous regions was made possible by Article 137 of the constitution of 1978, which permitted the organisation of the country into 'municipalities, provinces and any autonomous communities'. The system was subsequently extended to the whole of Spain from 1983. Each region – known as an 'autonomous community' – has an elected assembly and a regional government. These institutions have responsibility for policing, education, transport, language and cultural policy, energy and local government, either on an exclusive basis or as a concurrent responsibility with the Spanish government, depending on the terms of each separate 'autonomy statute'. The upper chamber of the Spanish legislature gives representation to the autonomous communities and provinces, and a constitutional tribunal upholds the autonomy of the regions *vis-à-vis* the central government. This arrangement brings Spain very close indeed to being a federal system. The autonomous communities are almost as 'protected' in their status as, say, the *Länder* of Austria or the language communities of Belgium. However, residual powers under the Spanish constitution remain with the central government, unlike, say, in Germany or Switzerland, and the second chamber representation of the autonomous communities is much weaker than in federal states (Agranoff 1995: 68).

Italy and France are other examples of western European states with significant regional structures.

The Italian system of regional organisation was created in 1970 (although five 'special regions', among them Sardinia, Sicily and Trentino-Alto Adige, had been nominated before that date). Regional assemblies are elected every five years. These assemblies elect executive governments, headed by the regional president. These governments have responsibility for certain functions (such as tourism, aspects of agricultural policy, cultural affairs, aspects of education, regional transport, and the environment) under Article 117 of the Italian constitution, and other functions may be delegated to regions by the central government under Article 118 of the constitution. The regions are dependent on the centre for financing, and much of their activity consists of administering policies decided in Rome. The central government has the right to veto regional legislation, and can dissolve regional legislatures. Unlike the system in federal states, the regions have no direct representation in the federal legislature. Special arrangements exist for Trentino-Alto Adige (also known as South Tyrol), incorporated in a statute of 1948. Here, protection is offered to the two existing cultural communities (the German-speaking and the Italian-speaking), under that 1948 statute as supplemented by later treaties and agreements. However, political forces in the area (some demanding the return of the area to Austria, others the dilution of special protection for the German-speaking community) indicate clearly that the situation is not fully acceptable to all sections of the population.

Regional authorities in France have evolved over many years. The system of administrative regions set up under decrees of 1950–60 was amended significantly by a law of 1972, which created regional councils, of which there are now twenty-six (including those overseas). However, the first direct elections for these councils only occurred in 1986; until then, they had been composed of the members of the French parliament and representatives of local government authorities in the area. Though the regions have considerable powers in matters such as training and education, environmental protection, regional arts funding and areas of economic policy, they have very limited budgets (compared to local authorities) and are the only 'level' of government not to have protected status in the constitution (Douence 1995:23). The lack of importance of the regional level of government is indicated by the preference of politicians to hold local authority offices (such as the position of mayor) alongside whatever national office they hold, rather than a position at regional level.

Although the UK is one of the few western European states lacking some form of regional political structure, special arrangements have existed for Northern Ireland, Scotland and Wales. Northern Ireland used to have the most far-reaching form of devolution – its own elected legislature (Stormont) – but the eruption of violence in Northern Ireland led to its suspension in 1972, and direct rule from London. Scotland has its own administration for matters such as local government, education, justice and policing, health and social security, and local transport, under the control of the Secretary of State for Scotland. Special arrangements also apply in the House of Commons, since many laws applicable to England and Wales do not apply to Scotland, and separate legislation is necessary. The situation for Wales is somewhat similar, though the range of powers under the authority of the Secretary of State for Wales is narrower, and generally separate legislation is not necessary for Wales. The special arrangements for Northern Ireland and Scotland are the consequence of the creation of the Irish Free State in 1922 and the Act of Union between Scotland and England in 1707. Pressure for either separation or home rule in Scotland, nationalist campaigns in Northern Ireland, and concern about the Welsh language and Welsh culture, led to proposals for constitutional reform, proposals given support by the findings of the Kilbrandon Report of 1973.[6] Referendums on the creation of elected assemblies for Scotland and Wales were held in 1979. In Wales the proposal was heavily defeated; in Scotland a narrow majority voted in favour, but the turnout was insufficient for the proposal to be taken further by the House of Commons. While the Liberal party is enthusiastic about the formation of regional authorities (including for England), and the Labour Party supports greater autonomy for Scotland and Wales, the Conservative party under Mrs Thatcher's and Mr Major's prime ministership has set itself decidedly against any such changes. In Northern Ireland, there is likely to be the institution of some form of elected assembly for the area, if talks about the future of Northern Ireland are successful.

Some other countries have regional structures. The Netherlands has twelve provinces, with limited political responsibilities. Greece has thirteen regions, but these have advisory responsibilities only, and there are no elected regional bodies. Portugal has provision in its 1976 constitution for the creation of regions, but, except for Madeira and the Azores, which have special autonomous status, the regions have few powers, though they are given responsibilities by the central government. The Scandinavian countries, by and large, use regional arrangements – where they exist at all – as administrative agencies, not as political structures with autonomous powers.

The importance of regions in various countries may perhaps be indicated by their allocation of seats on the new Committee of the Regions of the EU. Belgium sends its representatives solely from the regions. Germany, France, Italy and Spain send representatives mainly, but not exclusively, from the regions. The Netherlands sends representatives equally from regions and local government districts. However, Portugal sends them mainly from local government districts, while several countries, including Denmark, Ireland, and the UK, send their representatives only from local government organisations.

Regional devolution has advantages and disadvantages. It may serve to reinforce democracy, if regional legislatures have significant powers of their own, and if dependence on central government for resources is not too great. On the other hand, if regional autonomy is a reality, there may be variations in the levels of services, policies which run counter to those of central government (such as levels of public spending), and divisive political conflicts (such as the linguistic conflicts in Belgium) which complicate the national political process. But if regional authorities are primarily little more than implementational agencies for central government, if there is hardly any real autonomy, then their existence can hardly be regarded as a reinforcement of democracy, however useful they may be as a device for more localised administration.

Local government

Whether a state is organised on a federal or unitary basis, some kind of local government structure will be in place. In federal states, the pattern of local government, its financing and its powers will be broadly matters for the provincial levels of government to decide. In unitary states, central government will determine the structure and functions of local government, and will usually provide the greater share of local government's financial resources.

The detailed arrangements for local government will vary from country to country. However, in most states, functions of local government will include provision of local services such as primary and secondary education, refuse collection, some social services, libraries and cultural services, road maintenance, local planning controls, perhaps also some housing and local transport services. These will be financed by central or provincial government grants, local taxes of some nature, charges for services and perhaps predetermined shares of some forms of central taxation.

Indeed, financing is one of the principal problems of local government (some of the tasks of local government are very costly: education, for instance). So to what extent should the financing of local government be determined and the funds raised locally? Does excessive reliance on central government funding dilute local democracy? How can local government financing be brought into harmony with national economic policy? On the one hand, local democracy would seem to require a significant degree of autonomy for local authorities in matters of levying and spending local taxation. On the other hand, policies of a democratically elected central government could be vitiated or sabotaged by such autonomous local decision-making, especially by local authorities controlled politically by parties which form the opposition to that central government.

Another problem concerns the functions and powers of local government. What functions should be carried out locally? How much variation in local policymaking should be accepted? For example, can education in schools be organised independent of national standards? What functions should be regarded as 'discretionary' (leaving it to the local authority concerned to decide on whether, and how, it provides a particular service) and which functions should be 'mandatory'? Of course, this problem of responsibility links closely to that of financing: decreeing that local authorities should undertake certain functions means that central or provincial government must ensure that the resources are available for those functions. Care of old people in Britain and provision for asylum-seekers in Germany are just two examples of the imposition of expensive responsibilities on local authorities. Legislation from the EU places additional requirements on local authorities, without providing the financial resources to ensure its implementation.

Structure can also be a problem: as indicated by the numerous post-war revisions of local government structure in Britain (including the structural reforms undertaken in the 1990s), and by the reduction of the numbers of local authority districts in many countries (France and Germany in particular) over the past two decades. Local government units may vary greatly in size, and yet be required to undertake the same range of functions. There is an unresolvable dilemma about the need for local policies to be decided upon and local services to be provided *locally* (an extension of the 'subsidiarity' principle embraced by the EU[7]), yet for local government units to be of a sufficient size to be economically efficient. Should there be just one, or two or even three tiers of local government? How democratic is it to provide some services through joint single-purpose authorities, whose members are appointed by local authorities rather than elected by the voters?

Whether states are federal or unitary in their structure, whether unitary states have adopted regional devolution in some form or not, and whatever the pattern of local government arrangements, western European democracies face the ongoing challenge of combining effective and democratic central government with procedures for more local decision-making and administration. This is especially important today, with trends towards increased centralisation even in federal states such as Germany and Switzerland, and with more and more decisions affecting all member states being taken by the institutions of the EU. This growing importance of the EU as an additional level of government adds an extra 'layer' to whatever national political arrangements are in force.

Notes

1 For example, in Germany some *Länder* (such as Hessen, Baden-Württemberg and Bavaria) have directly elected mayors while in others (such as Lower Saxony) the mayor or other leader of the local authority acquires that position by virtue of being the leading candidate of the governing party (or, in a coalition, the largest governing party) in that city or district.

2 After reunification, Article 23 – providing for the inclusion in the Federal Republic of areas of Germany at the time outside the Federal Republic's borders – was no longer required, since no such areas remained. It was therefore replaced by one which contained new provisions concerning the relationship between the *Länder* and the EU.

3 These are soon to be located instead in Berlin, as progress is made to move the agencies of the federal government there.

4 'Half-cantons' have been produced by the division of previously existing cantons: for example, Basel was divided into Basel-Stadt (the urban area) and Basel-Land (its more rural hinterland). Half-cantons each have only one member of the Council of State; other cantons have two members each.

5 I am grateful to Kris Deschouwer (Free University, Brussels) for advice concerning changes in the Belgian constitution and the federal structure.

6 Lord Kilbrandon chaired a Royal Commission on the Constitution, which was primarily concerned with the status of the component areas of the UK.

7 The concept of *subsidiarity* derives from a doctrine of the Catholic church, which considers that decisions which affect people's lives should be taken as locally as possible. It is used now as a principle in the EU, though there is lack of clarity concerning what it means in the context of the EU. For example, it could be a reason for limiting EU decision-making to matters which national governments could not handle as well themselves, or it could be an excuse for greater autonomy at regional or local levels of government.

References

Agranoff, R. (1995) 'Asymmetrical and symmetrical federalism in Spain', in B. de Villiers (ed.) *Evaluating Federal Systems*, Juta, Nijhoff, pp. 67–70.

Alen, A. and R. Ergec (1994) *Federal Belgium after the Fourth State Reform of 1993*, Brussels, Ministry of Foreign Affairs, External Trade and Development Cooperation.

Douence, J.-C. (1995) 'The evolution of the 1982 regional reforms: an overview', in J. Loughlin and S. Mazey (eds) *The End of the French Unitary State*, Ilford, Frank Cass, pp. 10–24.

Hooghe, L. (1995) 'Belgian federalism and the European Community', in B. Jones and M. Keating (eds) *The European Union and the Regions*, Oxford, Clarendon Press, pp. 135–65.

Further reading

Burgess, M. (ed.) (1986) *Federalism and Federation in Western Europe*, London, Croom Helm.

Burgess, M. and A.-G. Gagnon (eds) (1993) *Comparative Federalism and Federation*, London, Harvester-Wheatsheaf.

Chandler, J. (ed.) (1993) *Local Government in Liberal Democracies*, London, Routledge.

de Villers, B. (ed.) (1995) *Evaluating Federal Systems*, Juta, Nijhoff.

Jeffery, C. and P. Savigear (eds) (1991) *German Federalism Today*, Leicester, Leicester University Press.

Levy, R. (1995) 'Governing Scotland, Wales and Northern Ireland', in R. Pyper and L. Robins (eds) *Governing the UK in the 1990s*, Basingstoke, Macmillan.

Loughlin, J. and S. Mazey (eds) (1995) *The End of the French Unitary State*, Ilford, Frank Cass.

Meny, Y. and V. Wright (eds) (1985) *Centre–Periphery Relations in Western Europe*, London, Allen & Unwin.

11

The European Union and the member states

Almost every aspect of European national politics described in this book is touched at some point by the activity of the EU. This organisation is the product of an ongoing process of European integration which began after the Second World War. It started on a small scale, as a body to coordinate the production and marketing of coal and steel. It has since evolved into a permanent organisation of fifteen members and has some of the characteristics of a sovereign state. It has its own constitutional framework and institutions of government. It has the authority, in agreed policy areas, to make decisions which are binding on the national governments and individual citizens of its member states. The implications of this are enormous. Membership of the EU has changed the way in which the conventional institutions of national government operate. National policy aims, always shaped in part by external relations, are increasingly influenced by the concerns of the EU. This chapter traces the development of post-war European integration. It describes the governing institutions of the EU and the way in which they work together. It considers the effect of the EU on the government and politics of the member states. Finally, it considers some of the issues and problems the EU must face in the near future in order to achieve its goals.

European integration in the post-war period

Seen from a pre-war perspective, the EU would have appeared a most unlikely development. Western Europe was made up of established, independent nation-states. Colonial powers with a proud history, these countries had fought wars with one another for the best part of four centuries rather than lose their territorial and cultural identity. Nevertheless, many of these countries have since chosen to work together at a very real cost to their independence. The most bitter enemies of all, France and Germany, have often proved the driving force in post-war European integration. What explains this unprecedented degree of voluntary cooperation between the countries of Europe? The answer lies in a series of crises, each of which has helped to shape the EU in the form in which it exists today (see Dinan 1994).

The first and most compelling of these was the Second World War, which left the countries of continental Europe with pressing economic and defence needs. These countries had lost much of their industrial capacity, housing and infrastructure, their overseas markets had collapsed with the loss of their colonies and their workforce had been decimated. Immediately after the war, there were fears that these nations would not be able to survive as independent economic units. Also, their military power was exhausted, leaving them vulnerable to attack. Following two world wars, defence fears centred on the 'German problem' – how was Germany to be prevented from ever again becoming a dominant and aggressive force within Europe? In the late 1940s the urgency of western Europe's defence needs was underlined by the onset of the cold war.

The ideological and political climate of the time strongly favoured a joint solution to these problems. Some of the political elite had lost confidence in the structures of the nation-state and the moral and philosophical ideas which underpinned it. The two devastating world wars of the twentieth century were, for thinkers such as Altiero Spinelli, the logical outcome of the existence of separate sovereign states.[1] The nation-states of Europe had failed to resolve their conflicts and had exposed their people to years of suffering and an uncertain future. Some believed that only a European federation would serve to uphold peace and prosperity where the nation-states had failed.

The rapid changes which took place between the immediate post-war period and the mid-1950s ensured that European integration did not take a federalist course. A French proposal for a far-reaching European Defence Community (EDC) was abandoned in 1954. By this time, western European leaders were less convinced of the need for full political and defence integration. National politics had reasserted itself on the model of parliamentary democracy. There no longer seemed to be the imminent threat of crisis in international relations. Stalin had died, the Korean War had ended and the Soviet Union appeared to present less of a threat to the non-Communist world. A range of new international organisations ensured regular communication among the western nation-states as they tried to adapt to a new world order dominated by the superpowers of the United States of America and the Soviet Union. These organisations included the Organisation for European Economic Cooperation (OEEC), the North Atlantic Treaty Organisation (NATO), the Western European Union (WEU) and the Council of Europe.[2]

The European Coal and Steel Community (ECSC)

By the 1950s, however, European integration had achieved a momentum of its own. There were still sound economic reasons for the pooling of resources between countries. Moreover, the countries of continental Europe, France in particular, were still deeply suspicious of Germany. They were wary of isolating the country, a policy which had proved disastrous after the First World War. Instead, they involved West Germany as an equal partner in the first of the European Communities: the European Coal and Steel Community (ECSC).[3]

It was a French initiative which led, in 1952, to the founding of the ECSC. Six countries became members: Belgium, France, Italy, Luxembourg, the Netherlands and West Germany. Britain chose not to join. The ECSC took over agreed areas of competence within the coal and steel sectors from the national governments. It controlled production, certain aspects of pricing, investment and social conditions. This organisation, planned by Jean Monnet and promoted by the French foreign minister, Robert Schuman, was a brilliant strategic device, combining two central aims. It gave a good grounding to the economic reconstruction in Europe while at the same time ensuring that no member country could divert vital resources into a war economy. It established a Franco-German partnership which has remained central to post-war European integration. Moreover, it was the first of the post-war European organisations to feature a supranational decision-making authority.

The European Economic Community (EEC)
The European Economic Community was established in 1957 by the Treaty of Rome and began operating in 1958. Its founder members were the six countries party to the ECSC. It has since been enlarged to take in fifteen countries, with further applications under consideration (see Table 11.1). The Rome Treaty established a customs union. Members agreed to a phased programme to remove all tariffs and quotas from trade among themselves while setting a Common External Tariff (CET) on imports from outside the EEC. They also agreed to formulate common policy on agreed areas, primarily agriculture and transport, to promote trade within the EEC. A common social policy was to help offset any hardship suffered in the transition to a more open market. The policy process was conducted through a set of governing institutions: a supranational Commission, a Parliamentary Assembly, a Court of Justice and a Council of Ministers made up of government representatives of the member states. Since 1974, the European Council, a regular summit of the member state heads of government, has evolved as a major institution of the EU. (These institutions are described in detail below.)

The membership of each institution of the EU strongly influences the way in which it operates. The Council of Ministers and the European Council are essentially intergovernmental institu-

Table 11.1   Member states of the European Union

Country	Joined
Belgium	1958
France	1958
Germany[a]	1958
Italy	1958
Luxembourg	1958
Netherlands	1958
Denmark	1973
Ireland	1973
UK	1973
Greece	1981
Portugal	1986
Spain	1986
Austria	1995
Finland	1995
Sweden	1995

[a] In 1990, membership was extended to the former East Germany, not in its own right, but as a part of unified Germany.

tions. They are made up of government representatives of the member states. The members of these institutions have to account for their decisions to their home constituencies and can therefore be expected to put their country's interests before those of the EU as a whole. Other institutions, such as the Commission or the Court of Justice, are essentially supranational. They are made up of members appointed to work for the EU itself and not for the member states. Members of the European Commission, for example, must give a solemn undertaking not to take instructions from any government (or any other body), but to perform their duties independently. Obviously, Commissioners can be expected to have some loyalty to their own member state and to be particularly aware of its concerns. Nevertheless, the Commissioners' stance is more impartial than those of the country representatives who participate in the Council of Ministers and the European Council.[4]

This distinction between the intergovernmental and supranational institutions helps to explain why the EU works as it does. While the founders of the EEC were motivated by their commitment to supranationality, many of the political leaders of the original six member states had reservations. They wanted to ensure that member state governments would not lose control of their countries' vital interests. In response to pressure from the member states, the Treaty of Rome established a network of governing institutions which was weighted in favour of intergovernmentalism. Ever since, the conflict between those who want to preserve an intergovernmental Community and those who want a more supranational Community has been one of the main sources of antagonism within the organisation. This issue divides political opinion within the member states, but some countries – for example, Britain, Denmark and, in some respects, France – are notably more hostile than others to moves towards supranationality. At the other end of the scale, Belgium, Germany and Italy are keen to promote further integration to the point of a future European federation.

Intergovernmentalism within the EEC was soon to be compounded by the formalisation of decision-making conventions which protected the interests of the individual member states. In 1965, France precipitated a crisis by walking out of the Council of Ministers. The French delegation objected to elements of a proposed institutional reform of the EEC and the manner in which they had been initiated. It was six months before France could be persuaded to return to the Council. The price was the convention known as the 'Luxembourg Compromise'. This established the right of any member state to veto a decision of the Council of Ministers if it felt that this decision would adversely affect its vital interests. In practice then, from 1966 onwards, important decisions of the Council of Ministers had to have the unanimous support of all member states or they could not be passed. The Council had already been accustomed to making most decisions on a unanimous basis, so the main effect of the formalisation of this convention was to raise the status of member state interests within the decision-making process.

During the 1970s, the EC was afflicted by a period of 'Eurosclerosis'. The European economy came under pressure from the quadrupling of oil prices in 1973–74. The governments of the member states had to contend with soaring inflation and unemployment. They were unable to reach agreement on a joint EC response to the energy crisis and became increasingly protectionist. At a procedural level, an increasing workload and the need for unanimity in the Council of Ministers slowed the decision-making processes within the EC and contributed to a severe loss of confidence in the organisation. Alarmed by the lack of political leadership within the EC, President Giscard d'Estaing of France and Chancellor Schmidt of West Germany proposed regular summit meetings between the heads of government of the member states. The summits were to provide a forum for economic planning and policy development within the EC. This forum became known as the European Council in 1974 and in 1987 gained formal recognition under the Single European Act. The European Council's contribution to European integration is paradoxical. Meeting as the European Council, the top political representatives of the member states have, by taking over political leadership, strengthened intergovernmentalism within the EU. Since the late 1980s, though, the European Council has been responsible for steering the Community towards closer integration, thereby increasing the potential for the development of a truly supranational EU.

The new challenges of the 1980s
By the 1980s, the EC was facing new challenges. Many were reminiscent of those which had launched European integration in the late 1940s. They included economic pressures brought about by new industries and changing patterns of international trade. By the 1980s, the EC's share of the world market in traditional sectors, such as steel or textiles, was under pressure from newly industrialising countries. Production costs are lower in

these countries because the workforce is less protected by legislation and trade-union activity than in western Europe. At the same time, the USA and Japan had come to dominate world trade in the new technologies. If the EC was to challenge that superiority, it would need to become a more efficient organisation. Meanwhile, dramatic developments in international relations led the EC to reconsider the need for defence integration. The collapse of communist rule in the eastern European countries in the late 1980s was soon followed by the break-up of the Soviet Union. The reunification process in Germany, formally concluded in October 1990, revived Europe's 'German problem'. These developments left the EC with the need to rethink its place in the world order.

The EC tried to meet these challenges as they arose, launching reforms which culminated in the Single European Act and the Treaty on European Union (Maastricht Treaty). These measures came into force in 1987 and 1993 respectively. As well as aiming to improve the efficiency of the EC, they represented a major constitutional revision of the Rome Treaties.

The Single European Act
The central aim of the Single European Act was to improve the economic efficiency of the EC by creating a single European market (SEM) between member states by 1992. While the Rome Treaties had removed tariff barriers among the member states, in practice non-tariff barriers were still impeding trade among them. This reduced the competitiveness of the EC in world trade. For example, sectors including steel, ship-building and textiles were heavily subsidised by the central governments of the member states. Each country had its own health and safety standards. These have often been abused by member states to effect an informal block on imports of a particular product from other countries and so protect their own industries. Each member state had developed its own national specifications for new technologies, which fragmented the market. The Cecchini Report commissioned by the EC and published in 1988 (see Cecchini 1988)

estimated that the achievement of a true single market could add nearly 5 per cent to the Community's gross domestic product (GDP).[5]

The SEM could not be created in a vacuum; it required a tighter control of EC economic policy and related areas. Here, the Single European Act prepared the ground by formally expanding the EC's policy competences to include environmental policy, research and technological development and regional policy (termed 'economic and social cohesion'). It established new legislative procedures to improve the efficiency and control of decision-making (the 'cooperation' and 'assent' procedures; see below). These gave the European Parliament (EP) slightly more influence in EC decision-making, but only in measures connected with the creation of the SEM, association agreements between the EC and third countries, and the accession of new member states to the EC.

The Maastricht Treaty and the EU
The Maastricht Treaty established the EU. This organisation is based on three 'pillars': the European Communities (the EEC, ECSC and Euratom); a Common Foreign and Security Policy (CFSP); and cooperation in the fields of justice and home affairs (JHA). While it has stopped short of placing foreign and security policies under the authority of the EU, there must now be systematic cooperation between member states on matters of general concern. On JHA, the Treaty lists a number of areas, until now the preserve of the national governments, which are to be coordinated at the level of the EU. These include immigration and asylum policy, police cooperation to combat drug trafficking and other serious crime, and judicial cooperation. The Treaty provisions on CFSP and JHA are open-ended, so as to allow for future moves towards integration in these areas if member states agree. Currently, neither CFSP nor the bulk of JHA is subject to the jurisdiction of the European Court of Justice. In these areas, then, the Maastricht Treaty provides more a statement of intent than a concrete framework for integration. It represents an uneasy compromise between the

supranationalist and intergovernmentalist factions within the EU.

The Maastricht Treaty consolidated the Single European Act by setting a strategy and timetable for implementing Economic and Monetary Union (EMU). This ambitious programme aims to create a single currency for the EU by 1999, managed by a European Central Bank (ECB), with close coordination of member states' economic policies.[6] (Denmark has opted out of EMU and Britain has reserved the right to do so.) Particularly for the French, EMU was conceived as more than a measure to improve the competitiveness of the EU. In a similar strategy to that of the European Coal and Steel Union, EMU was seen as a means of supervising the transition to a unified German state in the uncertain context of the collapse of the Soviet bloc. After unification, Germany accounted for 27 per cent of the Community's GDP and 25 per cent of its population (Dinan 1994:161). There were fears that united Germany, already in a dominant position through the strength of the Deutschmark, would soon be able to control EU affairs. EMU would absorb the Deutschmark with every other European currency and would require Germany to cooperate closely with the other member states over economic policy. Germany too was keen to subscribe to EMU, in order to reassure the Community about its intentions to forge a 'European Germany' rather than a 'German Europe'. The Maastricht Treaty also created the Cohesion Fund to channel financial support for the improvement of transport infrastructures and for environmental improvements in the poorer member states. All member states except Britain agreed to cooperate in the fields of social and employment policy under the Social Chapter. They hoped that Britain would join in later so that agreed aspects of these policy areas can become the full responsibility of the EU.

The institutions of the European Union

The EU is governed by a unique set of institutions. It is easy to be misled by the familiar names of some of these institutions – the

European Parliament, the Council of Ministers – into seeing them as counterparts of the national institutions of government in western Europe. In fact, their functions are quite different and can best be understood in relation to one another. The Treaty of Rome established the Commission primarily to propose legislation, the Parliamentary Assembly to advise, the Council of Ministers to legislate and the Court of Justice to interpret the law. However, the Community has changed considerably during its short life, both in size and in the scope of its activities. Its institutions of government have changed with it.

The European Commission

One of the key institutions of the EU is the European Commission. The Commission is in effect two organisations: the executive Commission and the administrative Commission. Headed by a president, the executive Commission was expanded following the 1995 EU enlargement from seventeen to twenty members. Commissioners are appointed by the member state governments for a renewable five-year term of office. Each country has one Commissioner and the largest (France, Germany, Italy, Spain and the UK) have a second. Jacques Delors, who held the presidency of the Commission from 1985 to 1994, ensured that this prestigious post acquired the highest profile of any office in the EU. The president represents the Commission in its dealings with the other EU institutions and outside bodies, supervises the Commission's administrative services at the highest level and may hold a policy portfolio. An active president can set an agenda for the work of the Commission as a whole. The president and each Commissioner is supported by a personal 'cabinet', a small team of officials.

Similar to the way in which policy areas are divided between ministries at national level, the policy areas dealt with by the administrative Commission come under Directorates General (DGs). These vary in size and the complexity of their internal organisation according to their current policy importance and workload. Some Commission portfolios – agriculture, or regional policy – change little from Commission to Commission, but others are determined by current needs.

The tasks performed by the Commission comprise policy-making, legislation, the kind of preparatory work and implementation carried out by the higher civil service at national level, a 'watchdog' role concerning the treaty framework of the EU, and the external representation of the EU to non-member states and international organisations. This formidable list would seem to leave nothing for the remaining institutions to do. This is far from the case, as the Commission must share its duties in clearly defined ways.

The Commission has the right to initiate and draft legislation and has the power to issue certain types of Community law. At first sight, then, it would appear to have even greater powers in legislation than the European national governments. However, the Commission is not an independent legislator. Most of its legislative proposals and recommendations can be rejected by the Council of Ministers, and, in certain limited circumstances, by the EP. So as not to waste time and effort, the Commission must be fairly confident that its proposals will be acceptable to these institutions. In fact, Commission proposals are the product of lengthy consultations through advisory committees with representatives of the member states and with interest-groups concerned with the issue at stake. Also, the Council of Ministers has encroached on the policy-making role of the Commission by effectively presenting legislative proposals to the Commission for initiation. These proposals can be so detailed that little is left for the Commission to do but to feed them into the decision-making process. Also, the Maastricht Treaty gave the EP the formal right to present proposals to the Commission concerning the implementation of the Treaty.

The Commission's power to issue laws is also less significant in practice than it might appear, as it is usually shared with the Council of Ministers. While the Commission issues the greater number of laws, these concern largely technical and administrative matters. The Council of Ministers is responsible for major legislation, setting the political priorities of the EU. In practice, the Commission is more a mediator in the policy process than a truly independent actor. Since the mid-1960s, the Commission has often been criticised for taking a reactive rather than a proactive approach. One reason for this is that the brusque treatment of individual member states could cause resentment, which in turn could easily stall the process of continuous negotiation and compromise necessary to the functioning of the EU. Within these constraints, the Commission can and does take initiatives. For example, some of the Commission proposals approved at meetings of the European Council from the mid-1980s onwards have been crucial in the development of the internal market and monetary policy.

In addition to its policy-making and legislative role, the Commission must keep the member states to their legal obligations to the EU. The Commission supervises both the payment of budgetary contributions from the member states and the EU's expenditure. It must check that appropriate legislation is being introduced in the member states' national parliaments and that EU policies are applied in a uniform manner throughout the member states. If the Commission believes a member state to be neglecting its obligations in this respect, it issues a warning to the national government. An established infringement procedure is followed which gives the member state in question the opportunity to rectify any problems identified by the Commission. If, however, the government in question shows no signs of cooperation, the Commission may pass the case to the Court of Justice.

In practice, the Commission, with its limited staff and resources, is simply not competent to exercise an effective control on the implementation of EU legislation. At the end of 1993, for example, only some 100 Commission officials were specifically employed to combat fraud (Nugent 1994:108). It is only able to follow up a tiny proportion of cases where a breach of member state obligations is suspected. As a result, member states are tempted to be negligent in implementing unpopular EU legislation. Environmental policy, the single market and agriculture

are the worst areas of non-compliance. While many governments may from time to time delay implementation, some member states, notably Italy, Greece, Spain and Portugal, are
notoriously lax (Dinan 1994:303). This inevitably leads to resentment in those member states with a good record in implementation. Failure at the implementation stage of legislation is a
growing problem for the EU, one which is often rather unfairly
blamed on the Commission.

As the external representative of the EU, the Commission con-
ducts diplomatic and trade negotiations with outside countries
and represents the EU at international organisations such as the
United Nations, the World Trade Organisation, the Organisation
for Economic Cooperation and Development (OECD) and the
Council of Europe. On behalf of the Council of Ministers, the
Commission carries out the greater part of the preliminary negotiations with states applying for membership of the EU.

The Council of Ministers
The Council of Ministers is the main legislative body of the EU.
It is the forum in which government ministers from the member
states meet, attending according to the policy area under discussion. For example, if measures concerning the CAP are on the
agenda, then the agriculture ministers of the national governments attend.[7] The meetings of the Council are chaired by the
representative from the member state holding the Council
presidency. This rotates among the member states on a six-
monthly basis. The General Affairs Council, comprising the foreign ministers of the member states, has informally adopted a
general coordinating role. It tends to take the lead in formulating
policy guidelines and deals with politically sensitive issues. However, it lacks the authority and resources to provide consistent
leadership of the work of the Council of Ministers. While it can
only act on the basis of Commission proposals, the Council alone
takes decisions on most politically sensitive matters. Institutional reform through the Maastricht Treaty has given the EP a
potential veto on Council legislation in certain specified circumstances. However, these powers are very recent and so far the

Council has been able to maintain its dominance of the legislative process.

Various delegations, committees and working parties help to prepare and conduct the work of the Council of Ministers. Each minister is supported in the Council by a small delegation of national experts and officials. Preparatory work is carried out by the Committee of Permanent Representatives (COREPER), a group of senior diplomats and policy experts who work on behalf of the member states, and many decisions are taken at this level. Administrative support is provided by the General Secretariat of the Council. The key policy area of agriculture has its own Special Committee on Agriculture (SCA).

Legal agreements such as the Single European Act and the Maastricht Treaty have played their part in the reform of the Community since the 1980s. Equally important, though, has been the growing recognition that the member states must work together to revitalise the EU. Perhaps the best example of the interplay between legal agreements and working practice has been the move to decision-making by qualified majority in the Council of Ministers. The use of the national veto through the 'Luxembourg Compromise' had reduced decision-making in the Council to the lowest common denominator. In a speech to the EP in 1984, President Mitterrand of France spoke for the greater use of majority voting to decide important issues. This stance became more acceptable as the EC expanded to twelve members in the 1980s, making unanimity increasingly difficult to achieve. The Single European Act and the Maastricht Treaty formalised the member states' commitment to majority voting and expanded the range of decisions to which it is applied.

In fact, Council decisions are agreed without a vote if at all possible, so that the new practices apply only if member states in a minority position wish to press an issue. Some measures are decided by a simple majority, but most are taken on the basis of a qualified majority. Each country's share of votes is roughly in proportion to its size, but the smallest have a greater than proportional share so that they are not at the mercy of the giants. Following the 1995 enlargement, there is a total of eighty-seven Council votes. Sixty-two votes are needed for a qualified majority, so a minority needs twenty-six votes to block a measure to be decided in this way.

The European Council

The European Council meets at least twice every year. Membership is confined to the prime minister and foreign minister of each member state (France sends the president and either the prime minister or foreign minister) plus two representatives of the Commission. These meetings develop longer-term policy on the process and direction of European integration, considering in particular constitutional issues, economic integration, proposed enlargements of the Community, and wider external relations (particularly with the USA and Japan). They also discuss politically sensitive internal issues. Reform of the CAP and the question of member state budget contributions have often featured at meetings of the European Council.

The European Council is sometimes viewed simply as an extension of the Council of Ministers, but this is potentially misleading. Unlike the Council of Ministers, the European Council was not part of the original constitutional framework of the EEC and its role has never been fully determined. This has given the European Council considerable freedom to decide its own competences without having to answer to any other EU institution – including the Court of Justice.[8] As a forum of the member state heads of government, the political legitimacy of the European Council owes more to national elections than to the EU treaties. Its political authority is greater than that of the Council of Ministers. In practice, the European Council has developed a role quite independent of the Council of Ministers. It has chosen not to meet as an extension of the Council of Ministers, and, therefore, does not legislate in its own right. Instead, it has emerged as the only body capable of giving political direction to the EU.

The European Parliament

Established in 1958 as the Assembly of the EEC, the EP adopted its current title in 1962. Since then, its formal powers have been upgraded, but its role is still largely advisory. Its influence extends to three areas which are traditionally part of a national parliament's work: legislation, the budget and control of the executive. Since the introduction of direct elections to the Parliament in 1979, it can also claim to represent the people of Europe.

The EP has made good use of the limited powers at its disposal to influence the legislative and budgetary processes. It has presented policy ideas and initiative reports to the Commission, even though in the past there has been no obligation for the Commission to act on these. It has cooperated with the Commission over the annual legislative programme. It must give its view on most of the important legislation passed by the Council of Ministers (but not by the Commission). If the Council of Ministers tries to pass legislation before the EP has expressed its view, the Court of Justice will rule the measure invalid.

The Single European Act of 1987 and the Maastricht Treaty have given the EP a number of opportunities to become more involved in EU decision-making. One is the right to suggest legislative proposals to the Commission, noted above. They also introduced three variations into the legislative process. The basic 'consultation procedure' requires the Council of Ministers to seek the opinion of the EP prior to passing legislation: this procedure remains in place for much of the legislation passed by the Council. However, in certain circumstances, proposed legislation must be channelled through the 'cooperation procedure', the 'assent procedure', or the 'co-decision procedure'. Under the cooperation procedure, proposed legislation must receive two separate readings in the EP. The assent procedure and co-decision procedure both give the EP a potential veto over Council legislation.[9] In spite of these developments, the EP's potential for initiating, developing and deciding legislation remains minimal when compared with that of the national parliaments. The

Council of Ministers can easily delay the legislative process if it does not like the EP's position.

The EP's budgetary powers have been increased since the 1970s. The budgetary process involves two readings in the EP, which has the right to propose amendments to raise or trim the budget within narrow limits. With a two-thirds majority (which must constitute a majority of all MEPs), the EP may reject a draft budget. It has used this right several times, negotiating with the Council of Ministers via the Commission to arrive at a mutually acceptable budget.

Weakest of all the EP's 'powers' has been its control function. The Maastricht Treaty has upgraded this slightly. The EP now has the right to be consulted about the choice of the president of the Commission, who is nominated 'by common accord' by the member state governments. The Commission as a body is subject to a vote of investiture in the EP before it can take office, bringing it more into line with conventions of executive-legislative relations in western European nation-states.[10]

A long-standing right of the EP has been to dismiss the Commission (but not individual Commissioners) – again, a right borrowed from the European practice of a national parliament's power of dismissal of the executive. The EP has never successfully used this right. In any case, it would not have gained any particular advantage by dismissing the Commission as long as it had no reciprocal rights of appointment. The threat of EP dismissal of the Commission may become more realistic now that the EP has the right to veto a Commission, if not to appoint one of its own choosing. Also, the EP's control function continues to be limited by the fact that there is no single institution representing the executive within the EU. As we have seen, executive functions are shared among the Commission, the Council of Ministers and the European Council. While the Maastricht Treaty has increased the ability of the EP to control the Commission, the EP remains very weak with respect to the Council of Ministers and the European Council. Currently, the members of these institutions are answerable only to their home parliaments. Any move to make them responsible to the EP would be resisted by those member states who reject a more supranational EU.

Committees of the EP may also actively supervise the work of the Commission, but have very limited resources with which to carry out an investigation. In the same way as a national parliament may question the government, the EP may ask written and oral questions regarding the Commission's activities. The Maastricht Treaty provided for the appointment of a parliamentary ombudsman to investigate citizens' claims of maladministration within the EU. The first EU ombudsman, Jacob Söderman, was elected by MEPs in July 1995 and received over 400 complaints during his first five months in office.

Members of the original European Parliamentary Assembly were selected from the sitting MPs in the member states' parliaments. It was envisaged from the start that this interim arrangement would be replaced by a system of direct elections. Some of the more 'Eurosceptic' countries, particularly France and later Britain and Denmark, were unhappy about this development. It would boost the legitimacy of one of the 'supranational' institutions of the Community and might lead to further reforms at the expense of member state influence. The introduction of direct elections was blocked until 1979 and then implemented in a way which limited the added legitimacy to the EP.

Instead of using a single electoral system to elect the 626 MEPs, each member state has devised its own. Britain uses its preferred 'first-past-the post' system in single-member constituencies. Northern Ireland uses the STV to ensure representation for its Catholic minority. The other member states have all adopted a variant of proportional representation. The result of this patchwork of electoral systems is that MEPs are chosen on a far from equal basis. Also, if the proportion of MEPs to constituents is an indication of the quality of representation, then some member states are better represented than others. In 1994, Germany had one MEP to 819,156 voters compared to Luxembourg's one MEP to 64,967 voters (Nugent 1994:188).[11]

Low voting turnouts in European elections have so far failed to provide the degree of legitimation hoped for by advocates of a more active EP. Turnouts have fallen steadily from 1979 (62 per cent) to 1994 (56.5 per cent). There would seem to be a vicious circle here. Active popular support is needed to justify reforms to strengthen the powers of the EP. However, there is little incentive for European voters, with their high expectations of what a parliament does, to vote for a body which seems so ineffective. Their vote will not determine the 'government' of the EU, as it would in a national election. For many European voters, the work of the EU seems in any case very remote from their daily lives. Particularly in those countries where the main parties are divided over European issues, European election campaigns tend to be used as a rehearsal for the more important national contests.

The European Court of Justice

The European Court of Justice (ECJ) is made up of one judge from each of the fifteen member states. The judges are appointed for six-year, renewable terms of office. They are assisted by nine advocates-general. The ECJ is responsible for the interpretation and application of EU law. This gives it a similar role to the constitutional courts of the member states. Where EU law conflicts with a law already in force in a member state, it is the EU legislation which takes precedence. This principle was established by the ECJ and is widely respected throughout the member states. The ECJ cannot initiate a case, but must wait for an action to be brought by a member state, an EU institution, or, under certain circumstances, by 'natural or legal persons'. The number of cases dealt with by the ECJ has increased dramatically. In the 1960s, some 50 cases were dealt with every year; now there are between 400 and 500 annually (Nugent 1994:230). In 1989 a Court of First Instance was created to deal with some of the workload. In 1993, its jurisdiction was expanded to enable it to filter most of the caseload of the ECJ. Only since the Maastricht Treaty has the ECJ had the right to impose a fine on a member state for refusing to comply with an ECJ judgment.

The ECJ deals with claims that a member state or an EU institution is in breach of its treaty obligations. It can also be asked to undertake judicial review, that is, to consider the legality of an EU law. In this area, a growing number of cases relate to procedural questions. As we have seen, various procedures can be used to make EU law. The choice of procedure is not optional, but is based on guidelines laid down in the Treaties. Often a case can be made for the use of alternative procedures and it is this uncertainty which is the basis of this type of legal action. The cases are brought because the use of different procedures has different implications for the institutions of the EU and for the individual member states. Obviously, the EP prefers the use of a procedure which gives it a potential veto in the legislative process. Where a member state supports a minority view, it will prefer the use of a unanimous vote, rather than have a decision made by the majority.

The ECJ decides cases involving both primary and secondary legislation. The primary legislation of the EU is made up of the treaties between member states which together form the EU's constitutional framework. The Maastricht Treaty is the latest and most comprehensive expression of primary legislation. Secondary legislation refers to laws passed by the Council of Ministers (sometimes in conjunction with the EP) or the Commission. These measures can take the form of regulations, directives or decisions. The decision-making institutions may also issue recommendations and opinions, which do not strictly have the force of law.

It was noted in Chapter 9 that the courts in western European countries have come to influence legislation and policy-making. In interpreting the law, they have gone well beyond a simple elucidation of technical or grammatical questions to set guidelines for future laws. This is also true of the ECJ. A number of pressures have pushed the ECJ into a policy-making role. One is familiar in those member states where the governing coalition tends to be unstable, such as the Netherlands. Here, and within the EU, legal measures are often framed in ambiguous terms – to clarify them would be to risk the fragile consensus between decision-makers. When it comes to the implementation of this legislation, the ambiguities must be resolved and the ECJ is called in to help. Other factors relate to the EU in particular. The EU is much younger than any of its member states. In consequence, its body of law is in the early stages of development and measures often require the ECJ's interpretation. As the primary legislation of the EU tends to be patchy and ambiguous, the ECJ has turned to the kind of case-law approach developed in England: the ECJ refers back to its own previous rulings to help it resolve the case in hand. In this way, it is making its own contribution to EU law.

Initially, the ECJ had no responsibility for individual and civil rights. (This is the preserve of the European Court of Human Rights, which is based in Strasbourg.) In 1967, however, the German *Bundesverfassungsgericht* (Federal Constitutional Court) challenged the supremacy of EC law, arguing that certain fundamental rights enshrined in the West German Basic Law could not be effectively protected under EC law, as the Treaty of Rome contained no provision for the protection of human rights. The ECJ responded to this challenge by developing a jurisprudence on fundamental rights (Wincott 1995:593–4).

The European Union and the member states

The idea of European integration runs counter to that of the sovereign nation-state, on which every country in western Europe is based. In order to be a member of the EU, a nation-state must give up its claim to full legislative sovereignty. This is a cost which affects member states both at a symbolic and a practical level. For some member states, the symbolic cost is harder to accept than for others. It is particularly hard for Britain, where parliamentary sovereignty has been equated with national sovereignty, and also for France. While some member states might have difficulty in understanding Britain's commitment to the abstract ideal of parliamentary sovereignty, the practical costs affect them all.

The fact that EU legislation takes precedence over member state laws clearly affects the legislative freedom of the national parliaments. A further constraint imposed on the national parliaments is the 'opportunity cost' involved in processing EU laws. EU draft legislation must pass through the member state parliaments before it can be implemented. Parliamentary time must be set aside for this in both plenary sessions and committees. In Britain, concerns have also been expressed that the government may take advantage of EU draft legislation to by-pass the normal channels of parliamentary scrutiny. Here, the convention is to pass EU proposals without amendment. It has been suggested that governments may occasionally have added details of their own before presenting the drafts to parliament, 'smuggling' their own provisions through under the cover of EU legislation.[12]

Governments too are being diverted from domestic concerns towards European concerns. The work of the Council of Ministers has expanded tremendously in recent years and makes increasing demands on the time of government ministers and top civil servants in the member states. A member state is particularly overburdened when it holds the presidency of the Council. Also, national governments have been reluctant to let the 'supranational' institutions of the EU (particularly the Commission) gain control of decisions which directly affect their citizens' interests. To avoid this, they have been determined to involve themselves wherever possible in the decision-making process. They have contributed to a bewildering maze of committees and specialist working parties concerned with the details of legislative proposals and their implementation. Ministries have increasingly resorted to forging direct contacts with the ministries of other member states, often by-passing the EU institutions altogether. These developments are stretching the resources of the national governments and are potentially damaging to the efficiency of the EU.

The work of the ECJ is contributing to the 'judicialisation' of politics noted in Chapter 9. The ECJ works increasingly closely with the courts of the member states. If a national court is conducting a case and requires the clarification of an item of EU law, it may (or, under certain circumstances, must) request a 'preliminary ruling' from the ECJ. The ECJ does not decide the case itself, but gives the national court the ruling it needs to arrive at a judgment. Preliminary rulings now comprise the largest category of cases undertaken by the ECJ. This practice helps to promote the authority of the ECJ within the member states. It also contributes to the standardisation of legal rulings even in those areas outside the direct reach of EU law. Preliminary rulings may in effect invalidate member state law, if the latter is found to contravene the Treaties of the EU (Weiler 1994:515). This applies even to those countries where the home courts may not challenge their own parliaments' laws, such as Britain and the Netherlands.

The EU has also had an impact on the subnational level of government: the *Länder*, regions and local authorities of the member states. The regional and social structural funds of the EU have attracted applications from regional and local authorities in the member states. In order to pursue their claims, subnational authorities have set up a lobbying network aimed at Brussels. The Committee of the Regions established by the Maastricht Treaty has given representatives of the regional and local authorities direct access to decision-making in the EU. Many have established offices in Brussels. Until the recent constitutional revision in Belgium and the accession of Austria in 1995, Germany was the only federal state in the Community. Membership proved problematic for the *Länder*. As the policy reach of the EC expanded, it was encroaching more and more on those policy areas falling under the competence of the *Länder*. In exchange for ratification of the Single European Act, the *Länder* demanded (via the Bundesrat) that the federal government consult them in future over any policy plans concerning the EU.

National and multinational pressure groups, firms and quangos are also learning to lobby the EU. Currently though, they cannot afford to neglect their national contacts. In Britain, for example, recent key policy developments such as privatisation, the restructuring of the health and education services and trade-union reform have been dominated by national government rather than the EU. Even if the policy reach of the EU should expand to cover more areas of economic and social life, it is likely that the EU will still depend on national and subnational governments for the implementation of its decisions (Mazey and Richardson 1993:246–9).

Membership of the EU and the future direction of European integration have become issues in the national political life of the member states. In Britain, ideas about the proper role of the EU have cut across party lines, at times posing a very real threat to party cohesion. Disagreements over Europe were a contributory factor in the split in the Labour Party which led to the formation of the SDP in 1981. Margaret Thatcher's leadership of the Conservative party foundered over Europe. John Major won his leadership on his promise to hold the party together over Europe and faced repeated challenges over his ability to do so. In some countries, single-issue parties concerned with the EU have formed to contest European elections. In Denmark, two anti-Maastricht groupings, the People's Movement against the EU and the June Movement, won over 25 per cent of the vote in the June 1994 European election. At the same election, two French parties also made a good showing: the pro-European Radical Energy and the anti-European Other Europe.

The European Union in the 1990s

The 'democratic deficit'

The EU faces a number of challenges as it works to consolidate the reforms of the Single European Act and the Maastricht Treaty. One problem which has caused growing concern since the 1980s is the EU's 'democratic deficit': decision-making powers are being transfered from the member state parliaments to EU institutions which are not democratically accountable. There are two aspects to this problem. One is that institutional checks on EU decision-making are inadequate. The other concerns public perceptions of an elitist EU, out of touch with the realities of life in the member states.

Within the EU, executive and legislative functions are not divided between a government and parliament according to a traditional parliamentary model of government. Instead, they are largely shared between the Commission, the Council of Ministers and the European Council. As the EU has no single 'executive', it is difficult to control by the traditional means of parliamentary scrutiny or a constitutional court. The Commission, which fulfils some of the EU's key executive functions, is a non-elected body and operates behind closed doors. Although members of the Council of Ministers are elected at the national level, they have more freedom of action than would the members of a national government. By convention, Council meetings have been considered confidential. This means that the government ministers who take part in them are not bound by the usual principle of ministerial accountability. While unanimous voting was the norm, national parliaments could reasonably hold their government representatives to account for failing to exercise their veto. However, qualified majority voting has increased since the 1980s, giving the national parliaments less of a hold on their ministers' actions in the Council. Government ministers have sometimes returned with conflicting reports of Council discussions, adding to concerns about the lack of transparency in Council decision-making.

The media has brought to public attention the problems of fraud, mismanagement and corruption within the EU. The Common Agricultural Policy and the regional aid funds are particularly difficult to police. Experts suggest that fraud and mismanagement within these funds cost the EU as much as one tenth of its total budget expenditure in 1993 (*The Economist*, 19 November 1994). The Maastricht Treaty obliges member states to take the same measures to counter fraud against the EU as they would against fraud affecting their own national financial interests, but, so far, little effort has been made to comply with this.

The EP has consistently argued for greater legislative, budgetary and supervisory powers to redress the institutional imbalance in the EU. However, there is no evidence that a stronger parliament would, in itself, solve the problem of democratic deficit. Most Europeans tend to see the EP as part of the problem rather than as part of the solution (Dinan 1994:259). Members of the EP enjoy generous allowances and some have flamboyant life-styles. Together with the fact that plenary sessions of the EP are often poorly attended, this does little to engender public respect. Low turnouts at European elections are indicative of the weak ties between the EU and the European electorate.

Ironically, although the Single European Act and the Maastricht Treaty contained measures to improve accountability within the EU, the way in which these treaties were concluded was in itself an example of the lack of transparency in European decision-making. In Britain, the question of European integration had become central to John Major's position as prime minister. In consequence, media attention on the issues of the Maastricht summit was inevitable. Elsewhere, though, there was little public debate on the Maastricht Treaty at the negotiation stage. This left government leaders and bureaucrats free to decide its radical measures largely sheltered from the public eye. Public disapproval of the complacency of EU decision-makers became painfully evident when the Maastricht Treaty barely survived the ratification process in the member states.[13] The Maastricht ratification crisis seemed to alert government leaders to the need to secure public favour for further European integration. Initial steps have been taken to make EU decision-making more accessible to the public. The Council of Ministers now reveals how member states vote (although most measures do not come to a formal vote). At the Birmingham summit of 1992, member state governments promised to consider holding some open discussions of the Council of Ministers (Dinan 1994:246, 254).

'Widening' versus 'deepening'

The future path of European integration depends in part on its membership. Currently an organisation of fifteen members, the EU is considering the applications of several other countries to join. Turkey applied for membership in 1987, Cyprus and Malta in 1990 and Hungary and Poland in 1994.[14] Further applications can be expected from the former Soviet satellite states in central and eastern Europe. These countries are keen to enjoy free access to EU markets and the security involved in being part of a major international organisation. For the EU, though, the prospect of further enlargement is problematic. At a practical level, the current and prospective applicants would prove a drain on the EU's budget. In many cases, they lack a well-established tradition of liberal democracy. This raises questions of compatibility with the existing member states.

Also, the experience of past enlargements has shown that the more diverse the EU, the more difficult decision-making can be. There are already fears, for example, that a twenty-member Commission might prove difficult to manage. In particular, the Commission and some of the more 'integrationist' member states are concerned that widening the EU with additional members might only be possible at the expense of deepening it. Earlier enlargements brought in countries which did not share the founder members' hopes for closer integration. Britain, Denmark and Ireland, which joined in 1973, had a pragmatic interest in being part of a common market, but remain averse to moves towards supranationality in the EU. Austria, Sweden and Finland, members since 1995, have a tradition of neutrality which is likely to influence the future development of any common defence strategy.

One possibility is for the EU to pursue integration on a differential basis, for example as a 'two-speed' or 'two-tier' community. This type of development would imply an EU with a prominent and highly integrated core group of member states and a secondary, less well-integrated group. The secondary group might be expected to include member states such as Britain and Denmark which have always viewed European integration as essentially a matter for cooperation rather than the transfer of competences to a supranational authority. It might also include those member states which are relatively underdeveloped and would be unable to meet the stringent conditions for participation in the core group. For the stragglers in the secondary group, the fear would be that the core group might then become established in a position of superiority. Although Britain has consistently resisted calls for this type of development, the decision to opt out of the Social Chapter of the Maastricht Treaty and to avoid a commitment on joining EMU have created the potential for Britain to be left behind.

An ever closer union?

The Rome Treaty committed the founder members of the EEC to a continuing process of integration, with the aim of forging an 'ever closer union'. Since then, the member states have seen substantial convergence in those policy areas under the competence of the EU. In the late 1980s, the pace of integration was spurred on by commitments made in the Single European Act and the Maastricht Treaty. However, some doubt remains as to how realistic some of these commitments are. Is the integration process open-ended, or will the EU one day meet the limits of integration? The Maastricht Treaty has prepared the way for an extension of the EU's authority to encompass traditional symbols of nationhood such as citizenship, currency and defence. Will Germany give up the Deutschmark for a shared European currency, or France accept a shared defence policy? It remains to be seen whether the member states will really be prepared to merge their identities to this extent.

Notes

1 The Italian anti-fascist Altiero Spinelli drafted his manifesto for a free and united Europe in 1941. The central theme was that conflicts between separate sovereign states would inevitably lead to global war.
2 The OEEC was established in 1948 as a channel for Marshall Plan assistance from the United States. In 1958, it became the Organisation for Economic Cooperation and Development (OECD), which is concerned with international economic research and analysis. NATO was founded in 1949 as a defence union for the western world. Its membership included the United States and western Euro-

pean countries. The WEU was created in 1955 by a number of western European countries after the failure of plans for an EDC. Membership of the WEU allowed West Germany access to NATO in 1955. The Council of Europe was founded in 1949 with the aim of promoting unity among European states on the basis of respect for individual freedom, political liberty and the rule of law.

3 The other two European Communities were the EEC and the European Atomic Energy Community (Euratom), established in 1957 by two separate treaties, known as the Treaties of Rome. The governing institutions of these communities were merged by a treaty signed in Brussels in 1965, which came into force in 1967. Since then, the EEC has usually been referred to as the European Community (EC). The Maastricht Treaty, which came into force in 1993, established the European Union (EU).

4 The joint loyalties of the Commissioners can be illustrated by the reform of the Common Agricultured Policy (CAP) devised by the Irish Commissioner, Ray MacSharry. Agriculture is Ireland's chief policy concern as a member of the EU. Although the MacSharry reform proved unpopular in Ireland, Irish farmers could have fared a lot worse under a Commissioner from another country (Dinan 1994:212, 331–3).

5 While the SEM might yet fulfil its promise, its first year in operation was disappointing: the EC's GDP shrank by 0.3 per cent while unemployment rose to 10.5 per cent of its workforce (*The Economist*, 22 October 1994). The EU Commission's annual assessment of 1995 reported some outstanding problems for the completion of the SEM, including the continued border controls on people travelling; the absence of tax harmonisation in some areas; insufficient liberalisation of some sectors, particularly energy and telecommunications; and delays in adapting company law to the requirements of the SEM.

6 Member states may only proceed to EMU if their economies meet an agreed standard of strict 'convergence conditions'. These pertain to levels of inflation, budget deficits, exchange rate stability and long-term interest rates. Progress towards EMU is to be evaluated before the end of 1996 at an Intergovernmental Conference. Since these plans were agreed, a number of developments has thrown some doubt on the timetable for EMU established by the Maastricht Treaty. These include the crises in the Exchange Rate Mechanism (ERM) of the European Monetary System (EMS) in the early 1990s and economic recession throughout the member states.

7 At least, this is true in principle. In addition to the main business in hand, each Council usually approves the 'A points' on its agenda. COREPER vets proposals submitted to the Council and divides them into 'A points' and 'B points'. B points are politically sensitive issues which must be resolved at the level of the Council. A points are those which have been agreed at COREPER level and are expected to be passed by the Council without further discussion. In this way, a Council can find itself adopting measures outside its own area of competence. For example, in October 1992, the Fisheries Council adopted a directive on the protection of pregnant workers (Dinan 1994:247).

8 The Maastricht Treaty requires the European Council to submit to the EP a report after each of its meetings and a yearly written report on the progress achieved by the Union. This is the only formal constraint on the European Council's activities.

9 The cooperation procedure and the assent procedure were introduced by the Single European Act; the co-decision procedure by the Maastricht Treaty. Nugent (1994) gives a detailed account of each of these legislative procedures and of the circumstances in which they apply.

10 When the EP first used its new right to approve the proposed president and Commission in 1994–95, it chose to make a show of strength by threatening to veto the nominations in each case. The new president of the Commission, Jacques Santer, had been hurriedly put forward as a second choice after Britain had vetoed the favoured candidate, Jean-Luc Dehaene. The EP threatened to veto Santer, on the grounds that members had not been consulted adequately on his nomination. In the event, they gave him a grudging vote of approval in July 1994 of 260 votes to 238, with 23 abstentions. The first vote of investiture of the Commission was held in January 1995. The EP had objected to the appointment of five of the Commissioners, but eventually accepted the proposed Commission by a comfortable margin of 416 votes to 103, with 59 abstentions.

11 The unequal distribution of seats is intended to protect the interests of very small member states against larger ones. The same principle is behind the weighting of qualified majority votes in the Council of Ministers.

12 One claim was that out of some eighty supposedly European regulations affecting the catering industry, fewer than twenty originated

with the EU and the remainder were placed by the British government (Hearl 1994:526).

13 In every member state, the Maastricht Treaty had to be approved by
the national parliament before it could come into force. The constitutions of Ireland and Denmark also required the approval of the
people through a national referendum. In addition, President
Mitterrand of France chose to hold a referendum on the Treaty. He
fully expected the French to give it their overwhelming support
and hoped that this would revive the voters' enthusiasm for his
party, the Socialists. However, in their referendum of June 1992,
the Danish people voted against ratification of the Treaty by 50.7
per cent to 49.3 per cent. A package of concessions to Danish concerns was hastily assembled and a second referendum was held in
May 1993 to give the Danes another chance to get it right. This time
the vote approved the Treaty by 56.8 per cent to 43.2 per cent.
Meanwhile, changing domestic politics in France meant that the
referendum campaign of September 1992 was hard-fought. The
French approved ratification, but only by 51.05 per cent to 48.95
per cent. This whisker-fine majority was almost as embarrassing as
the Danish rejection of the Treaty. In Britain, the government took
until July 1993 to have the Treaty approved by a rather sceptical
House of Commons. Finally, the German Federal Constitutional
Court investigated the claim that ratification would infringe
the German Basic Law, ruling in favour of the Treaty in October
1993.

14 Norway has applied twice to join the Community, but each time the
country's application has been rejected by a popular referendum. In
1972, 53.4 per cent of the electorate voted against joining: in November 1994, the rejection was sealed by 52.2 per cent.

References

Cecchini, P. (1988) *The European Challenge: 1992*, Aldershot, Wildwood
House.

Dinan, D. (1994) *Ever Closer Union? An Introduction to the European
Community*, Basingstoke, Macmillan.

Hearl, D. (1994) 'Britain and Europe since 1945', *Parliamentary Affairs*,
47:4, 516–29.

Mazey, S. and J. Richardson (eds) (1993) *Lobbying in the European Community*, Oxford, Oxford University Press.

Nugent, N. (1994) *The Government and Politics of the European Community*, Basingstoke, Macmillan, 3rd edn.

Weiler, J. (1994) 'A quiet revolution. The European Court of Justice and its interlocutors', *Comparative Political Studies*, 26:4, 510–34.

Wincott, D. (1995) 'The role of law or the rule of the Court of Justice? An "institutional" account of judicial politics in the European Community', *Journal of European Public Policy*, 2:4, 583–602.

Further reading

Dinan, D. (1994) *Ever Closer Union? An Introduction to the European Community*, Basingstoke, Macmillan.

Nugent, N. (1994) *The Government and Politics of the European Community*, Basingstoke, Macmillan, 3rd edn.

Urwin, D. (1995) *The Community of Europe: A History of European Integration*, London, Longman, 2nd edn.

12

Democracy in western Europe: stability and political change

This book set out to explore the liberal democratic form of government as it has developed in the countries of western Europe. A number of shared principles define these countries as liberal democracies (see Chapter 2). The principle of representation has played a fundamental role in the western liberal tradition. The symbolic importance of representing the people continues to give parliaments a special place in the democracies of western Europe, in spite of the fact that MPs as individuals now have very limited influence on government. Particularly since the Second World War, two other democratic principles have gained in prominence and help to characterise a contemporary western European style of liberal democracy. One is constitutionalism, a concept which encompasses commitment to the rule of law; standard procedures of government; and 'balanced' government, where institutions of government check each other's authority in a way which avoids a concentration of executive power. The other is pluralism. In practice, pluralism is expressed through procedures such as the selection of political leaders through competitive elections, and the competition among pressure groups to influence the decision-makers. Within these broad preferences, each country of our study has developed its own unique form of democratic regime.

In Chapter 1 it was noted that liberal democracy in western Europe is not the inevitable end-product of our history. In the past, the countries of our study have known other forms of government – feudalism, absolutism, fascism – and will no doubt know new forms in the future. Neither is liberal democracy a perfect system. In practice, the countries of our study are not always true to their principles. One unusual feature of liberal democracy is that it is not blind to this fact. It is more tolerant of criticism than other forms of regime. In fact, within limits, it goes so far as to encourage internal criticism (see Budge 1994).

Self-criticism is perhaps unavoidable in any system which attempts to uphold principles such as the freedom of speech and association and competitive entry to positions of power. But what are its implications for the stability of the regime? It could be argued that to invite criticism of the values and procedures of the system is to lay it open to attack. Many of the countries of our study have experienced the vulnerability of democracy at first hand, when earlier attempts to set up a democratic regime were frustrated by overtly repressive forces. On the other hand, once established, democratic regimes can boast a high level of internal stability. They are seen as legitimate by the vast major-ity of their population and political leaders. Changes in govern-ment have been possible without civil war or the overthrow of the regime. The regime has not died out with the founding generation of political leaders, but has peaceably passed on to the next generation. It is possible that the faculty of self-criticism inherent in liberal democracy has contributed to its staying power in western Europe. No system of government can survive indefinitely without responding to changes in the society on which it is based. The fall of the communist GDR in 1989 offers a recent example of what can happen when a system of government stagnates and loses any legitimacy it once enjoyed.

Far from being an unqualified danger, then, it is possible that challenges to the system can help to revitalise a flagging political community. Of course, the challenges faced by liberal democra-cies are not always limited to the kind of self-criticism invited by pluralist structures of government. Some challenges come from outside. During the years of the cold war, for example, the liberal democratic regimes of the western alliance confronted the socialist regimes of the Soviet bloc in an ideological conflict with the potential to launch a global war. Others are internal challenges, but are not conducted within the terms laid down by the state. This chapter considers some of the challenges faced by western European liberal democracies in recent years. These include calculated attempts to change the regime or even to destroy it, new demands raised by changing societies, and the problems of new democracies. Taken together, they help to demonstrate the extent to which these countries have been able to meet challenges and accommodate new interests.

Political terrorism in western Europe

Terrorism involves the deliberate and systematic use of physical or psychological violence to intimidate others. In Europe, it has been used by various groups in an attempt to resolve political conflicts in their favour. Although only very small numbers of people have resorted to terrorism, it has been a recurrent problem for the countries of our study and has at times caused the widespread disruption of social and working life. Various grievances can motivate terrorism against the state, and three categories in particular have recently affected western Europe: extreme ideologies of the left and right; centre–periphery conflicts; and single-issue conflicts. A notable example of single-issue conflict inspiring terrorist violence is the campaign for animal rights as espoused in Britain by the Animal Liberation Front (ALF).[1]

All of these conflicts have been the focus of legal party or pressure group activity. It is not the conflict itself, then, that defines terrorist activity, but the method of violent intimidation. Terrorist action has included arson, bombings, kidnappings, hijackings and killings. The use of terrorism as a means to an end goes against some of the most fundamental principles of liberal democracy. It ignores all the procedural norms designed to regulate conflict in a non-arbitrary fashion. It disregards the rule of law, the usual representative channels of pressure groups and parties and the norm of majority rule. Moreover, terrorists have displayed a chilling lack of respect for the fundamental human rights of their victims.

Ideological conflicts: the example of the extreme left
The case of the extreme left serves as an example of ideologically motivated terrorism in western Europe. Marxist-Leninist terrorist organisations have operated in western Europe since 1970 in Belgium, France, Germany, Greece, Italy, Spain and Portugal.[2] These 'fighting communist organisations' were most active during two periods: 1977–81 and 1985–86. Their central aim was to overthrow the liberal democratic regimes of their respective countries and to launch a Marxist revolution. They believed that the traditional communist parties of western Europe had failed. In their view, radical action was needed to reveal the repressive nature of the capitalist, imperialist state and to promote the revolutionary consciousness among the proletariat that would ultimately lead to the overthrow of the capitalist system. In an attempt to educate the masses and secure their support, the fighting communist organisations have publicised their activities, issuing statements and distributing leaflets. In spite of these efforts, the only activists to gain a measure of public support were the Italian Red Brigades (RB). This success can be explained by conditions of profound uncertainty affecting Italy during the 1970s.[3]

Most of the attacks of the fighting communist organisations have been against people who are somehow symbolic of the capitalist state, including politicians, industrialists and judges. The most notorious attacks against individuals included the kidnapping and murder, in 1977, of Dr Hanns-Martin Schleyer, a German industrialist and economic adviser to Chancellor Helmut Schmidt. Likewise, in 1978, the leading Italian Christian democrat politician Aldo Moro was kidnapped and eventually killed by the RB when the government refused to accept their demands. The groups have been prone to ideological splits and disagreements over strategy. Typical conflicts have centred on whether to initiate international activity or restrict action to the group's home nation; whether the group should seek to lead the masses or simply work together with them; and the use and treatment of hostages.

During the mid-1980s, the groups began to forge alliances across national boundaries to fight what they perceived as the imperialist European regimes. Fears of a 'Euroterrorist' threat have declined since the extensive police operations of the 1980s succeeded in neutralising some of the key groups, but those still active have continued to collaborate with one another on a more piecemeal basis. In 1990, for example, the German Red Army Faction (RAF) engaged in several proxy operations on behalf of the Spanish First of October Anti-Fascist Resistance Groups (GRAPO). These involved arson attacks and acts of vandalism against Spanish financial interests in Germany (Alexander and Pluchinsky 1992:9).

The centre–periphery conflict and the European separatist groups

The centre–periphery conflict, which helped to define modern European politics, re-emerged in the 1970s in the context of economic recession, social modernisation and cultural revival (see Chapter 3). It was channelled largely through the legal activity of regional political parties, but in some countries also found an outlet through terrorism. The groups associated with regional terrorism are separatists seeking complete independence from their respective nation-state. They see themselves as the liberators of their territory from 'foreign' occupation. In this, they challenge the unity of the nation-state.

The countries most affected by regional terrorism are the UK (with respect to Northern Ireland), France (Corsica) and Spain (the Basque country). Some of the most significant separatist organisations to engage in terrorist acts over these territories have been the Irish Republican Army (IRA), the Corsican National Liberation Front (FLNC), and Basque Homeland and Liberty (ETA). The IRA and ETA have been supported in their respective regions by the legal political parties Sinn Fein and Herri Batasuna (Popular Unity). This gives them a propaganda and organisational advantage over those organisations lacking a legal political arm. The separatist groups have targeted the national police and the military, which they view as forces of occupation in their territory. Their attacks have been carried out mainly within the regions they seek to liberate and in the national capitals of London, Paris and Madrid. The operations in the national capitals have tended to be more indiscriminate, including attacks on civilian targets such as railway stations.

The state against terrorism

Since terrorism poses a direct threat to democratic government, democratic government must be expected to fight back. The problem for western European governments has been finding an adequate response without themselves breaching the principles and procedures of liberal democracy. On a practical level, terrorist action is cheap and easy to organise, but expensive and difficult to counter. Terrorist organisations can exploit the inherent civil rights and freedoms of the liberal state. These include freedom of movement within and between western European countries, freedom of association, freedom of the media (which ensures publicity for terrorist actions) and judicial and constitutional restraints on state action against terrorist suspects (see Wilkinson 1977:102–4). With these advantages, terrorist groups with only a handful of core activists have been able to cause widespread disruption.[4]

The terrorist groups have seen their activity as essentially political. However, western European governments have preferred to treat terrorism as criminal activity and have dealt with it largely as a problem of public order. In times of heightened terrorist activity, governments have tended to adopt a centralised response, setting up special government offices, anti-terrorist squads and new security procedures (see Allum 1995:521). This approach succeeded in neutralising some of the key groups, including the Fighting Communist Cells (CCC) of Belgium, Direct Action (DA) of France and the RB of Italy. However, it has not always prevented successor groups from emerging, some based on networks established in prison. Also, some critics have questioned this type of police action on the grounds that heightened security and surveillance measures have done more to erode democratic freedoms than to protect them.

The most comprehensive police action against terrorist activity was mounted in West Germany during the 1970s. At this time, the internal secret services and criminal investigation offices were substantially expanded and given special tasks related to terrorism. Computerised surveillance techniques were introduced, together with centralised data-processing systems. New laws designed to combat terrorism addressed issues such as the hijacking of aeroplanes, the kidnapping of adults and hostage taking. More controversial was the 1972 *Radikalenerlass* (Radicals' Decree), which stipulated that any individual suspected of extremist activities could be banned from employment in the civil service, a broad category of employees including teachers. Critics argued that the Radicals' Decree could lead to a witch-hunt and that the country was well on the way to becoming a 'surveillance state' where civil rights were subordinated to an inflated perception of security needs. It was the late 1970s before tensions began to relax.

In conjunction with police operations, governments have sometimes engaged in cautious (and mostly covert) negotiations with extremists, seeking to resolve conflicts on the state's terms by offering concessions which address a group's substantive concerns. For governments, the main problem with this approach has been how to stay in control. Governments must contrive to give concessions in such a way that they do not appear to be responding directly to terrorist intimidation. For this reason, any negotiation is usually accompanied by a 'ceasefire'. Another problem has been the refusal of some extremist groups to compromise in any way on their demands. In recent years, some of the most prominent European terrorist groups, including the RAF, the IRA and ETA, have signalled that they might be prepared to negotiate an end to the hostilities. To date, though, no negotiated settlement has been achieved.

What would the terrorists stand to gain by engaging in a dialogue with the state? One suggestion is that some terrorist organisations are finding their resources too stretched to carry on their guerrilla activities. Certainly, the fighting communist organisations would appear to be in decline. By the early 1990s, only three significant groups were active in western Europe: the RAF in Germany, GRAPO in Spain and the Revolutionary Organisation 17 November (17N) in Greece. However, these organisations are still capable of striking at the system: in 1991, the RAF killed Detlev Rohwedder, president of the *Treuhandanstalt*, a German government agency in charge of privatising former East German state-owned firms.

Even if the current extremist groups should agree to accommodation with the state, the problem of terrorism will not necessarily be resolved. Terrorism is not linked to any particular cause but is simply a means to an end, one which can take advantage of the conditions of liberal democracy. As new conflicts replace those of the 1970s and 1980s, fanatical supporters of new causes might take to terrorism. In many European countries, the recent revival of extreme right-wing ideologies has been accompanied by coordinated attacks on foreigners by extreme right-wing fringe groups. However, the experience of the 1970s and 1980s has also shown that mass publics have been alienated from terrorists' causes by their extreme views and violent means. These two features, inherent in terrorist activity, are perhaps the best defence against terrorist attempts to undermine the western European liberal democracies.

The 'new social movements'

Social movements can be described as a conscious attempt to bring about a change in values in society and to have these new values reflected in national politics: an attempt which attracts some mass support. Social movements rarely last for long. Historically, they have tended to emerge at times of social upheaval or rebellion against established political elites, only to dissolve when a measure of consensus is restored. The demands of social movements are sometimes accommodated by the system, sometimes ignored. Occasionally, they can help to bring about regime change. The 'peaceful revolution' of 1989 in the GDR is a good illustration of this. Isolated groups of activists campaigning for civic rights attracted mass support, which led to a general rebellion against the values and structures of the communist state. Consensus was restored with German unification. The civic rights campaigners, whose demands were recognised but partly submerged by other unification issues, have since been relegated to a relatively marginal role in east German politics.

Throughout the period from the late 1960s to the early 1980s, social movements were particularly active across western Europe. The ideologies and issues which prompted protest action included feminism, nuclear disarmament and peace, and environmentalism (the 'green' movement). These 'new social movements' challenged their liberal democratic states in different ways. At the height of their activity, they posed a challenge to public order through their unconventional protest tactics. (Unlike terrorist tactics, these aimed largely to disrupt and attract attention rather than to destroy and intimidate.) Taken together, the movements shared a common outlook which amounted to an attack on the values of the western European democracies. In particular, they demanded a new interpretation of democracy. They wanted to promote individual participation in political decision-making in place of 'ritual' political activity, often limited to voting. This was a challenge to representative democracy, which rests on established channels of representation through parties and parliaments.

The feminist movement

The feminist movement that emerged in western Europe in the 1960s to 1970s was divided into two branches: the women's rights movement and the women's liberation movement. The women's rights movement had its historical roots in the suffrage movement at the turn of the twentieth century, which secured women's right of access to education and to professional qualifications. In the 1960s and 1970s, this branch of the feminist movement was particularly successful in France and Britain. At this time, the women's rights movement was concerned with promoting gender equality – that is, the same rights as men to work and participate in society. Women's rights activists tried to secure political reforms largely by traditional methods, often working through political parties and trade unions.[5] In contrast, adherents of the women's liberation movement adopted the idea of gender difference. Their aim was to develop a feminist counter-culture. For them, influencing the political establishment took second place to changing women's attitudes. The women's liberation movement was organised at the grassroots level and its campaigns were conducted through mass protests.

The feminist movement did succeed in starting an ongoing public debate on women's role in society, even if their values were accorded rather limited recognition within national politics. One area in which they were successful was in their demand for easier access to abortion. After a period of intense and emotive debate, abortion laws were passed in most western European countries between 1975 and 1985. It is perhaps an indication of the success of feminist attempts to change people's attitudes that it is now 'politically correct' to recognise women's issues. In their efforts to demonstrate their awareness, many political parties have now adopted a stance on women's issues. In this, parties of the left have been most responsive to feminist influence; only parties of the far right have been openly hostile. However, some feminists feel that parties are only paying lip-service to women's issues, are using feminist ideas for their own purposes, or have failed to reflect their ideas accurately.

In the 1970s and 1980s, the women's rights movement made its mark through the introduction of a range of state bodies to promote gender equality. Britain set up the Equal Opportunities Commission; France a ministry for women's rights; and Spain a Women's Rights Institute. This was the first institutionalisation of the gender conflict in the political systems of these countries. Some feminists doubted the value of the new institutions, believing that working through 'the system' might rob the women's lobby of its radicalism. Also, the French experience has shown that concessions made to feminism need not last. In France, the representation of women's issues has been strongly tied to the success of the PS. In sum, the democracies of western Europe accommodated feminist demands largely on their own terms. They made concessions on abortion law, an area in which there was wide public support for the feminist case. The political parties adopted a broadly supportive, if unspecific, stance on women's issues, and those in government made minor institutional adjustments to accommodate this 'new' interest.

The green movement

The green movement has taken a rather different course. In contrast to the feminist movement, which remained fragmented, the green movement extended its organisation to the national level in order to strengthen its political impact. This began with the formation of umbrella organisations of green activists. In 1971, the French group Amis de la Terre was formed; and in 1972, the West German Bundesverband Bürgerinitiativen Umweltschutz (BBU). Concern over the use of nuclear energy helped further to consolidate the green movement. After the 1970s oil crisis, many European governments decided to expand their civil nuclear energy programmes. Green activists found this alarming, because of both the potential for accidents and the chance that civil nuclear capacity might later be diverted to military uses. As energy policy is decided at the national level of government, the nuclear energy issue was a catalyst for the formation of national environmentalist protest lobbies. In the late 1970s, these concerns were compounded by the NATO dual-track decision on intermediate nuclear forces and the eventual stationing of cruise missiles and Pershing II in western Europe. In many countries, peace activists and environmentalists joined forces over the issue of nuclear power, creating a broad-based movement with links with other countries. The scale and organisation of these movements helped them to attract and channel considerable public support at key moments in their campaigns.

In the early 1980s, most green movements tried to persuade the socialists or social democrats in their national parliaments to take up their proposals. The anti-nuclear and environmentalist factions within the socialist parties were prepared to voice concerns over these issues, but the greens' more radical demands found no sympathy among the socialists or any other party. The main sticking point was the greens' claim that long-term environmental security could only be guaranteed if western nations were prepared to limit their economic growth. The established political parties have always seen constant economic growth as the key to improving the quality of life of the population and thereby to maintaining their support at elections. Finding their efforts blocked, many of the European green movements decided to set up their own parties to pursue their interests (see Chapter 3).

While these parties have rarely been in a position to influence government directly, their presence in European party systems has helped to secure prominence for green issues. Traditional parties in government have been most responsive to self-contained environmentalist proposals: for example, to ban the use of lead in petrol. They have been least responsive to proposals with more far-reaching implications over cost, security interests or ideology. The formation of green political parties has ensured that green issues have had a more consistent and lasting influence on western European politics than those of the movements which did not translate into party politics. Nevertheless, public interest in green issues is less intense now than it was in the 1980s. There are several explanations for this. The greens have already secured recognition within national politics for environmental protection, so there is less need for citizen protests. The nuclear issue appears less pressing. A decade has passed since the Chernobyl accident and there is less mass support for campaigns against the use of civil nuclear energy; the cold war ended with the collapse of the Soviet bloc. Some green parties have discredited themselves by fierce internal divisions which have made them seem ineffective. Also, the return of economic recession appears to have refocused the interests of European publics on material interests rather than the future quality of life.

The new social movements and the 'new politics'

Some theorists have argued that the shared outlook of the new social movements amounted to a new set of values, a 'new politics',which differed fundamentally from the 'old politics' of the established liberal democracies.[6] The 'old politics' values were a product of the years immediately following the Second World War, and included a desire for material security, to be achieved through sustained economic growth; law and order; rigorous national security; and traditional, family-based lifestyles. These values were articulated by the established political parties of western Europe. The characteristic values of 'new politics' were environmental quality; social equality; alternative lifestyles; minority rights; and direct, individual participation in political decision-making. These value priorities were those of a younger generation which had been sheltered from material hardship and had enjoyed the benefits of improving educational provision in post-war Europe.

While the liberal democracies of western Europe made some concessions to the substantive concerns of the new social movements, there was relatively little accommodation of the new values these movements advocated. In part this was because they did not strike the same chord with mass publics as did the more tangible aims of abortion on demand and fighting environmental pollution. In addition, the values of the 'new politics' came into conflict with the theory or practice of liberal democracy. One example has been noted above: that is, the conflict between the greens' vision of future quality of life and the traditional parties' perceived need for constant economic growth. The same goes for the demand for more grassroots democracy and more active participation in the political process. Established parties and political bodies would not stand to gain from mass participation. Western European government is based on an elite view of democracy. This assumes that active participation in the process of government should be limited to a small group of political leaders, and that mass participation might lead to instability.

Immigration: towards a multicultural Europe

Unlike terrorism and social movements, immigration does not represent a conscious, direct challenge to the values or political institutions of western Europe. Indirectly, though, it poses one of the most far-reaching collective challenges currently faced by the countries of our study. Since the Second World War, long-term immigration has been steadily changing the national, ethnic and cultural balance of the population in western European countries. By 1991, there were around 15.4 million legally resident foreigners in the countries of western Europe (see Table 12.1, which excludes asylum-seekers). In addition, some 2.6 million were living there illegally. Of the legal immigrants, 8 million were non-EU citizens and 4.3 million were Muslim (Böhning 1991: 449).

As the population diversifies, the potential for conflicts of interest in society grows. The governments of western Europe must reconcile the interests of foreign residents with those of the indigenous population. Since the mid-1970s, two arguments have been put forward against mass immigration. One is that immigrants contribute little to the economy, but place a burden on welfare services and housing. The other is that immigration threatens the national identity and civic culture of a country. This argument draws attention to cultural and religious differences between the indigenous communities of the host countries and immigrant communities. Muslims in particular are seen by some as a threat to the Christian basis of modern European society. Recent research suggests that both of these arguments are flawed (see Hollifield 1992). Nevertheless, they can appear plausible, and have formed the basis of conflicts between foreign and indigenous communities in western European countries. They have been developed and 'politicised' by the parties of the far right, such as the national front parties of Britain (1970s) and France (1980s), the German Republicans and the *Überfremdung* movement of Switzerland. At times, these parties have been permitted to set the terms of political debate on immigration. Parties of the far right use immigrants as

Table 12.1 Inflows of foreign populations into western Europe, excluding asylum-seekers (in thousands)

	1981	1982	1983	1984	1985	1986	1987	1988	1989	1990	1991
Belgium	41.3	36.2	34.3	37.2	37.5	39.3	40.1	38.2	43.5	50.5	54.1
France[a]	75.0	144.4	64.2	51.4	43.4	38.3	39.0	44.0	53.2	102.4	109.9
Germany[b]	451.7	275.5	253.5	295.8	324.4	378.6	414.9	545.4	649.5	649.3	664.4
Luxemb.	6.9	6.4	6.2	6.0	6.6	7.4	8.2	9.1	9.1	10.3	..
Neths.	49.6	39.7	34.4	34.7	40.6	46.9	47.4	50.8	51.5	60.1	62.7
Norway	13.0	13.9	13.0	12.5	14.1	13.8	15.2	16.4	14.0	11.7	11.5
Sweden	..	..	18.3	14.1	13.4	19.4	19.0	24.9	28.9	23.9	17.4
Switz.	80.3	74.7	58.3	58.6	59.4	66.8	71.5	76.1	80.4	101.4	109.8
UK	59.1	53.9	53.5	51.0	55.4	47.8	46.0	49.3	49.7	52.4	53.9

Source: Système d 'Observation Permanente sur les Migrations (1994:188, Table A.2).

[a] The way in which immigration was recorded in France changed in 1990. Before 1990, the figures include permanent workers, holders of provisional work permits and family reunification. As of 1990, they include spouses of French nationals, parents of French children, refugees, self-employed and others eligible for a residence permit, but exclude provisional work permits.

[b] 'Germany' refers to West Germany until 1990 and to the united Germany from 1991.

scapegoats for economic recession and problems of law and order.

Immigrants can be classified according to their motivation in entering another country and the status awarded them by this 'host' country. They may arrive looking for work (labour migration); to join family members already living in the host country (family reunification); or to escape political persecution in their own country (asylum-seekers). Assuming that they meet the current criteria for entry into the host country, these newcomers are classified as legal immigrants. Those who do not meet the entry requirements or whose applications are considered but turned down may attempt to live in the host country as illegal immigrants.[7] Since the 1980s, new developments in immigration have led western European governments to address a wide range of issues linked to immigration, including economic policies, asylum policy, electoral rights, social policy, security issues and civil rights. The current trend is for governments to perceive immigration as a serious problem and to take action to restrict it. In contrast, the national constitutional courts, acting on international agreements to protect human rights, have tended to uphold the rights of asylum-seekers, resident foreign workers and their families against attempts at more aggressive government policies to oust them.

New trends in mass immigration: asylum-seeking and illegal immigration

Since the 1980s, two forms of immigration, asylum-seeking and illegal immigration, have taken on mass proportions which are causing problems for western European governments. Immigration in these categories had been rising over a long period because of continued population growth and economic weakness in the developing countries of Africa and Asia. This is expected to contribute to migration into Europe for decades to come. Also, in the late 1980s, the political changes in central and eastern Europe created widespread economic uncertainty and a rise in nationalist feeling, spilling over into civil war in the former Yugoslavia. These pressures sent thousands to nearby western borders, particularly to Germany, and, to a lesser extent, Austria and Sweden. With the exception of Germany and Sweden, statistics from 1992 and the start of 1993 suggest that immigration into Europe has reached a peak, but it is too early to be certain (SOPEMI 1994:13).

The countries of western Europe have traditionally offered a safe haven to refugees and asylum-seekers fleeing political persecution. Belgium, Sweden, Switzerland and (West) Germany were especially popular because of their liberal asylum policies and good employment prospects. Until the mid-1980s, western European countries could afford to make a show of generosity as the numbers seeking asylum were modest. However, in the ten years from 1981 the annual number of asylum applications to European countries increased five-fold, exceeding half a million in 1991 (see Table 12.2), making asylum-seeking the largest single category of immigration to Europe (Coleman 1993:57). Illegal immigration had been widespread in western Europe throughout the post-war period. By definition, it is difficult to determine its scale, but there has been evidence of a recent upsurge in numbers. This can be explained in part by restrictions on legal labour immigration and by the growth and high failure rate of asylum applications.[8]

Government action against illegal immigration and the misuse of asylum provisions

By the early 1990s, concern about the numbers of asylum-seekers and illegal immigrants led governments to take action. One aim was to restore asylum provisions to their original purpose: that is, a refuge against political persecution rather than an alternative route to working abroad. New legal and administrative measures were adopted to this end. These included the tightening of border controls, stricter visa requirements, and sanctions against airlines which carry passengers without the required documents. Refugees arriving from countries deemed 'safe countries of origin' are no longer granted the status of asylum-seekers. Accordingly, some western European countries have recently refused entry to refugees from Romania, Poland

Table 12.2 Inflows of asylum-seekers into western Europe (thousands)

	1981	1982	1983	1984	1985	1986	1987	1988	1989	1990	1991	1992[a]
Austria	34.6	6.3	5.9	7.2	6.7	8.6	11.4	15.8	21.9	22.8	27.3	16.2
Belgium	2.4	3.1	2.9	3.7	5.3	7.6	6.0	4.5	8.1	13.0	15.4	17.6
Denmark	0.3	0.3	0.3	4.3	8.7	9.3	2.7	4.7	4.6	5.3	4.6	13.9
Finland	:	:	:	:	:	0.1	0.1	0.1	0.2	2.7	2.1	3.6
France	19.8	22.5	22.3	21.6	28.8	26.2	27.6	34.3	61.4	54.8	47.4	28.9
Germany	49.4	37.2	19.7	35.3	73.8	99.7	57.4	103.1	121.3	193.1	256.1	438.0
Greece	:	:	0.5	0.8	1.4	4.3	6.3	9.3	6.5	4.1	2.7	2.0
Italy	:	:	3.1	4.6	5.4	6.5	11.0	1.4	2.3	3.6	24.5	2.6
Netherlands	0.8	1.2	2.0	2.6	5.6	5.9	13.5	7.5	13.9	21.2	21.6	17.1
Norway	0.1	0.1	0.2	0.3	0.8	2.7	8.6	6.6	4.4	4.0	4.6	5.2
Portugal	0.6	0.4	0.6	0.2	0.1	0.1	0.2	0.3	0.1	0.1	0.2	0.6
Spain	:	:	1.4	1.1	2.3	2.8	3.7	4.5	4.1	8.6	8.1	11.7
Sweden	:	:	4.0	12.0	14.5	14.6	18.1	19.6	30.0	29.4	26.5	83.2
Switzerland	5.2	7.1	7.9	7.4	9.7	8.5	10.9	16.7	24.4	35.8	41.6	18.1
UK	2.4	4.2	4.3	4.2	6.2	5.7	5.9	5.7	16.8	38.2	67.0	–

Source: Système d'Observation Permanente sur les Migrations (1994:188, Table A.3).
[a] Provisional data.

and the Czech Republic. Steps have also been taken to speed up the processing of asylum applications. Britain, Switzerland and France have concentrated on reducing a backlog of applications. Since July 1993, German immigration police on duty at the borders may determine who is eligible to apply for refugee status.[9] Sanctions against employers of illegal immigrant labour have been tightened in Belgium, France and Germany and are being considered elsewhere.

It is now recognised that no country in western Europe can take action on immigration without affecting its neighbours, and some efforts have been made to coordinate immigration policies between countries. In 1990, for example, the EC countries (except Denmark) agreed to harmonise the procedures for registering asylum requests to prevent multiple applications. One problem in coordinating immigration policies has been the uneven distribution of new arrivals across western Europe. Whereas some countries, including Britain, have seen only modest increases, others have been faced with a massive increase (see Tables 12.1 and 12.2). Germany stands out as the country which has borne the brunt of the explosion of asylum-seekers in the early 1990s. In 1992, the number of asylum applications registered in Germany (438,000) exceeded the number for that year in all the other European OECD countries combined.[10] Governments have recently made bilateral arrangements to spread the load by applying the principle of 'safe countries of first asylum'. Refugees are expected to make application for asylum in the first country they enter which respects democratic principles and is a party to the Geneva Convention on Refugees. If they pass through this country to apply in a more popular destination, they may be returned to the first 'safe' country.

Promoting the integration of foreigners
Mass immigration in western Europe has been explained as the combined result of thriving markets (which attract labour) and the protected position of foreigners in regimes which uphold basic rights (Hollifield 1992:216, 222). This suggests that as long as the countries of western Europe keep their place in the world

economy and their liberal democratic identity, government attempts to restrict immigration flows will meet with only limited success. While trying to control the rate of fresh immigration into Europe, governments are now attempting to promote the integration of those foreigners already living in their country. This move is intended to reduce the potential for conflict between indigenous and immigrant communities. France, Italy, Spain and Portugal have introduced 'regularisation' policies to enable illegal immigrants to come out of hiding. (Germany has been reluctant to follow this course, arguing that it might encourage other refugees to enter Europe illegally.) Since the early 1980s, naturalisation laws have been amended, generally making it easier for long-term foreign residents and second-generation immigrants to become citizens of their host countries.[11] In spite of the hostility which has sometimes erupted between foreign and indigenous communities, there are signs that foreigners are becoming integrated into their host societies.[12]

Transitions to democracy

For all its flaws, democracy as a principle and system of government has been gaining ground throughout Europe over the last 200 years. There have been reversals as well as gains for democracy, but, since the Second World War, all of the western European countries have managed to consolidate democratic regimes. The more recent cases include the post-war re-establishment of democracy by Allied occupation in Austria, West Germany and Italy. In these countries, democracy has since developed under internal leadership. Of the three, only Italy is now experiencing difficulty in securing functioning democratic institutions which command the respect of the people. Here, it is not the principle of democracy which is in question, but the legitimacy of the current system (see the appendix). Spain, Portugal and Greece have all had experience of authoritarian rule since the Second World War and have only established their current democratic regimes since the mid-1970s. Since 1988, the countries of central and eastern Europe have also begun transitions to democracy.

Although these attempts demonstrate an increasingly wide acceptance of democratic ideals, they also show that forging a democratic society and system of government is a long and arduous process, and one which is not guaranteed to succeed. There are indications that central and eastern European countries will find it more difficult to establish themselves as democracies than did the western European countries in the immediate post-war period and the 1970s. For the eastern transitions, problem areas include economic adjustment to market conditions, popular acceptance of the new regimes, cultural adjustment and possibly misguided attempts by the west to steer the course of democratisation.

The success of West Germany's post-war consolidation of democracy owed much to the speedy recovery of the economy. International aid served as a basis for recovery and the economic policy known as the 'social market economy' quickly gained the support of the people. The resulting economic upturn helped to legitimise the new political structures of the Federal Republic. Recent research has shown that public support for democratisation in eastern Europe is based less on current satisfaction with the new regimes than on two other factors: fears of a return to a more repressive system and the anticipation of a satisfactory economic system in the foreseeable future (Mishler and Rose 1993). This suggests that a successful economy could have a similar legitimising effect in eastern democracies to that experienced in post-war West Germany.

Unlike the West German case, though, the central and eastern European countries were based on Soviet-style state-controlled economies immediately before their transitions. In these countries, the task of establishing democratic structures of government is complicated by the need to carry through a simultaneous reform of the economy to establish a free market (termed 'marketisation'). In practice, marketisation is resulting in widespread hardship as people adjust to new problems such as unemployment in the absence of adequate welfare provision. The question is whether satisfactory economic recovery can be achieved quickly enough to avert widespread disillusionment with democracy, thereby giving democratic institutions time to become established. Rapidly changing conditions in the countries of central and eastern Europe make it very difficult to judge what will happen. The cautiously optimistic note that the experience of socialist regimes has given their populations reserves of patience which would not be readily understood in the west and which might prove a stabilising factor as these countries edge their way towards a functioning democratic system (see Mishler and Rose 1993:24–8). Others hope for success, but stress that marketisation is only one of many serious problems faced by central and eastern European countries in transition (Pridham *et al.* 1994).

Gaining the confidence of the people might prove to be more difficult for the new eastern democracies than it was for the new western post-war and Mediterranean democracies. The western would-be democracies shared more of the liberal democratic tradition. They could look to the established western European countries for their model of democracy. In the east, there is no real certainty over the type of democracy to aim for. In common with many regimes in transition, notable elements in society remain indifferent or hostile to democratisation. Recent opinion polls conducted in ten central and eastern European countries reveal a wide range of different attitudes towards the new democratic regimes.

Only in the Czech Republic did a majority of respondents (63 per cent) show a clear commitment to democracy in that they both expressed approval of their new democratic regime and disapproval of the former communist regime. Nowhere were the 'reactionaries' in the majority (those who disapproved of the new regime and preferred the former communist system), but in Belarus this category comprised 48 per cent of respondents, and in Ukraine 43 per cent. In addition to the 'democrats' and 'reactionaries', the survey identified two further categories of respondent: the 'sceptics' and the 'compliant'. Respondents in these categories shared a lack of commitment either to the old or the new regime: sceptics expressed dissatisfaction with both and the compliant gave a positive evaluation of both. Only in two countries did the response in these two categories fall below 40 per cent (29 per cent in the Czech Republic and 39 per cent in Belarus). Elsewhere, these categories comprised between 41 per cent and 52 per cent of respondents (Rose and Haerpfer 1994).

For regimes in transition, mass indifference can be very dangerous, as there is always the possibility that the indifferent might be swayed against the new regime. It is particularly dangerous when, as in eastern Europe, a substantial minority of reactionaries remains active and the democratisation process lacks direction. In comparison with these countries, Spain had a relatively clear view of its democratic aims and yet it has fallen prey to a number of attempted coups during the consolidation of democratic rule. Opinion polls can only give a snapshot view of a country's political life. In times of rapid change, their value lies less in their specific findings than in their anticipation of potential trends. While the process of democratisation in central and eastern Europe seems to have gained momentum, these findings show that it might take different paths in different countries and that its outcome cannot be guaranteed.

The USA and established western democracies have taken an active interest in democratisation in Europe, first in the western and now in the central and eastern European countries. During the cold war years, this interest stemmed in part from a desire to have the basic values of democracy affirmed. Their level of interest and willingness to intervene have also depended on the particular strategic and security interests concerned. As far as the democratising states are concerned, western attempts to sponsor democracy have proved a mixed blessing.

The western allies of the Second World War sponsored and closely supervised the early stages of the West German and Italian transitions. In the context of the cold war, it was considered essential that these countries should align themselves with the west. Italy occupied a strategic position in the Mediterranean and West Germany bordered on the Soviet-controlled GDR. In Italy, American and Soviet interference during 1947–48 helped to sour relations between the main political forces of the left and right and entrench a lasting cold war mentality which was later to prove damaging for the country's stability. The USA 'won' the allegiance of Italy for the western block by giving financial assistance to the Christian Democrats. In effect, this secured the permanent dominance of the centre-right in Italian politics. In spite of a significant level of popular support for the communist left, there was no alternation of government, which eventually became a source of malfunctioning in Italy's system. These problems should be kept in perspective. In the immediate post-war period, the main priorities for the countries of Europe were stability and security. It is impossible to say what problems the sensitive territories of West Germany and Italy might have experienced had there been no outside intervention at this time.

As far as central and eastern Europe is concerned, there is a danger that misplaced attempts to 'encourage' democracy might destroy respect for constitutionalism. It may be that some of the standard features of a western liberal democracy are inappropriate to the culture or circumstances of an emerging eastern European democracy. The imposition of multi-party systems, for example, which have done so much to contain conflicts in the West, might serve only to escalate the deep ethnic conflicts in areas of central Europe and the Balkans (Rengger 1994: 68–73). While the central and eastern European countries are taking steps to join western European organisations such as the Council of Europe and the EU, there is a danger that delays in forging such links, combined with a resurgence of ethnic nationalism, might dissuade some countries from wider European contacts in favour of more localised allegiances.[13] The international military involvement in the former Yugoslavia has certainly done little to promote confidence in western organisations.

Democracy in western Europe: adaptation and accommodation

In spite of the challenges and setbacks discussed in this chapter, democracy has proved a workable system of government for the countries of western Europe. Perhaps its greatest strength has been its capacity for responsiveness and evolution. The post-war communist parties of western Europe serve as an example of the way in which democratic government has 'domesticated' internal opposition without state repression. After the Second World War, communist parties were vociferous opponents of liberal democracy and market economy and advocated revolutionary change. In spite of ideological views which were inimical to the post-war western order, many countries included them in democratic procedures, allowing them to compete in elections and take up seats in parliaments or councils. This enabled communist parties to represent an often significant sector of society, which in turn helped to legitimise the democratic regime.

In time, both the rhetoric and actions of electorally significant communist parties showed that these had become reconciled to pursuing their policy aims within the framework of liberal democracy. In France, for example, the PCF did not take advantage of the 1968 student unrest to launch a revolutionary attack on the regime. In the early 1980s the PCF was briefly involved in a coalition government with the socialist PS. While this proved an unhappy experience for the PCF, it did nothing to threaten the integrity of liberal democracy in France. Despite the revolutionary Marxist rhetoric of the 1976 Portuguese constitution, party competition in this country has since been dominated by the centre-left PS and the centre-right PSD. In 1989, Portugal's constitution was revised to remove the state's commitment to Marxist principles. In Italy, since the corruption scandals of 1993, the reformed communist PDS has played an important role in acting as a stabilising force in the party system and in promoting democratic reform (see the appendix).

While some European countries have undergone a transition to democracy in the post-war period, some of the longer-established democracies have also experienced dramatic change. One of the most remarkable of these 'transitions within democracy' has been Belgium's phased transition from a 'unitary decentralized state' to a federal state (Alen and Ergec 1994). This process, begun in 1970 and completed in 1993, was a constitutional reform which evolved in response to mounting conflicts between Belgium's main linguistic communities, Flemish and Walloon. Given the strength of feeling within the communities and the fragmented nature of Belgian party politics, the peaceful resolution of the conflicts through a new constitutional consensus was a remarkable achievement. It owed much to the efforts of Wilfried Martens, prime minister almost continuously from 1979 to 1992, and his successor, Jean-Luc Dehaene. The bilingual King Baudouin, who reigned from 1951 to his death in 1993, was an integrating force during the years of constitutional uncertainty.

The collapse of the Soviet bloc after 1988 pushed Germany into the most extraordinary process of state transition in Europe since the Second World War: the 1990 unification of the Federal Republic of Germany with the GDR. Many aspects of the unification process did not bode well for the future social and political stability of the new Germany. It was not a merger of equals. The circumstances of 1989–90 allowed West Germany to absorb the smaller East Germany largely on its own terms. The new eastern *Länder* of the federation are considerably poorer than their western counterparts. How long eastern Germans must wait to enjoy a standard of living equal to those in the west remains uncertain. Eastern Germans have been expected to adapt virtually overnight from a socialist society and economy to a western system. These factors combined to produce the impression of eastern Germans as 'second-class citizens'. In spite of these problems, the unified Germany has survived its first years without a major social or political backlash. The Basic Law has been extended to the former territories of the GDR, and efforts are under way to make the promise of equality between eastern and western citizens a reality. With the exception of the new PDS, the reformed communist party of the GDR, the party system of West Germany remains virtually unchanged and has helped to stabilise a potentially difficult period of transition. The activities of fringe right-wing extremists are worrying, but have to date not translated into party politics at the federal level.

To date, western liberal democracy has proved capable of adaptation without the loss of its distinguishing features of constitutionalism, pluralism and representation. The most recent wave of democratic transitions in central and eastern Europe shows that constitutional democracy need not, possibly cannot, be a mirror image of the standard model of liberal democracy which has evolved in western Europe. With the cold war over, closer contacts between the countries of western and eastern Europe are certain to develop. A mutual exchange of information and ideas can be expected to influence not only the process of democratisation in the east, but also the further evolution of democratic ideas and institutions in the west.

Notes

1 A further type of terrorist activity affecting western Europe is carried out by middle Eastern terrorist groups. These are often state-sponsored, by countries including Libya, Syria, Iran and Iraq. In this type of terrorist activity, western European territory is used as a substitute battlefield for conflicts originating elsewhere. The attacks of these groups are mainly directed at opposing groups, rather than at the government or regime of the western European states in which they are carried out.

2 In many cases, several groups have been active. Within each country, the most significant have been: the CCC, Belgium; DA, France; the RAF, Germany; 17N, Greece; the RB, Italy; GRAPO, Spain; and, FP-25, Portugal (Alexander and Pluchinsky 1992:16–17).

3 In Italy, a period of rapid social and economic modernisation during the 1960s had resulted in severe social conflicts. These came to a head with the 'hot summer' of 1969, marked by strikes and student protests. The government seemed unable to control the situation. The legal parties on both sides of the ideological spectrum – the MSI

on the extreme right and the PCI on the extreme left – were in the process of moderating their position at a time when public opinion was sharply polarised, leaving the extremes of political opinion unrepresented though legal political channels. Extremist groups on the right took to terrorist actions in the hope of intensifying the existing social unrest and fears of a Marxist revolution, to pave the way for a government takeover by the extreme right. Their activity was countered by the RB, which enjoyed some public sympathy for limited periods, mainly in the cities. The early actions of the RB were aimed against right-wing trade unionists, managers and foremen. From 1977–78, though, they adopted a 'strategy of annihiliation', targeting 'servants of the state', including policemen, magistrates and journalists. There was a public outcry over the murder of Aldo Moro in 1978 and the RB had lost their public support by the early 1980s (Ginsborg 1990: Chapters 9–10, esp. 383–7).

4 When the Belgian CCC and French DA were neutralised by police operations in 1988, each was found to have only four hardcore terrorists. The two factions of the Italian RB had fewer than twenty members each (Alexander and Pluchinsky 1992:40).

5 These activists became professional lobbyists, working within the structures of the political establishment they were seeking to challenge. For this reason, the 'new social movement' theorists would not consider this branch of the women's movement to be a true new social movement. They argue that the new social movements target their activities *away* from the state and reject traditional lobbying tactics (Cohen 1985:667; Melucci 1980:794; Offe 1985:819, 830, 832). Nevertheless, the women's rights activists were attempting to change those values and structures of western European society which discriminated against women.

6 These 'new social movement' theorists or 'identity-oriented' theorists include Alain Touraine, Jean Cohen and Alberto Melucci.

7 Unfortunately, there is no standard classification for immigrants. The classification used in this chapter follows the publications of SOPEMI (Système d'Observation Permanente sur les Migrations), a body which produces an annual report on international migration. SOPEMI (1994:23) distinguishes between refugees and asylumseekers as follows: refugees are generally channelled through government programmes negotiated with specialised international

agencies, whereas asylum-seekers arrive and make application on their own initiative.

8 Some 90 per cent of asylum applications are refused on the grounds that the motivation for entry is primarily economic and not 'well-founded fears of persecution'. It has been suggested that over 75 per cent of applicants refused asylum in western Europe have stayed illegally. Other illegal immigrants enter as tourists or students. By 1991 there were some 2.6 million illegal residents in western Europe, bringing the total foreign population to 18 million (Böhning 1991:447, 449).

9 In Germany, the new asylum legislation came into force on 1 July 1993. The principle of the right of asylum remains as defined in Article 16 of the Basic Law, that 'Persons persecuted for political reasons shall be granted asylum', but the new Act states that nationals from the EC, EFTA, Poland and Czech Republic (countries respecting the Geneva Convention on Refugees and the European Convention for the Protection of Human Rights and Fundamental Freedoms) cannot claim asylum. In addition, an application for asylum from a foreigner whose country of origin respects the fundamental principles of human rights shall not be considered unless the applicant can prove that he or she is being persecuted for political reasons. Countries classified as 'safe' include Bulgaria, Romania, Slovakia, Hungary, Gambia, Ghana and Senegal (SOPEMI 1994: 45).

10 Many factors account for the enormous influx of immigrants into Germany at this time. Germany's share of immigrants has always been relatively high. Without the colonial links of the other northern European countries, West Germany pursued expansive labour recruitment programmes in the 1960s and early 1970s, founded on treaties with labour-exporting countries. Since the Second World War, it has encouraged the return of ethnic Germans from eastern Europe and Russia. This source of immigration dwindled after the Berlin Wall went up in 1961, but rose sharply in the late 1980s with the collapse of the Soviet Union and German unification. Until July 1993 (see note 8 above), Germany's asylum laws had been exceptionally liberal. The country's geographical position can account for much of the recent influx; asylum-seekers and illegal immigrants from eastern Europe have headed for Austria and Germany as the closest countries to their own.

11 Citizenship is not automatically conferred on resident immigrants in western European countries, but depends on national laws. In the past, some countries, including France, have made it relatively easy for resident immigrants and their children to become naturalised citizens. Others have adopted a more restrictive approach. Germany, for example, has made naturalisation very difficult except for those who have German blood relatives or ancestors. The question of naturalisation is politically significant. Immigrants who become citizens are given the full rights of indigenous citizens, whereas resident immigrants who do not enjoy this status do not automatically qualify for all the rights and benefits provided by the country in question. (At the least, though, they are given protection by the universal recognition of fundamental human rights, as enforced by the courts.) In spite of the differences in approach adopted by different European countries, the current trend is to facilitate naturalisation for resident legal immigrants.

12 Mixed marriages are on the increase and now account for some 10 per cent of marriages in Belgium, France and Germany. Foreign labour grew in all OECD countries between 1981 and 1991, between 4 per cent in France and 62 per cent in Luxembourg. There has been a tendency for foreign workers to be concentrated in low-paid jobs. While this is still true, foreigners began to become better integrated into the economic structure during the 1980s, moving into all economic sectors but particularly into services. (Eurostat Labour Force Survey, 1991, cited in SOPEMI 1994:35. The Eurostat study included Germany, Belgium, France, Luxembourg, the Netherlands, and the UK, and covered the period between 1983 and 1991.)

13 The eastern European countries lost their former external links when Comecon and the Warsaw Pact were disbanded. The Czech Republic, Estonia, Lithuania, Romania, Slovakia and Slovenia have now joined the Council of Europe. In 1994, the following countries applied for full membership: Albania, Belarus, Croatia, Latvia, Macedonia, Moldova, Russia and Ukraine. The EU requires that its member states have democratic systems. While the principle is not new, the conditions it associates with 'democracy' are becoming more stringent. During the Mediterranean enlargement, which brought in Spain, Portugal and Greece, the EC demanded evidence of a democratic consitution and of procedures such as the holding of free elections. Also, there should be a reasonably stable government

and a predominance of pro-democracy parties. Now, for the eventual entry of eastern European countries, the EU is demanding more evidence of democratic values.

References

Alen, A. and R. Ergec (1994) *Federal Belgium after the Fourth State Reform of 1993*, Brussels, Ministry of Foreign Affairs.

Alexander, Y. and D. Pluchinsky (1992) *Europe's Red Terrorists. The Fighting Communist Organizations*, London, Frank Cass.

Allum, P. (1995) *State and Society in Western Europe*, Cambridge, Polity Press.

Böhning, W. (1991) 'Integration and immigration pressures in western Europe', *International Labour Review*. 130:4, 445–58.

Budge, I. (1994) 'Comparative politics and reflexive democracy', in I. Budge and D. McKay (eds) *Developing Democracy*, London, Sage, pp. 1–5.

Cohen, J. (1985) 'Strategy or identity: new theoretical paradigms and contemporary social movements', *Social Research* 52:4, 663–716.

Coleman, D. (1993) 'Western Europe: a region of mass immigration?, *Western Europe 1993*, London', Europa Publications, pp. 57–67.

Ginsborg, P. (1990) *A History of Contemporary Italy. Society and Politics 1943–1988*, London, Penguin.

Hollifield, J. (1992) *Immigrants, Markets and States. The Political Economy of Postwar Europe*, Cambridge, MA, Harvard University Press.

Melucci, A. (1980) 'The new social movements: a theoretical approach', *Social Science Information*, 19:2, 199–216.

Mishler, W. and R. Rose (1993) *Trajectories of Fear and Hope. The Dynamics of Support for Democracy in Eastern Europe*, Studies in Public Policy no. 214, Glasgow, Centre for the Study of Public Policy.

Offe, C. (1985) 'New social movements: challenging the boundaries of institutional politics', *Social Research*, 52:4, 817–68.

Pridham, G., E. Herring and G. Sandford (eds) (1994), *Building Democracy? The International Dimension of Democratisation in Eastern Europe*, London, Leicester University Press.

Rengger, N. (1994) 'Towards a culture of democracy? Democratic theory and democratisation in eastern and central Europe', in G. Pridham, E. Herring and G. Sandford (eds) *Building Democracy? The International Dimension of Democratisation in Eastern Europe*, London, Leicester University Press, pp. 60–86.

Rose, R. and C. Haerpfer (1994) *New Democracies Barometer III: Learning from What is Happening*, Studies in Public Policy no. 230, Glasgow, Centre for the Study of Public Policy.

SOPEMI (1994) *Trends in International Migration*, Annual Report 1993, Paris, Organisation for Economic Co-operation and Development.

Wilkinson, P. (1977) *Terrorism and the Liberal State*, Basingstoke, Macmillan.

Glossary

ALF	Animal Liberation Front
Basic Law (*Grundgesetz*)	Constitution of Federal Republic of Germany since 1949
BBU (Germany)	Bundesverband Bürgerinitiativen Umwelt-schutz: green activists
Benelux countries	Acronym for Belgium, Netherlands and Luxembourg
Bundesrat (Austria)	Austria's upper chamber of the legislature
Bundesrat (Germany)	Germany's upper chamber of the legislature
Bundesrat (Switzerland)	Swiss executive government council
Bundestag	Germany's lower chamber of the legislature
canton	Constituent province of the Swiss federal state: equivalent to 'state' in the USA
CAP	Common Agricultural Policy (EU)
CCA (Belgium)	Fighting Communist Cells (Belgian terrorist group)
CDA	Christian Democratic Appeal
CDU (Germany)	Christian Democratic Union
CET	Common External Tariff
CFSP	Common Foreign and Security Policy (EU)
chancellor	Title of head of government in Germany and Austria
cohabitation	Situation in France when the president has to select, and then work with, a prime minister from a party in opposition to his

	own (as occurred in 1986 and then in 1993)
COREPER	Committee of Permanent Representatives
CSU (Germany)	Christian Social Union (Bavaria: sister party of CDU)
DA (France)	Direct Action (French terrorist group)
EC	European Community
ECB	European Central Bank
ECJ	European Court of Justice
ECSC	European Coal and Steel Community
EDC	European Defence Community
EEC	European Economic Community
EFTA	European Free Trade Area
EMU	European Monetary Union (EU)
EP	European Parliament
ETA	Basque Homeland and Liberty (a Basque separatist organisation)
EU	European Union
Euratom	European Atomic Energy Community
EVSSG	European Values Systems Study Group
FCC (Germany)	Federal Constitutional Court
FDP (Germany)	Free Democratic Party: Germany's liberal party
FIFA	International football federation
FLNC	Corsican National Liberation Front
FN (France)	National Front: French extreme right-wing party
FP-25 (Portugal)	Popular Forces of 25 April: Portuguese
formateur	Politician given the task, as prime minister-designate, by the head of state of attempting to form a coalition government
Forza Italia	'Come on, Italy!': the name of a party formed by Berlusconi in 1993, which emphasises deregulation, market forces and political reform.
GCHQ	Government Communications Headquarters
GDP	Gross domestic product
GDR	German Democratic Republic
GRAPO (Spain)	First of October Anti-Fascist Resistance Group (Spanish terrorist group)

green parties	Political parties (under various labels) which promote ecology and environmental protection as their priorities
informateur	Politician given the task by head of state of discovering which political leader could successfully form a coalition government
IRA	Irish Republican Army
JHA	Justice and Home Affairs Cooperation (EU)
JO	Justitieombudsman
KPD	Communist Party of Germany: banned by Constitutional Court in 1956.
Land (pl.: *Länder*)	Regional component of German Federal Republic and of Austria's federal structure; equivalent to 'state' in USA
MEP	Member of European Parliament
MP	Member of Parliament
MSI	Italian Social Movement: extreme right-wing party; successor to Fascist party
Nationalrat	Lower chamber of Austrian and Swiss legislatures
NATO	North Atlantic Treaty Organisation
OECD	Organisation for Economic Cooperation and Development
OEEC	Organisation for European Economic Cooperation
ombudsman	Officer responsible for investigating complaints of maladministration (originally a Swedish term, now used more widely)
PCA	British parliamentary commissioner for administration
PCI	Italian Communist Party
PDS (Germany)	Party of Democratic Socialism (successor party to the former ruling communist party in East Germany, the SED)
PDS (Italy)	Democratic Party of the Left (successor party to the PCI).
PR	Proportional representation system of election
PS (France)	Socialist Party
PvdA (Netherlands)	Labour Party

RAF	Red Army Faction (German left-wing terrorist organisation)
RB	Red Brigades (Italian terrorist group)
Reichstag	Lower chamber of German parliament, 1871–1945
SCA	Special Committee on Agriculture
SDLP	Social Democratic and Labour Party (Northern Ireland)
SDP (Britain)	Social Democratic Party (broke from Labour Party in Britain in the 1980s)
SED	Socialist Unity Party: the ruling communist party in East Germany, 1949–89
SEM	Single European market
17N (Greece)	Revolutionary Organisation 17 November: Greek terrorist group
SOPEMI	Système d'Observation Permanente sur les Migrations
SPD	Social Democratic Party of Germany
SRP	Socialist Reich Party: a West German neo-Nazi party banned by the Constitutional Court in 1952
STV	Single Transferable Vote (electoral system)
Third Reich	Regime in Germany under Hitler and Nazism, 1933–45
UK	United Kingdom of Great Britain and Northern Ireland
USSR	Union of Soviet Socialist Republics
Vichy regime	Regime in south east France (1940–42) based at the town of Vichy. While the rest of France was subjected to occupation by the Germans following the fall of France, the Vichy government consisted of French politicians who ruled in collaboration with the Germans.
Weimar Republic	Regime in Germany, 1919–33
WEU	Western European Union

Further reading

In addition to the suggestions for further reading presented at the conclusion of each chapter, there are several sources which cover western European politics in general, or which deal with political systems of particular countries. This listing draws the attention of the reader to such sources, as well as to two other kinds of sources: reference works, and academic journals devoted wholly or in part to western European politics.

Books

Andeweg, R. and G. Irwin (1993) *Dutch Government and Politics*, Basingstoke, Macmillan.

Budge, I. and D. McKay (1988) *The Changing British Political System: Into the Nineteen-Nineties*, London, Longman, 2nd edn.

Collins, N. and F. McCann (1991) *Irish Politics Today*, Manchester, Manchester University Press, 2nd edn.

Fitzmaurice, J. (1991) *Austrian Politics and Society Today. In Defence of Austria*, Basingstoke, Macmillan.

Furlong, P. (1994) *Modern Italy. Representation and Reform*, London, Routledge.

Ginsborg, P. (1990) *A History of Contemporary Italy. Society and Politics 1943–1988*, London, Penguin.

Hall, P., J. Hayward and H. Machin (eds) (1994) *Developments in French Politics*, Basingstoke, Macmillan, rev. edn.

Heywood, P. (1995) *The Government and Politics of Spain*, Basingstoke, Macmillan.

Hine, D. (1993) *Governing Italy. The Politics of Bargained Pluralism*, Oxford, Oxford University Press.

Merkl, P. (ed.) (1995) *The Federal Republic of Germany at Forty-Five*, Basingstoke, Macmillan.

Morris, P. (1994) *French Politics Today*, Manchester, Manchester University Press.

Paterson, W. and D. Southern (1991) *Governing Germany*, Oxford, Blackwell.

Peele, G. (1995) *Governing the UK*, Oxford, Blackwell, 3rd edn.

Pyper, R. and L. Robins (eds) (1995) *Governing Britain in the 1990s*, Basingstoke, Macmillan.

Smith, G., W. Paterson, P. Merkl and S. Padgett (eds) (1992) *Developments in German Politics*, Basingstoke, Macmillan, rev. edn.

Stevens, A. (1992) *The Government and Politics of France*, Basingstoke, Macmillan.

Reference sources

Bogdanor, V. (ed.) (1987) *Blackwell Encyclopaedia of Political Institutions*, Oxford, Blackwell.

Jacobs, F. (ed.) (1989) *Western European Political Parties: A Comprehensive Guide*, Harlow, Longman Current Affairs.

Keesing's *Record of World Events* (monthly), Harlow, Longman Current Affairs.

Nicholson, F. (ed.) (1990) *Political and Economic Encyclopaedia of Western Europe*, Harlow, Longman Current Affairs.

Roberts, G. and A. Edwards (1991) *A New Dictionary of Political Analysis*, London, Edward Arnold.

Academic journals

The Economist
Electoral Studies
German Politics
Government and Opposition
Journal of Common Market Studies
Parliamentary Affairs
Party Politics
Representation
West European Politics

Appendix

Countries and international organisations in western Europe

Austria

Population	7.8 million (1994)
Capital	Vienna
Territory	83,857 sq.km
GNP per capita	US$23,120 (1993)
Unemployment	4.2 per cent of workforce (1993)
State form	Republic. The Austrian constitution of 1920, as amended in 1929, was restored on 1 May 1945. In May 1955, the four Allied powers signed the State Treaty with Austria, ending the occupation and recognising Austrian independence.
	Current head of state: President Thomas Klestil (took office 8 July 1992).
State structure	A federation with nine provinces (*Länder*), each with its own constitution, legislature and government.
Government	The president appoints the prime minister (chancellor), and, on the chancellor's recommendation, a cabinet (Council of Ministers) of around fifteen members. The Council of Ministers is responsible to the lower chamber of parliament, the 183-member National Council (Nationalrat). The second chamber, the 64-member Federal Council (Bundesrat), is elected by the parliaments of the *Länder*. The

Austrian presidential elections, 26 April and 24 May 1992

	First ballot (%)	Second ballot (%)
Rudolf Streicher (SPÖ)	40.7	43.2
Thomas Klestil (ÖVP)	37.2	56.8
Heide Schmidt (FPÖ)	16.4	–
Robert Jungk (Green Alternative)	5.7	–

Election to the Austrian Nationalrat, 17 December 1995

	Votes (%)	Seats
Social Democratic Party (SPÖ)	38.1	71
Austrian People's Party (ÖVP)	28.3	53
Freedom Party (FPÖ)	21.9	40
Liberal Forum (LF)	5.5	10
Greens	4.8	9
Others	1.4	0
Total		183

government, or individual ministers, can be removed from office by a vote of no confidence in the National Council. The Federal Council has the power to delay legislation, but not to veto it. For certain important matters, the two chambers meet together as the Bundesversammlung. Certain matters may be subject to a referendum. The constitutional court (Verfassungsgerichtshof) determines the constitutionality of legislation and executive acts.

Current government: In October 1995, the ruling coalition between the Social Democratic Party of Austria (SPÖ) and Austrian People's Party (ÖVP) collapsed amid fears that the end of their nine-year partnership would destabilise Austrian politics.

However, in the elections to the National Council which followed in December, the right-wing nationalist Freedom Party (FPÖ) failed to make anticipated gains, and in early February 1996, the SPÖ and ÖVP agreed to renew their coalition partnership under the leadership of Franz Vranitzky of the SPÖ.

Electoral systems   The president is elected by direct universal suffrage for a term of six years and may not serve more than two terms.

Elections to the Nationalrat are based on a system of proportional representation. Term of office: four years.

Party system   Since the Second World War, the Austrian party system has been dominated by the SPÖ and ÖVP, which, until the general election of 1990, together took 90 per cent of the vote. The Greens emerged in the early 1980s, and, in 1986, the FPÖ became a serious electoral force under the charismatic leadership of Jörg Haider.

Belgium

Population   10.0 million (1994)

Capital   Brussels

Territory   30,519 sq. km

GNP per capita   US$21,210 (1993)

Unemployment   9.1 per cent of workforce (1993)

State form   Constitutional monarchy. Belgium seceded from the Netherlands in 1830, and the constitution of 1831 established Belgium as a 'unitary decentralised state'. Between 1970 and 1993 a four-stage process of constitutional reform transformed the country into a federation and culminated in the new Belgian constitution of 1994.

Current head of state: King Albert II (sworn in 9 August 1993).

State structure   A federation characterised by three linguistic communities (French-, Flemish- and German-
speaking), three regions (Walloon, Flemish and
Brussels) and four linguistic regions (French-speaking, Flemish-speaking, German-speaking and the
bilingual region of Brussels-Capital). The unusually
complex federal arrangements are designed to contain the conflicts between the country's linguistic
communities.

Government   The monarch appoints a formateur to negotiate the
formation of a new government. The monarch ap-
points the prime minister, and, on the prime minister's advice, a cabinet of up to fifteen members
comprising an equal number of Flemish and French
speakers. Executive power is nominally held by the
monarch, but in practice is exercised by the cabinet.
The cabinet is responsible to the lower chamber of
parliament, the Chamber of Representatives. Since
the constitutional reform of 1993, the upper chamber of parliament, the Senate, has had only limited
legislative powers.

Current government: Following the general election of 21 May 1995, a largely unchanged centre-
left coalition cabinet took office under Jean-Luc
Dehaene, prime minister since 1992. The coalition
comprised the two Christian social parties (Flemish
CVP and Walloon PSC) and the two socialist parties
(Flemish SP and Walloon PS).

Electoral systems   The constitutional amendment of 1993 altered the
membership of the two chambers of parliament.
The Chamber of Representatives formerly had 212
members and now has 150; the Senate formerly
had 182 members and now has 71.

Elections to both chambers are by a system of
proportional representation for a four-year term.
However, only forty of the Senate's seventy-one
members are directly elected; the remaining thirty-
one are co-opted from the councils of the linguistic
communities. In May 1995 elections were held for
the first time to the new assemblies for the regional/

Elections to the Belgian parliament, 21 May 1995

	Votes (%)	C of R seats	Senate seats
Christian People's Party (CVP)	17.2	29	7
Social Christian Party (PSC)	7.7	12	3
Flemish Liberals and Democrats (VLD)	13.1	21	6
Liberal Reform Party (PRL-FDF)	10.3	18	5
Flemish Socialist Party (SP)	12.6	20	6
Walloon Socialist Party (PS)	11.9	21	5
Flemish Bloc	7.8	11	3
People's Union	4.7	5	2
National Front (FN)	2.3	2	–
AGALEV (Flemish greens)	4.4	5	1
ECOLO (Walloon greens)	4.0	6	2
Total		150	40

linguistic communities and to the Brussels assembly. These assemblies each have a term of office of five years.

Party system Reflecting Belgium's linguistic divide, each of the main ideological families in Belgium is represented by two separate parties: the christian democrats by the Flemish CVP and Walloon PSC, the socialists by the Flemish SP and Walloon PS, the liberals by two recently 'renovated' groupings, the Flemish VLD (formerly PVV) and Walloon PRL-FDF, and the greens by the Flemish Agalev and Walloon Ecolo. In addition, there are many protest and fringe groups, of which the most significant are the extreme right-wing Flemish Bloc, the more moderate Flemish nationalist People's Union, and the extreme right Walloon National Front.

Denmark

Population 5.2 million (1994)

Capital Copenhagen

Territory	43,075 sq. km
GNP per capita	US$26,510 (1993)
Unemployment	10.4 per cent of workforce (1993)
State form	Constitutional monarchy, based on the constitution of 5 June 1953.
	Current head of state: Queen Margrethe II (succeeded to the throne 14 January 1972).
State structure	Unitary. Home rule was granted to the Faeroe Islands in 1948 and to Greenland in 1979.
Government	The monarch appoints the prime minister and, on the advice of the prime minister, the cabinet of around twenty members, which is responsible to the unicameral parliament (Folketing). Legislative authority rests jointly with the monarch and parliament. A bill adopted by the Folketing may be submitted to referendum on the request of one-third of the members of the Folketing. The bill is invalid if it is rejected by a majority of the votes cast, if this represents at least 30 per cent of the electorate.
	Current government: A minority centrist coalition of the Social Democratic Party (SD), the Centre Democrats (CD) and the Social Liberals (SL), led by Poul Nyrup Rasmussen (SD). This coalition is a continuation of the outgoing one, minus the Christian People's Party, which lost its representation in the election of 1994.
Electoral systems	The Folketing has a maximum of 179 members, two of whom are elected in the Faeroe Islands and two in Greenland. The Folketing is elected by a system of proportional representation for a term of office of four years.
Party system	The main parties are currently grouped into three alliances: the governing coalition of centrist parties (SD, CD and SL), a left-wing alliance (Socialist People's Party (SF) and Unity List) and a centre-right alliance (Liberal Party (V), Conservative People's Party (KF) and Progress Party (FP)).

Election to the Danish Folketing, 21 September 1994 (excluding representatives from the Faeroes and Greenland)

	Votes (%)	*Seats*
Social Democratic Party (SD)	34.6	62
Liberal Party (V)	23.3	42
Conservative People's Party (KF)	15.0	27
Socialist People's Party (SF)	7.3	13
Progress Party (FP)	6.4	11
Social Liberals (SL)	4.6	8
Unity List	3.1	6
Centre Democrats (CD)	2.8	5
Others	2.8	1
Total		175

Finland

Population	5.0 million (1994)
Capital	Helsinki
Territory	338,145 sq.km
GNP per capita	US$18,970 (1993)
Unemployment	17.7 per cent of workforce (1993)
State form	Republic, based on the constitution of 17 July 1919. Finland was part of the Kingdom of Sweden until 1809 when it became an autonomous Grand Duchy under the Russian Empire. During the Russian Revolution of 1917 Finland claimed its independence, and, after a brief civil war, the republic was founded in 1919.
	Current head of state: President Martti Ahtisaari (took office 1 March 1994).
State structure	Unitary
Government	The president appoints the prime minister and a cabinet (Council of State) of around fifteen ministers, which is responsible to the unicameral parliament (Eduskunta). The president holds supreme executive power and in practice has a more promi-

Finnish presidential elections, 16 January and 6 February 1994

	First ballot *(%)*	*Second ballot* *(%)*
Martti Ahtisaari (SDP)	25.9	53.9
Elisabeth Rehn (SFP)	22.0	46.1
Paavo Väyrynen (Kesk)	19.5	–
Raimo Ilaskivi (Kok)	15.2	–
others	17.4	–

nent executive and legislative role than most western European heads of state. The president appoints a chancellor of justice, who ensures that the Council of State acts legally. The president may depart even from the unanimous opinion of the Council of State and must approve all matters concerning foreign affairs. In certain circumstances, the president may issue decrees, grant pardons and dispensations, and call new elections to the Eduskunta. Both the Eduskunta and the president may initiate legislation and the president has the right of veto over all bills. A presidential veto can be overturned by the Eduskunta's immediate successor, as long as the successor Eduskunta adopts the proposed legislation without amendment. The Eduskunta has the right to interrogate the government and can impeach a member of the Council of State or the chancellor of justice, if he or she acts unlawfully. The Court of the Realm is responsible for impeachment trials. The Eduskunta appoints a parliamentary ombudsman for a four-year term of office.

Current government: In the general election of 19 March 1995, the moderate Social Democratic Party (SDP), in opposition since 1991, recorded its best election result since 1945 and emerged as the largest party in the Eduskunta. The leading party of the outgoing centre-right government coalition, the moderate Centre Party (Kesk), was the main loser. Within the context of Finnish electoral politics, the

Election to the Finnish Eduskunta, 19 March 1995

	Votes (%)	*Seats*
Social Democratic Party (SDP)	28.3	63
Centre Party (Kesk)	19.9	44
National Coalition Party (Kok)	17.9	39
Left-Wing Alliance (VL)	11.2	22
Swedish People's Party (SFP)	5.1	12
Greens (Vihreät)	6.5	9
Finnish Christian League (SKL)	3.0	7
Young Finns (NS)	2.8	2
Finnish Rural Party (SMP)	1.3	1
Ecological Party	0.3	1
others	3.7	–
Total		200

shifts in voting support were unusually large. On 13 April 1995, Paavo Lipponen of the SDP took office as prime minister at the head of a broad-based five-party coalition, comprising the SDP, the conservative National Coalition Party (Kok), the Swedish People's Party (SFP), the Left-Wing Alliance (VL) and the Greens (Vihreät).

Electoral systems Following constitutional amendments from 1987, the president is elected by direct universal suffrage for a term of six years. If no presidential candidate obtains more than 50 per cent of the vote, a second ballot is held to determine the winner, in which only the two leading candidates of the first ballot may compete.

The 200-member Eduskunta is elected by a system of proportional representation for a four-year term.

Party system In common with other western European countries, Finland's parties are largely divided by the class cleavage, with the Left-Wing Alliance, Social Democrats and Greens on the left, and the Centre Party, National Coalition Party (Kok), Swedish People's

Party and Christian League (SKL) on the right. Unlike the practice in other countries, though, it was common for the parties to cooperate across the class divide in broad-based coalition governments. The four-party centre-right government of 1991–95 broke with this tradition, which was restored after the election of 1995. Among the smaller parties is the right-wing Rural Party (SMP) and a new radical free-market party, the Young Finns (NS), which entered parliament in 1995 at its first attempt.

France

Population	57.4 million (1994)
Capital	Paris
Territory	543,965 sq. km
GNP per capita	US$22,360 (1993)
Unemployment	11.6 per cent of workforce (1993)
State form	Republic, based on the constitution of 1958 establishing the Fifth French Republic. Following the liberation of France from German occupation in 1944 and a brief provisional government led by General Charles de Gaulle, the Fourth French Republic was founded in 1946. This regime, which proved unstable, was replaced in 1958 by the current regime. Current head of state: President Jacques Chirac (took office 17 May 1995).
State structure	Unitary, comprising 96 metropolitan departments and 10 overseas departments. Corsica has its own directly elected legislative assembly.
Government	The president appoints the prime minister and a cabinet (Council of Ministers) of around twenty members, which is responsible to the bicameral parliament. Executive power is vested in the president, who is in practice the most politically powerful head of state in western Europe. The president 'presides' over the Council of Ministers and may, under speci-

French presidential elections, 23 April and 7 May 1995

	First ballot (%)	*Second ballot (%)*
Jospin (PS)	23.3	47.4
Chirac (RPR)	20.8	52.6
Balladur (RPR)	18.6	
Le Pen (FN)	15.0	
Hue (PCF)	8.6	
Laguiller (Worker's Struggle)	5.3	
De Villiers (Other Europe)	4.7	
Voynet (Greens)	3.3	
Cheminade (far right)	0.3	

fied circumstances, dismiss the goverment ministers and accept the resignation of the prime minister, submit a bill to a referendum, declare emergency powers, and dissolve the lower chamber of parliament, the National Assembly (Assemblée Nationale), once in a twelve-month period. The president makes appointments to senior civil and military posts. Throughout most of the Fifth Republic, the electorate has returned a majority supporting the party or coalition of the president to the National Assembly. This has enabled the president to be the effective executive leader of France. Exceptionally, the electorate has returned a majority from the opposing 'bloc'. During these periods of 'cohabitation' (1986–88, 1993–95), executive power has been shared between the president and the prime minister, with the latter commanding the support of the majority in the National Assembly. The constitutionality of bills is determined by the Constitutional Council.

Current government: The election of March 1993 brought the centre-right, previously in opposition, back into power, initially governing in conjunction with the Socialist president, François Mitterrand, for the remainder of his term of office. The govern-

Elections to the French National Assembly, 21 and 28 March 1993

	First ballot (%)	Second ballot (%)	Seats
Rally for the Republic (RPR)	20.4	28.3	247
Union for French Democracy (UDF)	19.1	25.8	213
Socialist Party (PS)	17.6	28.3	54
French Communist Party (PCF)	9.2	4.6	23
Left Radical Movement (MRG)	0.9	1.2	6
National Front (FN)	12.4	5.7	–
Greens (les Verts)	4.0	0.1	–
Ecology Generation	3.6	0.1	–
Other right	5.0	3.6	24
Other left	3.6	2.3	10
Others	4.2	0.2	–
Total			577

ment coalition comprises the neo-Gaullist Rally for the Republic (RPR), centre-right Union for French Democracy (UDF) and an independent. Prime Minister Alain Juppé took office in May 1995.

Electoral systems Since a constitutional amendment of 1962, the president has been elected by direct universal suffrage. If no presidential candidate obtains more than 50 per cent of the vote, a second ballot is held to determine the winner, in which only the two leading candidates of the first ballot may compete. The president's term of office is seven years.

The National Assembly has 577 members: 555 for metropolitan France and 22 for the overseas departments. Members are elected by a single-member constituency system of direct election, using a second ballot if the first fails to produce an absolute majority for any one candidate. The term of office is five years.

The upper chamber of parliament, the Senate, has 321 members, 296 for metropolitan France, 13 for the overseas territories and 12 for French nationals

Elections to the French Senate, 24 September 1995 (resulting total distribution of seats in the Senate)

	Seats
Union for French Democracy (UDF)	129
Rally for the Republic (RPR)	94
Socialist Party (PS)	75
French Communist Party (PCF)	15
Independents	8
Total	321

abroad. It is elected by an electoral college composed of members of the National Assembly and delegates from the councils of the departments and municipal authorities. Senators are elected for a nine-year term of office, but the Senate is not elected as a single body. Instead, one-third of the senators is elected every three years.

Party system During the years of the Fifth Republic, an initially fragmented party system has developed into a bipolar system of two main 'blocs' of parties on the centre-right and centre-left. For a time, these blocs were almost balanced in terms of electoral support, but recent elections show that support for the centre-left is currently very unpredictable. The landslide defeat of the Socialist Party (PS), the main party of the centre-left, in the 1993 general election was followed by an impressive recovery in the first round of the presidential elections of 1995. Each bloc comprises many parties which frequently splinter and merge. Currently, the most significant parties of the centre-right are those in government: the RPR, and the UDF, itself an umbrella organisation of parties which includes the Republican Party (PR), the Centre Social Democrats (CDS), the Radical Party, and Perspectives and Realities. The left bloc encompasses the Socialist Party (PS), the Communist Party of France (PCF) and the Left Radical Movement (MRG). Other parties include the far-right National Front (FN), Ecology Generation, the Greens (les Verts), and the Independent Ecologist Movement (MEI).

Germany

Population	80.6 million (1994)
Capital	Berlin
Territory	356,959 sq.km
GNP per capita	US$23,560 (1993)
Unemployment	11.0 per cent of workforce (1996)
State form	Republic, based on the Basic Law of 1949, with subsequent amendments. The Federal Republic of Germany was founded in 1949 from the three western zones of occupied Germany. On 3 October 1990, the territories of the former German Democratic Republic and Berlin joined the federation and accepted the authority of the Basic Law.
	Current head of state: President Roman Herzog (took office 1 July 1994).
State structure	Federation of 16 *Länder*, each of which has its own constitution, legislature and government.
Government	The federal prime minister (chancellor) is elected by an absolute majority of the parliament (Bundestag) and can only be dismissed if a successor is elected on the same occasion (a 'constructive vote of no confidence'). The chancellor selects a cabinet of around twenty members and the president formally appoints the chancellor and cabinet ministers. Executive authority rests with the federal government, which is responsible to the Bundestag. The Federal Council (Bundesrat) is composed of representatives of the governments of the *Länder*. Each *Land* sends between three and six delegates according to the size of its population, and may only vote *en bloc*. Under specified circumstances, the Bundesrat may veto legislation. The president's activities are strictly defined and observed and include, under

specified circumstances, the dissolution of the Bundestag. The federal constitutional court (Bundesverfassungsgericht) determines the constitutionality of legislation and executive acts.

Current government: A centre-right coalition led by Helmut Kohl of the Christian Democratic Union (CDU) and including the Christian Social Union (CSU) and Free Democratic Party (FDP) has been in power since 1982.

Electoral systems The president is elected by the Federal Convention (Bundesversammlung), comprising the members of the Bundestag and an equal number of delegates elected by the parliaments of the *Länder*. The candidate who wins an absolute majority of votes is elected. If no candidate secures an absolute majority in two ballots, a third ballot is held in which a relative majority is sufficient to win. The term of office is five years. A president may not serve more than two successive terms.

The Bundestag is elected by direct universal suffrage. The Bundestag has a standard complement of 656 seats, but the electoral system sometimes allocates surplus mandates (the election of 1994 resulted in a Bundestag of 672 members). Half of the 656 seats are allocated to constituency candidates

Election to the German Bundestag, 16 October 1994

	Votes (%)	*Seats*
Social Democratic Party (SPD)	36.4	252
Christian Democratic Union (CDU)	34.2	244
Christian Social Union (CSU)	7.3	50
Alliance 90/The Greens	7.3	49
Free Democratic Party (FDP)	6.9	47
Party of Democratic Socialism (PDS)	4.4	30
Republican party	1.9	–
Others	1.7	–
Total		672

on the simple majority plurality ('first-past-the-post') principle and the remainder by proportional representation based on party lists. Parties receive a share of seats in the Bundestag proportional to their share of party list votes, so that the electoral system is effectively one of proportional representation. The term of office is four years.

Party system   From 1961, only three parties won seats in the Bundestag: the CDU-CSU, the SPD and the small liberal FDP. The Greens entered the Bundestag in 1983 and the former East German reformed communists, the Party of Democratic Socialism (PDS), followed after German unification in 1990.

Greece

Population	10.2 million (1994)
Capital	Athens
Territory	131,957 sq.km
GNP per capita	US$7,390 (1993)
Unemployment	9.8 per cent of workforce (1993)

State form   Republic, based on the constitution of 1975. The liberation of Greece from German occupation in 1944 was followed by a civil war which lasted until 1949, when the communist forces were defeated and the constitutional monarchy restored. In 1967, a coup led by right-wing army officers took over the government and set up a façade democracy. The king went into exile, and, in 1973, Greece was declared a republic. In 1974, after a period of violent instability, former prime minister Konstantinos Karamanlis was invited to form a civilian government. A return to constitutional monarchy was rejected by referendum in December 1974. In June 1975, a new republican constitution was introduced, establishing a parliamentary democracy.

Current head of state: President Konstantinos Stefanopoulos (took office 10 March 1995).

State structure	Unitary, with 10 regions.
Government	The president appoints the prime minister, and, on the prime minister's recommendation, the cabinet of around twenty members. In 1986, constitutional amendments reduced the office of president to a largely ceremonial one and transferred many of the president's former executive powers to the unicameral parliament (Vouli ton Ellinon). The amendments restricted the president's right to call a referendum, transferred the right to call a state of emergency to parliament, and removed the president's right to dismiss the prime minister. In addition, the president may now dissolve parliament only if the resignation of two governments in rapid succession demonstrates a lack of political stability. The president may still ask parliament to reconsider legislation, or to pass it with an enhanced majority.

Current government: The general election of 10 October 1993 saw the return to power of the Panhellenic Socialist Movement (PASOK) after four years in opposition. Andreas Papandreou was appointed prime minister, but fell ill and was replaced in January 1996 by Kostas Simitis. Following Papandreou's death in June 1996, Simitis was elected leader of PASOK.

Electoral systems	The president is elected by parliament for a term of five years.

Election to the Greek Vouli ton Ellinon, 10 October 1993

	Votes (%)	Seats
Panhellenic Socialist Movement (PASOK)	46.9	170
New Democracy (ND)	39.3	111
Political Spring (POLA)	4.9	10
Communist Party (KKE)	4.5	9
Others	3.1	–
Total		300

The Vouli ton Ellinon has 300 members and is elected by direct universal suffrage for a term of four years.

Party system   The main parties are PASOK and the centre-right New Democracy (ND). On the left are the Greek Communist party (KKE) and other small groups. Political Spring (POLA) is a centre-right party.

Iceland

Population   300,000 (1993)

Capital   Reykjavik

Territory   102,820 sq. km

GNP per capita   US$23,620 (1993)

Unemployment   5.2 per cent of workforce (1993)

State form   Republic, based on the constitution of 17 June 1944, when Iceland declared its independence from Denmark.

Current head of state: President Ólafur Ragnar Grímsson (took office 1 August 1996).

State structure   Unitary

Government   The president appoints the prime minister and a cabinet of around ten members. Executive power is vested in the president and the cabinet, but in practice is exercised by the cabinet. The cabinet is responsible to the parliament (Althingi), unicameral since 1991. Ministers may be impeached by the

Icelandic presidential election, 29 June 1996

	Votes (%)
Ólafur Ragnar Grímsson	41.4
Pétur Hafstein	29.6
Gudrún Agnarsdóttir	26.4
Ástthor Magnússon	2.7

Election to the Icelandic Althingi, April 1995

	Votes (%)	*Seats*
Independence Party	37.1	25
Progressive Party	23.3	15
People's Alliance	14.3	9
Social Democratic Party	11.4	7
People's Movement	7.2	4
Women's Party	4.9	3
Total		63

Althingi and are tried by a court of impeachment. The president may dissolve the Althingi. The president may be dismissed by the Althingi by a resolution supported by three-quarters of its members and confirmed by referendum. If the president disapproves a law passed by the Althingi, it must be confirmed by referendum.

Current government: The general election of April 1995 led to the formation on 23 April 1995 of a new centre-right coalition of the conservative Independence Party and the formerly agrarian Progressive Party, led by Davíd Oddsson of the Independence Party.

Electoral systems   The president is elected by direct universal suffrage for a term of four years.

The sixty-three-member Althingi is elected by a system of proportional representation in eight constituencies. The term of office is four years.

Party system   Four main parties have competed in Icelandic elections since the 1930s. These are the Independence Party, the Progressive Party, the left socialist People's Alliance and the Social Democratic Party. The radical Women's Alliance entered parliament in 1983. The new People's Movement, a leftist breakaway group from the Social Democratic Party, was formed in 1994.

Ireland

Population	3.5 million (1994)
Capital	Dublin
Territory	70,283 sq.km
GNP per capita	US$12,580 (1993)
Unemployment	15.8 per cent of workforce (1993)
State form	Republic, based on the constitution of 29 December 1937. Ireland was formerly part of the United Kingdom. In 1920 the island was partitioned, the six north-eastern counties remaining part of the UK. In 1922 the twenty-six southern counties achieved dominion status, under the British Crown, as the Irish Free State. In 1937, the new constitution was adopted by referendum, giving the Irish Free State full sovereignty within the Commonwealth. Formal ties with the Commonwealth were ended in 1949, when the twenty-six southern counties became the Republic of Ireland (Eire).
	Current head of state: President Mary Robinson (took office 3 December 1990).
State structure	Unitary
Government	The president summons and dissolves the bicameral parliament on the advice of the government or prime minister (Taoiseach). On the nomination of the lower chamber of parliament (Dáil Éireann), the president appoints the prime minister, and, on the

Irish presidential election, 7–9 November 1990

	First count (%)	Second count (%)
Mary Robinson (LP and Worker's Party)	38.9	51.9
Brian Lenihan (FF)	44.1	46.4
Austin Currie (FG)	17.0	–

advice of the prime minister and the Dáil, the cabinet of around fifteen members. The president is advised by a Council of State. The president may refer certain bills to the Supreme Court for a ruling on their constitutionality. With the support of a prescribed proportion of members of both chambers of parliament, the president may refer certain bills to a referendum.

Current government: The coalition government between the Republican party (Fianna Fáil, FF) and the Labour Party (LP) which formed after the 1992 general election broke down in November 1994. The LP withdrew from the coalition following a dispute about a controversial senior legal appointment and the government was forced to resign. A new coalition took office on 15 December 1994, headed by John Bruton of the United Ireland party (Fine Gael, FG) and comprising the FG, LP and the radical socialist Democratic Left (DL).

Electoral systems   The president is elected by direct universal suffrage for a term of office of seven years.

The Dáil Éireann has 166 members and is elected by STV for a term of five years.

The upper chamber of parliament, the Seanad Éireann, has sixty members. Eleven are nominated by the prime minister, six are elected by the univer-

Election to the Irish Dáil Éireann, 25 November 1992

	First preference votes (%)	*Seats*
Republican Party (Fianna Fáil, FF)	39.1	68
United Ireland Party (Fine Gael, FG)	24.5	45
Labour Party (LP)	19.3	33
Progressive Democrats	4.7	10
Democratic Left (DL)	2.8	4
Others	9.6	6
Total		166

Election to the Irish Seanad Éireann, February 1993

	Seats
Republican Party (Fianna Fáil, FF)	25
United Ireland Party (Fine Gael, FG)	17
Labour Party (LP)	9
Progressive Democrats	2
Democratic Left (DL)	1
Others	6
Total	60

sities and forty-three by a broad-based electoral college. The term of office is five years.

Party system   The two main parties, FF and FG, are both right of centre. Their differences stem from their positions on the Anglo-Irish Treaty establishing the Irish Free State (1921). The anti-treaty FF formed in 1926, the pro-treaty FG in 1933. The LP emerged in the 1920s and became established in the party system. Other parties include the DL and the Progressive Democrats.

Italy

Population   57.8 million (1994)

Capital   Rome

Territory   301,277 sq. km

GNP per capita   US$19,620 (1993)

Unemployment   10.2 per cent of workforce (1993)

State form   Republic, based on the constitution of 1948. The constitutional framework of the previous regime, a constitutional monarchy, had remained in place throughout Mussolini's fascist dictatorship (1922–43) and was terminated by a national referendum held in June 1946.

Current head of state: President Oscar Luigi Scalfaro (took office 1992).

State structure   Unitary, with twenty regions, five with a special status. The regions each have an elected legislature and regional executive and enjoy a large degree of autonomy.

Government   The president of the republic appoints the prime minister, and, on the prime minister's advice, the other members of the cabinet (Council of Ministers). The cabinet has around fifteen full ministers and is responsible to parliament. The bicameral parliament has a lower chamber, the Chamber of Deputies (Camera dei Deputati), of 630 members and an upper chamber, the Senate (Senato), of 315 elected members plus ten life senators, appointed by the president of the republic. The two houses of parliament have equal powers. A Constitutional Court carries out the judicial review of legislation and judges accusations brought against the president of the republic or government ministers.

For many years, a crisis of legitimacy had been building up in the Italian republic. This centred not on the constitutional framework itself, but on the failure of the Italian parties to work within the institutions to provide strong, democratic government. The crisis broke in 1993 with a series of scandals linking government at the highest levels with crime and corruption. By the end of the year, hundreds of members of parliament, party officials and industrialists were either under investigation or under arrest. Among those implicated were the Christian Democrat (DC) President Cossiga who resigned early in 1992; Bettino Craxi, leader of the Socialist Party (PSI), who resigned in February 1993; and Giulio Andreotti, one of the country's most influential politicians of the 1970s and 1980s (DC). The parties which had ruled the country for forty years were thoroughly discredited. This crisis set in motion an ongoing attempt to bring about a fundamental reform of the country's political system. Central to this 'democratic revolution' have been the governments of the non-party prime ministers Ciampi (from April 1993 to May 1994) and Dini (from January 1995 to January 1996), members of the judiciary, the Constitutional Court, President Scalfaro, and some of the new radical reform parties. In spite of their efforts, there have been setbacks. The populist government of Silvio Berlusconi (from April 1994 to December 1994) compromised the reform movement by making inappropriate appointments to high-ranking positions and by manipulating the media through Berlusconi's personal financial interests. Many entrenched interests are threatened by reform and have managed to hamper the relevant decision-making processes. In view of these setbacks, some believe that the reform movement has lost its impetus.

Current government: After the 1994 election, a right-wing government took office under Prime Minister Silvio Berlusconi. The government proved unstable because of the conflict between Berlusconi's government position and his financial interests, an ongoing conflict between the government and the judiciary, and splits within the government coalition. The government fell in December 1994 and was replaced in January 1995 by an interim government of technocrats (nonpartisan experts) led by Prime Minister Lamberto Dini, a former director-general of the Bank of Italy. President Scalfaro accepted Dini's resignation in January 1996 under the threat of resolutions of no confidence tabled by the centre-right parties and the hardline Refounded Communist Party (PRC).

After the general election of 21 April 1996, a government was formed by the centre-left Olive Tree

Election to the Italian Chamber of Deputies, 21 April 1996

	Votes (%)	*Seats*
Olive Tree Alliance[a]	34.8	284
Freedom Alliance[b]	44.0	246
Northern League (LN)	10.1	59
Refounded Communist Party (PRC)[a]	8.6	35
others	2.5	6
Total		630

[a] The Olive Tree Alliance included: the Democratic Party of the Left (PDS); the christian democrat Popular Party (PPI)/Prodi List; the Dini List; Greens and other small parties. The hardline Refounded Communist Party (PRC) campaigned with the Olive Tree against the right, but would not endorse its programme.
[b] The Freedom Alliance included: Forza Italia; the National Alliance (AN); the new centre-right Christian Democratic List, United Christian Democrats (CDU)/Christian Democratic Centre (CCD); and other small parties, including liberals.

Election to the Italian Senate, 21 April 1996

	Votes (%)	*Seats*
Olive Tree Alliance[a]	41.2	157
Freedom Alliance[a]	37.3	116
Northern League (LN)	10.4	27
Refounded Communist Party (PRC)	2.9	10
Independents	3.4	4
Fiamma[b]	2.3	1
Socialists	0.9	0
others	1.6	0
Total		315

[a] For party alliances, see table of elections to the Chamber of Deputies.
[b] Neo-fascist, formerly the Italian Social Movement (MSI).

Alliance, a coalition of moderates committed to constitutional reform, under the leadership of Romano Prodi. The Prodi government was formed with the voting support of the PRC.

Electoral systems   The president of the republic is elected for a seven-year term of office by an electoral college made up of both chambers of parliament and fifty-eight regional representatives.

New electoral systems for elections to the Chamber of Deputies and the Senate were introduced in 1993. These symbolised the reform process in Italy and were hailed by some as the start of a new Republic. The Chamber of Deputies has 630 members. Three-quarters (475) are elected on the single-member, single-ballot, plurality principle, as in the UK. The remaining 155 members are elected on a system of proportional representation based on twenty-seven districts, with a 4 per cent threshold.

The senate has 315 elected members. The seats for these electoral posts are allocated on a regional basis. Three-quarters (238) are elected by a majority vote and the rest by proportional representation on a regional basis. The term of office for both the Chamber of Deputies and the Senate is five years.

At the 1996 elections, these new electoral arrangements proved so unsatisfactory that they are expected to be replaced with another alternative.

Party system   Italy's party system is currently in a state of flux. Widely discredited by the corruption scandals of 1993, the traditional parties found it impossible to continue under their old names and identities and were forced to reinvent themselves. In spite of this dramatic upheaval, there are strong elements of continuity in the emerging party system. In the 1994 general elections, the 'new' parties banded into three alliances based on familiar ideologies: the Progressives consisted of parties of the left and radical reformers; the Pact for Italy was a grouping of the centre right; and the Freedom Alliance represented the new right in Italian politics. The parties continue to change in their attempt to regain the voters' confidence. The following summary traces the development of the traditional parties and the more significant new parties in the emerging party system.

The christian democratic DC had dominated Italian government throughout the post-war period and was perhaps most directly affected by the corruption scandals. The main liberal wing of the DC became the Popular Party (PPI) in 1994, but was already under strain by early 1995. Italy's main party of opposition had been the Communist Party (PCI). The PCI began to change its stance in 1989 in response to the collapse of communism as a viable government ideology. In 1991, the bulk of the party became the social democratic Democratic Party of the Left (PDS) while the remaining hardliners formed the PRC. These two parties were the backbone of the alliance of Progressives in the 1994 general election. Of all the traditional parties, the reformed communists were best placed in this election. The other parties had contrived to keep the PCI out of government during the post-war period. Also, the PCI began its process of party reform well in advance of the scandals of 1993. Together, these factors shielded the PDS and the smaller PRC from the taint of corruption and gave particularly the PDS a popular reformist image. The Socialist Party (PSI), another traditional party of the left, was less fortunate. In 1992 it was found that the PSI in Milan had broken the party finance laws. This discovery launched a more thorough investigation into party and government affairs (the Mani Pulite, or 'clean hands' operation) which snowballed in 1993. The PSI became Socialist Italy (SI) in late 1994. The traditional liberal groupings, such as the PLI (now Union of the Centre) and PRI, promise to be overshadowed by new, pro-market liberal parties such as Segni's Pact. The Radical Party continues to campaign on civil rights issues. New radical reform groups include the Green Federation, formed in 1987, and The Network (La Rete), formed in 1991 as an anti-Mafia party. The main change in the party system is the current significance of the new right. The rise of the new right began in the early 1990s in conjunction with a revival in regional movements demanding more autonomy or even secession. The Northern League (now Northern League-Federal Italy) linked their regional demands with an anti-immigrant stance. In 1994, two newly formed right-wing parties rose to prominence. One was the populist, pro-market Forza Italia (the party name sounds like a football chant) formed by business tycoon Silvio Berlusconi. The other was the National Alliance (AN), which in 1995 absorbed the traditional neo-fascist party, the MSI-DN. (The AN has distanced itself from a neo-fascist stance, denouncing racism and anti-semitism.) Together with the Northern League and some breakaway groups from the old centre-right parties, these two new parties of the right won the 1994 general election under the banner of the Freedom Alliance.

The political parties, still undergoing considerable changes in identity and direction, forged new alliances to contest the general election of 21 April 1996. Two main groupings fought the election: the reformist centre-left Olive Tree Alliance and the new-right Freedom Alliance, which this time campaigned without the support of the separatist Northern League. With no separate alliance representing the centre, christian democratic parties divided to support one of the other alliances. The most significant progressive christian democratic group, the PPI/Prodi List, joined with the Olive Tree Alliance to win the first election victory for the left in the history of the post-1946 Republic.

Luxembourg

Population	400,000 (1993)
Capital	Luxembourg-Ville
Territory	2,586 sq. km

GNP per capita	US$35,850 (1993)
Unemployment	2.6 per cent of workforce (1993)
State form	Constitutional monarchy, based on the constitution of 17 October 1868, as amended in 1919.
	Current head of state: Grand Duke Jean (crowned 12 November 1964).
State structure	Unitary
Government	After consulting the parliamentary party leaders, the grand duke nominates the prime minister (president of the Council) who must receive a vote of confidence from parliament. The prime minister heads a cabinet (Council of Ministers) of around ten ministers, who must not simultaneously hold seats in parliament. In theory, parliament may dismiss the cabinet, but early dissolution is not now seen as a realistic option. The unicameral parliament (Chamber of Deputies) has sixty members (since 1989). An advisory body of twenty-one members, the Council of State, reviews legislative proposals before they can be adopted by parliament. The Council of State may delay legislation for up to three months and require parliament to vote on it a second time.
	Current government: In the general election of 12 June 1994, the coalition between the Social

Elections to the Luxembourg Chamber of Deputies, 12 June 1994

	Votes (%)	Seats
Socialist Party (LSAP/POSL)	30.4	17
Social Christians (CSV/PCS)	29.5	21
Democratic Party (DP/PD)	14.5	12
Green Party	10.1	5
Action for Democracy and Justice (ADR)	7.7	5
National Movement (extreme right)	3.0	–
Communist Party (KPL)	2.4	–
Others	2.4	–
Total		60

Christian Party (CSV/PCS) and Socialist Party (LSAP/POSL) which had governed since July 1984 was returned to power. Prime Minister Jacques Santer (CSV) resigned to become president of the Commission of the European Union in December 1994 and was replaced by Jean-Claude Juncker.

Electoral system   The Chamber of Deputies is elected on a system of proportional representation based on four districts. The parties put forward lists of candidates and voters may choose to vote for a party list *en bloc*, or for individual candidates across party lists. Voting is compulsory. The term of office is five years (since 1959).

Party system   The three main parties date from the turn of the twentieth century. The CSV/PCS have been in almost every government since 1945, with either the liberal Democratic Party (DP/PD) or the LSAP/POSL. Other parties include the Green Party (déi Gréng), formed in December 1994 from a merger of existing green groupings, and a single-issue party which campaigns for pension reform, Action for Democracy and Justice (ADR). The Communist Party (KPL) lost its one seat in the 1994 election and was ousted from parliament for the first time in 50 years.

Malta

Population	400,000 (1993)
Capital	Valletta
Territory	316 sq. km
GNP per capita	US$7,300 (1992)
Unemployment	3.8 per cent of workforce (1992)
State form	Republic, based on the constitution of 1964, subsequently amended. Malta was a Crown Colony of the United Kingdom from 1814. In 1964 it adopted the Independence Constitution, becoming an independ-

ent sovereign state within the British Common-wealth. The constitution was amended in 1974, establishing Malta as a democratic republic within the Commonwealth. Further amendments in January 1987 protect Malta's neutrality and ensure that the party with the majority of votes forms the government.

Current head of state: President Ugo Mifsud Bonnici (elected 4 April 1994).

State structure	Unitary
Government	The president appoints the prime minister, and, on the prime minister's advice, a cabinet of ten to fifteen ministers, the chief justice, the judges and the attorney-general. The cabinet can be dismissed by the unicameral, sixty-five-member parliament (House of Representatives).

Current government: With the general election of 22 February 1992, the Nationalist Party (NP) was returned to office with thirty-four seats and a slightly increased lead over its opponent, the Malta Labour Party (MLP).

Electoral systems The president is elected by the House of Representatives for a term of five years.

The House of Representatives is elected by STV, based on thirteen constituencies. The term of office is five years.

Elections to the Maltese House of Representatives, 22 February 1992

	Votes (%)	Seats
Nationalist Party (NP)	51.77	34
Malta Labour Party (MLP)	46.50	31
Democratic Alternative (AD)	1.69	–
Independent	0.04	–
Total		65

Party system   The major parties are the NP and the MLP. Minor
                      parties include the Democratic Alternative (AD)
                      and the Malta Democratic Party (PDM).

The Netherlands

Population   15.3 million (1994)

Capital   The Hague

Territory   33,937 sq.km (land only)

GNP per capita   US$20,710 (1993)

Unemployment   8.3 per cent of workforce (1993)

State form   Constitutional monarchy, based on the constitution
                      of 1814 and later revisions of 1848 and 1983.

                      Current head of state: Queen Beatrix (took the
                      throne 30 May 1980).

State structure   Unitary. The twelve provinces are each adminis-
                      tered by a directly elected council, provincial ex-
                      ecutive and a sovereign commissioner, who is
                      appointed by royal decree.

Government   The monarch appoints a senior politician
                      (informateur) to identify a potential prime minister,
                      who, as a formateur, will form a coalition govern-
                      ment. The monarch appoints the prime minister,
                      and, on the advice of the prime minister, the other
                      members of the cabinet. There is no formal vote of
                      investiture for the cabinet, which consists of some
                      fifteen members. Government ministers must not
                      simultaneously hold seats in parliament, but may
                      attend parliament and take part in debates there.
                      The cabinet, under the prime minister, is responsi-
                      ble to parliament. The parliament (States-General)
                      is bicameral. The lower chamber, confusingly
                      termed the Second Chamber, has 150 members; the
                      upper house (First Chamber) has 75. Legislation
                      may be proposed by the Crown (as advised by a
                      Council of State) and the lower chamber of parlia-
                      ment. The Council of State must be consulted on all

bills and draft general administrative orders. The First Chamber may approve or reject legislation, but not amend it.

Current government: a coalition of the Labour Party (PvdA) (Prime Minister Wim Kok), the liberal People's Party for Freedom and Democracy (VVD) and the left-wing liberal Democrats '66 (D66). This government broke with Dutch coalition traditions. It is the first government to be formed since universal suffrage was introduced (1918) not to include the Christian Democratic Appeal (CDA) or its predecessors. For the last thirty-five years, the PvdA and VVD have refused to work together in government.

Electoral systems   The Second Chamber is elected by a system of proportional representation based on national party lists. Its term of office is four years.

The First Chamber is elected by members of the twelve provincial councils. Its term of office is six years, with half its members retiring every three years.

Election to the Netherlands Second Chamber, 3 May 1994

	Votes (%)	*Seats*
Labour Party (PvdA)	24.0	37
Christian Democratic Appeal (CDA)	22.2	34
People's Party for Freedom and Democracy (VVD)	19.9	31
Democrats '66 (D66)	15.5	24
SGP/RPF/GVP	4.8	7
AOV	3.6	6
Green Left	3.5	5
CD	2.5	3
Socialist Party (SP)	1.3	2
55+ Union	0.9	1
Others	1.8	–
Total		150

Party system	There are now four main parties: the PvdA, CDA, VVD and D66. There are also numerous small parties including the Green Left and three right-wing protestant parties, SGP, RPF and GVP.

Norway

Population	4.3 million (1994)
Capital	Oslo
Territory	323,878 sq. km
GNP per capita	US$26,340 (1993)
Unemployment	6.0 per cent of workforce (1993)
State form	Constitutional monarchy, based on the constitution of 17 May 1814. Norway was formerly linked to the Swedish throne, but declared its independence in 1905 and elected its own monarchy. Current head of state: King Harald V (took the throne on 17 January 1991).
State structure	Unitary, with nineteen counties (*Fylker*)
Government	The king appoints the prime minister, and, on the prime minister's advice, the cabinet (Council of Ministers) of around twenty members. The cabinet is responsible to parliament. Ministers must not be members of parliament, but they may attend and speak there. The unicameral parliament (Storting) has 165 members. The Storting is elected *en bloc*, and then chooses one-quarter of its members to form the upper chamber (Lagting) while the remainder form the lower chamber (Odelsting). Legislation is proposed in the Odelsting and requires the consent of both houses, but, if the houses disagree, can be passed by a joint session of the Storting by a two-thirds majority. Constitutional amendments must be passed by a two-thirds majority of a joint session. The king may veto legislation, but his veto may be overturned by three successively elected Stortings.

Election to the Norwegian Storting, 13 September 1993

	Votes (%)	*Seats*
Labour	36.9	67
Conservative	17.0	28
Centre	16.7	32
Christian People's Party	7.9	13
Socialist Left Party	7.9	13
Progress Party	6.3	10
Others	7.3	2
Total		165

	Current government: After the election of 13 September 1993, the minority Labour cabinet under Gro Harlem Brundtland, which had taken office on 3 November 1990, resumed without significant changes.
Electoral systems	The Storting is elected by proportional representation based on district party lists; 157 members are elected as constituency representatives, while the remaining eight are elected so as to achieve a greater degree of proportionality among the parties. The four-year term of office is fixed by the constitution and cannot be terminated early.
Party system	The main parties are Labour, the agrarian Centre, Conservative, the Christian People's Party, the Progress Party and hard left Socialist Left Party. Since the early 1960s, government has usually fallen either to a coalition of centre-right parties or to a Labour minority government. The election of 1993 was unusual in that it reversed the swing to the right which had been evident since the 1970s.

Portugal

Population	9.9 million (1994)
Capital	Lisbon
Territory	92,072 sq. km

GNP per capita	US$7,890 (1993)
Unemployment	5.5 per cent of workforce (1993)
State form	Republic (since 1976). Portugal's First Republic was declared in 1910, but in 1926 fell to a military takeover. This had given way by 1932 to the right-wing dictatorship of Antonio de Oliveira Salazar, led by Marcello Caetano after 1968. In April 1974, this regime was overthrown by the military group, the Armed Forces Movement (MFA). A liberal democratic regime was established with the constitution of 1976. The substantial constitutional revision of 1982 removed the direct political influence of the military and reduced the president's powers; a further revision of 1989 removed the constitutional commitment to Marxist principles. Current head of state: President Jorge Sampaio (took office 9 March 1996).
State structure	Unitary; the Azores and Madeira are autonomous regions.
Government	The president appoints the prime minister, and, on the prime minister's advice, a cabinet (Council of Ministers) of around fifteen members. The cabinet's programme must win a vote of confidence from parliament within ten days of taking office. The cabinet may be dismissed by the parliament following a vote of no confidence. The unicameral parliament, the Assembly of the Republic (Assembléia da República) has 230 members. The president may dissolve the parliament. Legislation passed by parliament is subject to judicial review by the Constitutional Court. The president may veto legislation.

Portuguese presidential election, 14 January 1996

	Votes (%)
Jorge Sampaio (PS)	53.8
Anibal Cavaco Silva (PSD)	46.2

Parliament can overturn a presidential veto with an absolute majority of all its members. The Council of State is the political advisory body of the president.

Current government: With the election of October 1995, the Socialist Party (PS) returned to power after ten years in opposition, forming a minority government with Antonio Guterres as prime minister.

Electoral systems Presidential elections are by direct universal suffrage. The candidate who wins more than half of the valid votes is elected. If no candidate wins under these terms, a second ballot is held to decide between the two leading candidates of the first ballot. The term of office is five years. The president may not be re-elected for a third consecutive term of office.

The Assembly of the Republic is elected by a system of proportional representation, with a term of office of four years

Party system Despite the revolutionary rhetoric of the 1976 constitution, party competition has been dominated by the centre-left PS and the centre-right Social Democratic Party (PSD). The other main parties are the Portuguese Communist Party (PCP) and the conservative Democratic Social Centre/ People's Party (CDS/PP).

Elections to the Portuguese Assembly, 1 October 1995

	Votes (%)	Seats
Socialist Party (PS)	43.9	112
Social Democratic Party (PSD)	34.0	88
Democratic Social Centre/ People's Party (CDS/PP)	9.1	15
CDU (communist-led alliance)	8.6	15
Others	4.4	0
Total		230

Spain

Population	39.2 million (1994)
Capital	Madrid
Territory	504,782 sq. km
GNP per capita	US$13,650 (1993)
Unemployment	22.4 per cent of workforce (1993)
State form	Constitutional monarchy. The constitution was adopted by national referendum in December 1978. The previous dictatorship of General Franco, established in 1939 following the three-year civil war, effectively ended on Franco's death in 1975.
	Current head of state: King Juan Carlos I de Borbón (sworn in 22 November 1975).
State structure	Unitary, but with considerable devolution of executive and administrative powers to seventeen elected regional assemblies.
Government	After consultation with the parliamentary party groups, the king appoints the prime minister (president of the government), who must win a vote of confidence on his proposed government programme in the lower house of parliament, the Congress of Deputies (Congreso de los Diputados). On the prime minister's advice, the king appoints a cabinet (Council of Ministers) of fifteen to twenty members. The cabinet is responsible to, and may be dismissed by, the Congress of Deputies. The parliament (Cortes Generales) is bicameral, consisting of the 350-member Congress of Deputies and an upper chamber, the Senate (Senado) of 256 members. The prime minister may dissolve either or both houses of parliament once in a twelve-month period. Legislation passed by the Cortes Generales is subject to judicial review by a Constitutional Court.
	Current government: The moderate left Spanish Socialist Party (PSOE) had been in government from 1982 until 1996, with Felipe González

Márquez as prime minister. After the election of 3 March 1996, the centre-right Popular Party (PP) emerged as the largest party. On 5 May 1996, the PP formed a government with the votes of three regional parties, the Catalan Convergence and Union (CiU), the Basque Nationalist Party (PNV) and the Canary Islands Coalition. The prime minister is José María Aznar of the PP.

Electoral systems   The Congress of Deputies is elected by proportional representation for a four-year term. The electoral district is the province.

As to the Senate, 208 members are elected by a majority system on a provincial basis (with four

Elections to the Spanish Congress of Deputies, 3 March 1996

	Votes (%)	*Seats*
Popular Party (PP)	38.9	156
Spanish Socialist Party (PSOE)	37.5	141
United Left (IU)	10.6	21
Convergence and Union (CiU)	4.6	16
Basque Nationalist Party (PNV)	1.3	5
Others	7.1	11
Total		350

Elections to the Spanish Senate, 3 March 1996

	Seats
Popular Party (PP)	111
Spanish Socialist Party (PSOE)	81
Convergence and Union (CiU)	8
Basque Nationalist Party (PNV)	4
Canary Islands Coalition (CC)	2
Others	2
Total	208

senators for every mainland province). The remaining senators, currently 48, are chosen by the assemblies of the autonomous regions. The term of office is four years.

Party system

The main parties are the PP and the PSOE. Also significant is the far left coalition, the United Left (IU), which includes the Communists. The main regionalist parties are the CiU and PNV. Numerous other small parties contest elections, many representing regional positions.

Sweden

Population	8.7 million (1994)
Capital	Stockholm
Territory	449,964 sq.km
GNP per capita	US$24,830 (1993)
Unemployment	8.1 per cent of workforce (1993)

State form

Constitutional monarchy. The constitution of 1975 replaced the outmoded version of 1809. It was revised in 1979 to incorporate a new bill of rights.

Current head of state: King Carl XVI Gustaf (took the throne 15 September 1973).

State structure

Unitary

Government

After consultation with the parties represented in parliament (Riksdag), the Speaker of the Riksdag proposes a candidate prime minister. The prime minister must receive a vote of confidence in the Riksdag before taking office. The prime minister appoints a cabinet (Council of State) of around twenty ministers, which is responsible to parliament. Individual ministers may also be dismissed by parliament. The Riksdag is unicameral (since 1969) and has 349 members.

Current government: After the election of 1994, the Swedish Social Democratic Labour Party (SAP) re-

Election to the Swedish Riksdag, 18 September 1994

	Votes (%)	*Seats*
Swedish Social Democratic Labour Party (SAP)	45.25	161
Moderate Unity Party (M)	22.37	80
Centre Party (C)	7.65	27
People's Party (Fp)	7.19	26
Left Party (VP)	6.17	22
Green Party (MpG)	5.02	18
Christian Democratic Community Party (KdS)	4.06	15
New Democracy (ND)	1.23	0
Others	1.06	0
Total		349

turned from three years in opposition to form a minority government with Ingvar Carlsson as prime minister. Carlsson retired in March 1996, and was replaced as prime minister by Göran Persson.

Electoral system The Riksdag is elected by a system of proportional representation based on districts. In order to win seats, parties must secure 4 per cent of the total vote or 12 per cent in one district. Of the 349 seats, 310 are permanent constituency seats and thirty-nine are 'adjustment' seats, allocated to ensure that the distribution of seats in the Riksdag is proportionate to the total votes cast for each party. The term of office is four years (since 1994).

Party system The main parties are SAP, the Moderate Unity Party (M), the People's Party (also known as the Liberal party) (Fp), the Centre Party (C) and the Christian Democratic Community Party (KdS). Also significant are the Left Party (VP) (the former Communist party, which changed its name in 1990), and the Green Party (MpG). The right-wing New Democracy (ND) lost all of its twenty-five parliamentary seats in the 1994 election.

Switzerland

Population	6.9 million (1994)
Capital	Bern
Territory	41,293 sq.km
GNP per capita	US$36,410 (1993)
Unemployment	3.7 per cent of workforce (1993)
State form	Republic, based on the constitution of 29 May 1874.

Current head of state: President Jean-Pascal Delamuraz (1996). The president and vice-president of the federation hold office for one year only and are chosen from the seven members of the Federal Council, the Swiss executive. They are elected by the parliament, the Federal Assembly. The president's role is not comparable with any other western European presidency. The Swiss president has no special political privileges, but performs the formal duties of a head of state together with formally chairing the Federal Council.

State structure   Federation of twenty cantons and six half-cantons.

Government   The executive body, the Federal Council, consists of seven members, each from a different canton, who act as government ministers. These members represent a coalition of four parties which has been in power since 1959. The members of the Federal Council are elected by a joint session of the bicameral parliament (Federal Assembly) for a term of office of four years. Although the Federal Council is held 'responsible' to the Federal Assembly, the Federal Council may not be dismissed before the end of its term of office. The Federal Council is a collegiate body: there is no prime minister and most decisions are agreed by the Federal Council as a whole. The lower chamber of parliament (National Council) has 200 members and represents the Swiss people. The upper chamber (Council of States), representing the cantons, has forty-six members, two from each canton and one from each half-canton. The lower and upper chambers have equal powers.

Current government: The government does not hinge directly on election results, as in other western European countries, but comprises the formula coalition, noted above, of the Christian Democratic People's Party of Switzerland (CVP), Social Democratic Party (SPS), the liberal Radical Democratic Party (FDP) and the agrarian right Swiss People's Party (SVP).

Electoral systems   Elections to the National Council are by proportional representation based on party lists. Each canton or half-canton forms one electoral district. The term of office is four years.

The method of election to the Council of States varies from canton to canton.

Party system   In addition to the four main parties which make up the government coalition (CVP, SPS, FDP and SVP), a number of other parties contest federal elections. These include the Liberal Party (LPS), Green Party

Election to the Swiss National Council, 22 October 1995

	Votes (%)	Seats
Social Democratic Party (SPS)	21.8	54
Radical Democratic Party (FDP)	20.2	45
Christian Democratic People's Party of Switzerland (CVP)	17.0	34
Swiss People's Party (SVP)	14.9	29
Green Party of Switzerland (GPS)	5.0	9
Motorist's Party (APS)	4.0	7
Liberal Party of Switzerland (LPS)	2.7	7
Swiss Democrats (SD)	3.1	3
Alliance of Independents (LdU)	1.8	3
Evangelical People's Party (EVP)	1.8	2
Others	7.7	7
Total		200

(GPS), the anti-ecologist Motorists' Party (APS), Swiss Democrats (SD, formerly known as National Action against Foreign Infiltration of the People and Homeland party) and the Evangelical Party (EVP).

United Kingdom

Population	57.8 million (1994)
Capital	London
Territory	244,103 sq. km
GNP per capita	US$17,970 (1993)
Unemployment	10.3 per cent of workforce (1993)
State form	Constitutional monarchy, without a written constitution.
	Current head of state: Queen Elizabeth II (acceded 6 February 1952).
State structure	Unitary
Government	The monarch appoints the prime minister, usually the leader of the largest party in the lower house of parliament, the House of Commons. The prime minister chooses a cabinet of around twenty members, who are appointed by the monarch. The House of Commons has 651 members. The upper house, the House of Lords, has a variable membership of around 1,200. The House of Lords is a non-elected body with three categories of member: hereditary and non-hereditary peers appointed by the monarch; archbishops and senior bishops of the Church of England; law lords, who act within the House of Lords as a final court of appeal. Legislation must be passed by both houses and obtain royal assent. The House of Lords may delay legislation by up to a year. The prime minister may ask the monarch to dissolve parliament at any time.
	Current government: Conservative, led by John Major. The Conservatives have been in power since 1979. With the election of 9 April 1992, they were

Election to the UK House of Commons, 9 April 1992

	Votes (%)	*Seats*
Conservative Party	41.9	336
Labour Party	34.4	271
Liberal Democrats	17.9	20
Scottish National Party	1.9	3
Plaid Cymru	0.5	4
Northern Ireland parties	2.2	17
Others	1.3	0
Total		651

	returned for their fourth consecutive term of office with a reduced majority.
Electoral system	The House of Commons is elected for a five-year term of office by a simple majority system of voting in single-member constituencies (first-past-the-post system).
Party system	The main parties are the Conservative and the Labour parties. The Liberal Democrats are the third national force. The Scottish National Party (SNP) and the Welsh nationalist Plaid Cymru attract regional support. Within Northern Ireland, the main parties are the Protestant Unionist parties (OUP, DUP, PUP and the Alliance Party) and the mainly Catholic Social Democratic and Labour Party (SDLP). The extreme nationalist Sinn Fein also contests elections.

Council of Europe

Established in 1949 in Strasbourg to promote unity between its members, to encourage their economic and social progress and to uphold the principles of parliamentary democracy and respect for human rights. The ten founding members were: Belgium, Denmark, France, Ireland, Italy, Luxembourg, the Netherlands, Norway, Sweden and the United Kingdom. There are now thirty-three members including all the countries of western Europe and a number of eastern European countries. Other countries of eastern Europe have applied to join.

The Council of Europe has an intergovernmental Committee of Ministers, whose members are usually the foreign minister of their respective member states, and which makes decisions unanimously. It usually meets twice a year. The consultative Parliamentary Assembly has 236 members and meets four times a year. The current secretary-general of the Council of Europe is Daniel Tarschys (Sweden).

The European Convention for the Protection of Human Rights and Fundamental Freedoms was drawn up in 1950 on the recommendation of the Assembly and came into force in 1953. Under the Convention, the European Commission of Human Rights was established in 1954 to investigate alleged violations of human rights, and the European Court of Human Rights was set up in 1959.

European Union (EU)

The European Union (see Chapter 11) has fifteen member states. Its institutions are in three sites: Brussels, Luxembourg and Strasbourg. The EU is regulated by the Treaty of Rome (1957), the later accession agreements for new member states, and the Treaty on European Union (1993).

The decision-making process within the EU is as follows: proposals originate in the Commission or European Parliament (EP) and are passed to the Council of Ministers (representing the member states), which must agree the proposals before they can come into effect. Once passed by the Council of Ministers, the Commission oversees the implementation of decisions. The EP debates issues, questions Commissioners and ministers, may amend parts of the budget and accept or reject the budget as a whole. It can dismiss the Commission *en bloc*. The current president of the Commission is Jacques Santer (Luxembourg), who took office on 18 January 1995.

Direct elections to the EP were introduced in 1979. Each member state uses its own electoral system. The election of 1994 produced a European Parliament of 567 members. This was increased to 626 with the accession of Austria (21 MEPs), Finland (16) and Sweden (22) in 1995. Similar to the development in the member state parliaments, 'party groups' have formed within the EP. The main groupings are: Socialists, Christian Democrats (European People's Party), Liberal Democrat and Reformist Group, Conservative (European Democrats), the Confederal Group of the United Left and the Greens.

North Atlantic Treaty Organisation (NATO)

The Atlantic Alliance was established on the basis of the 1949 North Atlantic Treaty to provide common security for its members through cooperation in military, political and economic matters. The objectives of the Alliance are implemented by NATO, based in Brussels. The twelve founding members in 1949 were: Belgium, Canada, Denmark, France, Iceland, Italy, Luxembourg, the Netherlands, Norway, Portugal, the United Kingdom and the United States of America. Greece, Spain, Turkey and (West) Germany joined subsequently. The status of France is somewhat unusual. It is a member of the Atlantic Alliance but opted out of the integrated military structure of NATO in 1966 and does not attend these meetings. Since the dissolution of the Soviet-led Warsaw Pact in 1991, formerly regarded as the main adversary of the Atlantic Alliance, NATO has undergone radical restructuring in an attempt to meet the new security challenges in Europe.

NATO has an intergovernmental North Atlantic Council. It is attended on a weekly basis by permanent representatives of the member states, and at least twice a year by member state foreign ministers, or their heads of government and state. At all levels, it has effective decision-making authority and decisions are taken by common consent. NATO's Defence Planning Committee is convened twice a year at ministerial level and is attended by member state ministers of defence (although France does not send a representative). The current secretary-general of NATO is Javier Solana Madariaga (Spain).

References

Alen, A. and R. Ergec (1994) *Federal Belgium after the Fourth State Reform of 1993*, Brussels, Ministry of Foreign Affairs.

Electoral Studies 11:2 (1992) to 14:4 (1995).

The Europa World Yearbook 1994 (35th edn) and 1995 (36th edn), London, Europa Publications.

Koole, R. and P. Mair (eds) *Political Data Yearbook 1994 (1 January 1993–1 January 1994)* Special issue of *European Journal of Political Research*, 26:3, December 1994.

Keesing's Record of World Events, Vols 36 (1990) to 42 (1996), Harlow, Longman.

Index